AUTUMN ACROSS AMERICA

THE AMERICAN SEASONS

THE FIRST SEASON

NORTH WITH THE SPRING

THE SECOND SEASON

JOURNEY INTO SUMMER

THE THIRD SEASON

AUTUMN ACROSS AMERICA

THE FOURTH SEASON

WANDERING THROUGH WINTER

AUTUMN
ACROSS
AMERICA

EDWIN WAY TEALE

A NATURALIST'S RECORD OF A 20,000-MILE JOURNEY
THROUGH THE NORTH AMERICAN AUTUMN.
WITH PHOTOGRAPHS BY THE AUTHOR

INTRODUCTION BY ANN H. ZWINGER

ST. MARTIN'S PRESS
NEW YORK

Library of Congress Cataloging-in-Publication Data

Teale, Edwin Way
     Autumn across America : a naturalist's 20,000-mile journey through autumn / Edwin Way Teale.
        p.   cm.
     Reprint. Originally published: New York : Dodd, Mead, 1981. (The American seasons ; 3rd season).
     ISBN 0-312-04455-0
     1. Autumn—United States. 2. Natural history—United States.
3. Natural history—Outdoor books. I. Title. II. Series: Teale, Edwin Way American seasons ; 3rd season.
QH104.T355   1990 3rd season
574.5'43'0973 s—dc20   90-8004
[574.5'43]   CIP

First published in the United States by Dodd, Mead & Co.

Dedicated to
DAVID
Who Traveled with
Us in Our Hearts

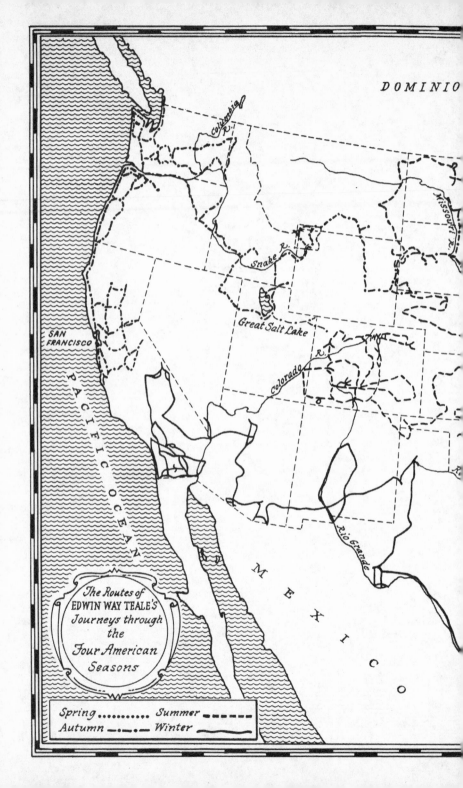

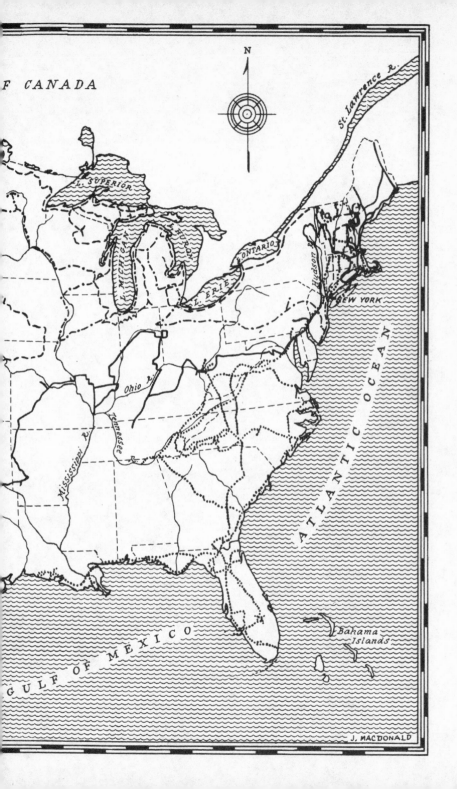

ACKNOWLEDGMENTS

WHEN William Wood published his *New England's Prospect* in 1634 he introduced the book with a note to the reader:

"Thou mayest in two or three houres travaile over a few leaves, see and know that which cost him that writ it yeares and travaile . . . before he knew it."

Those who travel over the leaves of this book, I trust, will find there something of the enjoyment we knew as well as what we learned during the days of our autumn journey.

So many were the kindnesses shown us during this adventure with a season that it is impossible to acknowledge them all. My indebtedness is transcontinental. For reading portions of the manuscript, aiding in problems of identification, offering me the benefit of their specialized knowledge or providing aid in various forms during or after the trip I am particularly under obligation to:

John W. Aldrich, Dean Amadon, Charles Anderson, Harold E. Anthony, John Bauman, Emily J. Bedell, Mervin Bedell, Charles M. Bogert, Oliver E. Bowen, Jr., Donald Braun, Maurice Broun, Wayne W. Bryant, Rachel L. Carson, Mont Cazier, Ray Chapman, William T. Clapp, Lucy Claussen, Lee Crandall, Homer Croy, Allan D. Cruickshank, Helen G. Cruickshank, C. H. Curran, Bernard DeVoto, George Dock, Jr., Frank Dufresne, Oren C. Durham, John J. Elliott, Avery Fisher, James L. G. FitzPatrick, James Forbes, Jacob Freedman, Willis J. Gertsch, Sheldon L. Glover, Ludlow Griscom,

Elizabeth C. Hall, Robert Harris, Philip Heywood, Bob Hines, Ruth Hopson, William R. Horsfall, John Thomas Howell, Donald G. Huddleston, James A. Humphreville, Thomas H. Kearney, Don Greame Kelley, John Kieran, George F. Knowlton, Ken Legg, A. Starker Leopold, Helen MacDonough, Harold F. Mayfield, Ernst Mayr, J. T. McNeill, Jr., Edmund Morgan, Henry M. Neely, Peter K. Nelson, John T. Nichols, John Pallister, George H. Peters, Roger Tory Peterson, Richard H. Pough, H. E. Prentice, Hugh Rice, Harold W. Rickett, T. C. Schnierla, Herbert F. Schwarz, J. Harold Severaid, Grace B. Selzer, Lucia Shepardson, Orlo Stephens, Reginald G. Thorpe, Josselyn Van Tyne, Percy L. Verity, Alma J. Verity, Roman Vishniac, Farida Wiley, M. Woodbridge Williams, Vanez T. Wilson, Robert G. Wind, Mary V. Wissler, Stanley P. Young, Howard Zahnizer.

For invaluable assistance in checking manuscript pages and proofs I am indebted to Benjamin T. Richards. I also would like to express my gratitude to the authors of some 800 books, articles and scientific papers who have helped me round out my information or have aided me in understanding more clearly the events of autumn seen along the way.

The chapter on "The Long Valley" and portions of "Butterfly Trees" originally appeared in *Audubon Magazine*. Parts of "Mystery Sleep" and "Warbler River" were published by *Coronet* and *Natural History* respectively. I wish to express my thanks to the editors of these publications for permission to include the material in this book. In the editing and production of the volume my debt is great—as it has been on many occasions during twenty years of cordial relationship between author and publisher—to the Dodd, Mead staff, particularly to Edward H. Dodd, Jr., Raymond T. Bond, S. Phelps Platt, Jr., John Blair and Ruby Carr.

August 1, 1956
EDWIN WAY TEALE

INTRODUCTION

*E*DWIN Way Teale sits in the stern of the canoe, paddle hooked under the thwart in front of him. A small spiral notebook rests on his right knee, stubby pencil in hand, recording the immediate details of what he has just seen in a few words, or perhaps noting something to look up, or even jotting down a philosophical comment on the beauty he sees but, always, catching the freshness of the moment. This picture is indelible for me not only because I saw him so often in this pose when we worked together on a book about the Assabet and Sudbury rivers in Massachusetts, but because it catches the quintessence of Teale as the ultimate meticulous nature writer.

Edwin Way Teale's shirt pocket notebook was always with him, a lifelong habit that turned trips anywhere into vivid and lively accounts. When he translated his notes into finished text, he fretted about the "bridges" needed to join disparate passages. It was that concern for smooth reading that gave his writing such a seamless, deceptively effortless quality and allowed his words to fall with great calmness on the page.

Dr. Teale left assignment magazine writing in October 1941 to become what he had set his heart on, a nature writer, and forever after celebrated his "freedom day." He had prepared for a career in nature writing for years, neatly and methodically as he did almost everything in his life. As an uncommonly good black-and-white photographer, he made the lens an extension of his learning. He began by writing about the world close by, and widened his horizons through the years, culminating in the four books in which he followed the seasons throughout the United States.

Although the first Earth Day in 1970 came eleven years before Dr. Teale's death, his writing never left the center of the pure nature writing tradition. Although he was an ardent champion to Rachel Carson's *Silent Spring* and was deeply disturbed by the damage he saw being done to the environment, his books never became "environmental writing." During his forty-year career of writing and editing more than thirty volumes, all embellished with his fresh insights and lucid prose, he won both the John Burroughs Award and, for *Wandering through Winter,* a Pulitzer Prize in 1966, the first in more than fifty years given to a nature book.

His books on the seasons are as expansive in design and character as Edwin Way Teale was. He always saw them as a whole, and that is how they read, despite the years between their publication: spring, 1951, summer, 1960, autumn, 1956, and winter, 1965. His delightful and beloved Nellie accompanied him on all these trips through "the great days of our lives," and all four books are dedicated to "DAVID, Who Traveled with Us in Our Hearts," their only son, who was lost in World War II.

The itineraries for each trip were thoroughly organized through months of extensive and meticulous research of who and what to see where and when, yet he was always able to take advantage of the unexpected adventure. He kept notes of every single travel day and transcribed them on a portable typewriter at night, turning skeletal observations into sentences and paragraphs of near-perfect prose. At the end of each book he had the typescript pages bound into volumes that now reside at the Rare Books Room in the Library of the University of Connecticut. They are voluminous, Herculean accomplishments of devotion and self-discipline; they have to be leafed through to understand the care and attention to detail that went into them, and the sheer labor, all accomplished while driving about 17,000 miles per book.

We find reassurance as well as pleasure in reading these books today, for Teale's values are rooted in the natural world. He writes of green leaves and clear summer skies over the lakes of Minnesota, of the glossy ibis and a spring sunset over Lake Okeechobee, of an ice storm in Indiana and a flooding Ohio River, of a luminous larva on a barrier beach and fireflies lighting the dusk, of harvester ants foraging on the Little Bighorn battlefield in Montana.

The seasons herein are not only those of the countryside, but seasons of the heart. We reap a pleasure in the reading from a goodness of the heart, a keenness of the mind, and an excellence of the writing.

—ANN HAYMOND ZWINGER
Colorado Springs, Colorado

CONTENTS

CONTENTS

CONTENTS

ILLUSTRATIONS

AUTUMN ACROSS AMERICA

ONE

MONOMOY: TURN OF THE TIDE

WHERE low dunes roll their yellow waves inland from the shore on Monomoy; where the shifting blues and greens and purples of the open Atlantic stretch away unbroken to Europe from Monomoy; where slow waves trip and spill and slide in foam up the shining incline of the beach and sanderlings flow, on scurrying feet, up and back with every wave on Monomoy; there, under the late-August sun, amid the sparse marram grass and seaside goldenrod, on Cape Cod's far-eastern tideline of the continent, our long adventure with the fall began.

The tide rose to full and made its turn. And all across the continent behind us another tide, a greater tide—the tide of the seasons—was also at its turn. Summer, during these last of the August hours, was accelerating its yearly slide into autumn. Curlew and godwit, dowitcher and plover already were moving southward along the narrow flyway of the shore. And on the mainland, in the waning summer nights, bobolinks were taking wing for far-off South America. These were the early ripples of migration, ripples we would later see mount into the great waves of the autumn flight.

Not many miles from where we stood, Henry Thoreau once faced the Atlantic on an outer beach of Cape Cod and observed that there a man had put all America behind him. For us, rather, all America lay before us.

Here where Monomoy points its ten-mile finger of sand

from Cape Cod toward the island of Nantucket we were at the beginning of 20,000 miles of wandering through autumn, the third season, the most colorful of the year. Before us stretched glorious days of drifting in that time described on an ancient page as "these golden weakes that doe lye between the thunderous heates of summer and the windy gloomes of winter."

Our car was packed—binoculars and cameras and field guides stowed away, marked maps cramming the glove compartment, tramping shoes and raincoats ready in the trunk. The pleasures of preparation were over. The days of dreaming, the evenings of planning, the months of anticipation were behind us. Nellie and I were starting again on an adventure with a season.

When we had come north with the spring, some years before, Monomoy had been veiled in sheets of falling rain. Now the air was shining with the haze of summer's ending and the slow beat of the sea was in our ears. In spring we had journeyed north, following the path of the season, keeping pace with its progress up the map from Florida to Canada. Now we were cutting across the advancing front of a season, across the whole continent-wide sweep of the North American autumn— across the four great flyways of the migrating birds, through the multicolored forests of the hardwoods, over the prairie fall, through the high autumn of the Rockies and the desert autumn of the salt flats and the rain-forest autumn of the Northwest. We would see a thousand moods and facets of the season. We would see new birds, new lands, new trees, all in the surroundings of fall. Nowhere in the world is autumn more beautiful than in America. And we would witness it all—across the land from east to west, as the sun shines on it, as the pioneers saw it trekking to Oregon, as the flow of American history crossed the continent.

Only in very recent years has such a trip as my wife and I planned been possible, carrying us, as it would, into out-of-the-way corners of more than half of the states in the Union, all a single season. Audubon and Bartram and Muir traveled on foot or on horseback or by stagecoach. Many autumns—and every autumn is different—would have been required to witness the coming of the season from coast to coast. To see it in one continuous flow we depended upon innumerable innovations of the restless present, on highways and filling stations and radio weather reports. We talked that day, as we stood amid the seaside goldenrod and sparse marram grass on Monomoy, of all the people to whom we were indebted for bringing within our grasp this dreamed-of journey through autumn—the steel workers, the automobile makers, the road menders, the glass-factory technicians, even those old, old innovators, the first men to use fire and employ wheels and devise cloth and leather to keep themselves warm and dry. They all had contributed something to the travels that lay before us and to them all we were profoundly grateful.

There is a midsummer. There is a midwinter. But there is no midspring or midautumn. These are the seasons of constant change. Like dawn and dusk they are periods of transition. But like night and day and day and night they merge slowly, gradually. As Richard Jefferies once wrote, broken bits of summer can be found scattered far into the shortening days of fall. Only on calendars and in almanacs are the lines of division sharply defined. Just as in the far reaches of the Everglades we had found a pre-spring spring, a season that was still winter on the calendar but already showing evidences of change, so now, while summer still officially ruled, we were in a pre-autumn autumn surrounded by the signs of coming fall.

During the first days of our wanderings we followed the pointing finger of Monomoy to Nantucket where on the high moors John Kieran showed us golden plover that soon would head across the open sea with landfall on another continent—spanning, without a pause, the distance to Argentina. In the midnight stillness of a Woods Hole laboratory, Rachel Carson introduced us to plumed worms and moss animals, to the bizarre, fascinating creatures that people her book, *The Edge of the Sea.* Then, in the warm sunshine of early afternoon, we rode west on U.S. 6, the longest continuously marked highway in America. Oak leaves, here and there, had fallen and yellow was creeping into the foliage of the locust trees as we left the Cape behind.

Across New England the summer-long pageant of the wildflowers was drawing to a close. Over the lowlands spread the pinkish-purple of the joe-pye weed. Chicory blue, that bluest of blues, shone from the roadside amid the violet-blue of the New England asters. The massed yellow of goldenrod—to the English "farewell-summer"—ran up the hillsides and the madder-purple of ironweed gleamed from the higher pasturelands. These were the varied flower hues that would be replaced in the weeks to come by the blazing colors of the autumn leaves. In New England fall comes as the glorious, flaming sunset of the year.

Already, as we crossed lower Massachusetts and Rhode Island and Connecticut, we could see this brilliance in its initial stages. Scarlet enveloped an occasional sumac. Deeper red ran across the leaves of poison ivy. Along old stone walls, where chipmunks scurried with cheek pouches bulging with seeds, the berries of the bittersweet were yellow, still to split and reveal the brilliant red of the inner coating. Once we rounded a turn and came upon the glorious coloring of the branch of a sugar maple prematurely clad in autumn leaves. Although we were skirting New England along its southern border, although we were in advance of its autumn glory, we could remember from past years that beauty, unsurpassed anywhere around the world.

We could see in our mind's eye the gorgeous tapestry of its rolling countryside, the multicolored ridges curving away mile on mile, the long vistas from its mountaintops. We could see the vivid hues reflected in quiet river reaches and mirrored in the still water of the innumerable ponds and lakes of Massachusetts and Connecticut. We could see the village greens, the white-spired churches, the winding roads, all surrounded by the incomparable pageantry of the autumn leaves. Soon the elms would be scattering golden leaves across the well-cut grass of the village greens, the sugar maples would be lifting upward like sheets of flame and all the breath-taking beauty that envelops this region in the fall would be at its height.

The acid soil of New England, its wide stretches of hardwoods, its numerous sugar maples, its rolling or mountainous character, the sunshine of its autumn weather, all these contribute to the glory of this annual display. The birches of Maine, the aspens of the White Mountains, the sugar maples of Vermont, the long rainbow of the Connecticut River Valley cutting from top to bottom through New England, the Berkshires—mention these to anyone who has traveled widely through a New England fall and you will evoke instant memories of superlative beauty.

This beauty was still to come as we rode west. But other signs of the season were apparent along the coast. Beach plums were ripening close to shore and across all the sea meadows ran a wash of russet-gold. Other plums were ripening, other sea meadows were russet, when, late that day, we crossed to the far-eastern end of Long Island, riding the ferry from the Connecticut shore to Orient Point. Thirty miles away, below the Shinnecock Hills, spread the shallow waters of an extensive bay. Under its surface, as in the sea and along the tideline, fall would give rise to innumerable changes. In one of the memorable adventures of the trip—in the night, in the eelgrass jungles of the bay—I was to see some of this hidden underwater life that autumn so soon would affect.

TWO

FORESTS OF THE SEA

I ADJUSTED my face mask. Through the oval of its tempered glass I looked up at the nearly full early-September moon. Then I snapped on my underwater flashlight, took a quick, deep breath, kicked with the rubber frog-foot of a swim-fin and followed the beam of my torch down into a strange and silent forest of the sea.

It was ten o'clock at night. We were near the eastern end of Long Island. Monomoy lay 150 miles behind us. Between the low dark line of the seaward dunes and the high dark line of the landward hills, Shinnecock Bay extended in an expanse of moonlit waters. For more than two hours I had been alternating between this upper world of moonlight and a torch-lit submerged world where the multitudinous ribbons of the eelgrass waved in the current breezes of the bay bottom.

Acre after acre, on and on across the shallows of the bay, the eelgrass extended. Its strands, about three-eighths of an inch wide, were often a yard or more in length. And all this multitude of slender ribbons of green ascended in buoyant, sinuous curves toward the surface. My flashlight, for nearly a minute at a time, would wind among the swaying strands like a luminous eel, its beam sending a play of shadows running over the ribbons beyond. Then I would surface, see the moon through the streaming veil of water running down my face mask, stand chest-deep in the shallows, store up oxygen and dive once more. Half a hundred times I had emerged thus and descended again into the underwater night of this eelgrass jungle.

The ribbons that slid like slippery seaweed along my legs belonged to no ordinary plant. Everything connected with eelgrass—its associations, its past as well as its recent history—all are remarkable. It is not a grass. It is not related to the sea-weeds. It belongs to the fresh-water pondweed family. It is a flowering plant, one of the very few flowering plants found in salt water. Like the whale and the dolphin, the eelgrass, *Zostera marina*, has gone back to the sea.

Bays and estuaries where it is protected from the most violent action of the waves, shallows where the water is between two and six feet deep at high tide, a bottom that is formed of mixed mud and sand—these provide the eelgrass with its favored habitat. But sometimes it is found at depths of more than forty feet, and where sluggish rivers join the sea it often ascends the streams to a point where the salinity of the water drops to twenty-five per cent that of the adjacent ocean.

A perennial, the plant reproduces both by seeds and by rhizomes. These creeping, jointed rootlike stems ramify until as many as 2,000 of the eelgrass ribbons may rise from a single square yard of bay bottom. Its capacity for multiplication is so great that scientists have calculated that from one seed the possible total of flowering shoots at the end of twenty-five years would be 8,388,608. The flowers are minute, naked, submerged and rarely seen. They are fertilized by currents that distribute tiny threads of pollen that have a density almost exactly that of water.

Swimming among the strands, as among slender carnival streamers, I might have been anywhere in a thousand bays on either side of the Atlantic. Wherever eelgrass grows—whether it is along the coast of Europe, the northern Pacific shore of Asia or the upper part of either seaboard of North America—the underwater scene is much the same. Around the world it is a plant of many names: sea grass, ribbon grass, mallow, drew, sea wrack, bell ware, barnacle grass, sea moss, brant grass, sea oar, glass wrack and tiresome weed—the latter name bestowed, no doubt, by baymen forced to row their boats through its clinging beds or to disentangle the strands from their propellers.

The dry eelgrass that is piled in silver-brown windrows on the shore by storms is variously called sea hay, sea wrack and alva marina. Analysis of ashes found on sites of ancient villages in Denmark suggest it was a source of soda and salt for early men. In Europe it has been used as fuel and fertilizer. It has gone into the thatching of French houses and into the construction of dikes in Holland. New England pioneers used it to bank their houses and barns for winter. It has been employed in the manufacture of paper, for bedding domestic animals, for packing glass and china and for stuffing mattresses and chairs. In the first world war Germany turned to eelgrass as a substitute for cotton in making nitrocellulose. During the 1920's it was rather widely employed in soundproofing and insulating. The year of maximum commercial use probably was 1929 when the Netherlands exported 3,000 tons, Nova Scotia shipped an equal amount and production in the United States exceeded 5,000 tons.

Then disaster, a mysterious catastrophe that is still something of a riddle, brought death to the eelgrass up and down both sides of the Atlantic.

It began late in 1930. First the leaves discolored, then the stems died and finally the roots decayed. Gradually wasting away, the plants were washed ashore. Some scientists blamed the dumping of oil from ocean tankers, others thought a mycetozoan parasite was responsible, others suggested the cause was a fungus while still others maintained some highly infectious bacteria was the source of the swiftly spreading plague. By the summer of 1931 the eelgrass was dying all the way from North Carolina to Cape Cod. The following year the mysterious epidemic swept northward up the Canadian coast and, on the other side of the Atlantic, began devastating the eelgrass beds of England, Holland and France. By 1933 less than one per cent of the eelgrass along the east coast of North America—from southern Labrador to Beaufort, North Carolina—was still alive. As Clarence Cottam says in his excellent summary in the 1934 *Yearbook of Agriculture*, such rapidity of spread and destructiveness by a plant disease is unknown elsewhere in botanical history.

And as the eelgrass was stricken, creatures whose lives depended on it were stricken also. First the brant, those sea geese whose diet is often nearly ninety per cent eelgrass, were brought to starvation. Already reduced by gunning, the flocks shrank so alarmingly that the government declared a year-round closed season along the eastern seaboard. Then the scallops, those remarkable swimming clams that live largely in the eelgrass beds, grew scarce. The shellfish industry was affected. Companies that specialized in eelgrass for soundproofing and stuffing furniture went out of business. Erosion occurred in places where the matted roots previously had anchored down the mud and sand. In the vicinity of Plymouth, England, two species of small sea snails, formerly found clinging to eelgrass, disappeared entirely from the coastal waters and swans, accustomed to feed on the ribbon leaves, began appearing at remote fishing villages in search of scraps. Even some of the plankton of the coastal seas, minute organisms that had found rich fare among the detritus of eelgrass on bay bottoms, became reduced in numbers. Thus, in its effects, the catastrophe that had overwhelmed a single plant carried on and on through the innumerable links of the close-knit chains of natural life.

By the early 1940's, after ten years, the slow comeback of the eelgrass had begun. Brant, grown accustomed to eating sea lettuce, found their favorite food once more in small patches in Shinnecock Bay. For here, at the exact spot where I was exploring on this moonlit September night, the returning eelgrass had gained one of its earliest footholds. Here, in the years since its reappearance, it had spread into one of the most lush and flourishing beds on the eastern coast.

Swimming amid the maze of its sinuous strands I found that now as in the long past it signified home and food to a host of creatures. My torch-beam picked them out—a blue crab as large as my hand sculling in a swift, sidewise dash into a denser tangle; prawns, almost transparent, like creations of glass with eyes that shone pink in the glare; a baby starfish, an inch and a half across, curled around six strands of eelgrass, holding them together like a dull-gold ring on a green finger. Once I nosed out over a little opening so thickly strewn with mud snails that it seemed paved with small cobblestones. Another time I came upon a pipefish motionless and vertical and wonderfully camouflaged among the interlacing ribbons. And always, wherever I went that night, there were the drifting, insubstantial ovals of the little comb jellies, the sea walnuts, entangled like living bubbles in the strands of eelgrass.

At one place I came upon thirty or more of them caught in the upper eelgrass as though among the treetops of a forest. They ranged from half an inch to three inches in length. So transparent were they that I could see the green eelgrass beyond as though looking through clear crystal glass. When I caught one and carried it in my hand to the surface it seemed no more substantial than the white of a raw egg and just as colorless. Yet each time one of these drifting ovals came into the direct line of my flashlight, spots of metallic brilliance glowed on the slender riblike plates that ran lengthwise down the sides of the little ctenophore. Each had eight such plates with cilia, or swimming hairs, extending out from the sides like the teeth of a comb. It was these rapidly moving cilia that were breaking up the rays of light, and by refraction—somewhat as minute striations in the shards of certain beetles produce their vivid colors—were creating the metallic greenish-purple sheen I saw. In brilliant sunshine prismatic colors pass rhythmically down the length of these plates to produce a rainbow-tinted flashing as the transparent creatures propel themselves slowly and deliberately through the water.

Emerging at the end of each successive dive I would hear the bandsaw chorus of the conehead grasshoppers in the beach grass a quarter of a mile away. Sometimes, farther out on the bay, I would catch the barking cry of a black skimmer winging its way just above the water, fishing in the moonlight. Then I would slip down again into that still, submerged world where the spotlight of my torch revealed noiseless movement all around me. Snail shells on the bottom advanced with sudden starts and the tiny ribbon of tracks they left behind showed they were inhabited by hermit crabs. Killifish and needlefish— with heads slender and drawn out like the noses of supersonic planes—shot away from their great hiding grounds, the denser tangles. They turned and twisted, navigating expertly the mazes between the strands, moving in unison like flocks of shorebirds on the wing. Once, where all the eelgrass tilted to one side in a current like trees leaning in a wind, and I was standing still with my flashlight pointed down into the water, the dark sliding form of an eel flowed across a small opening toward me. It was two or two and a half feet long with rounded little fins projecting out on either side just behind its head. Like an underwater blacksnake it nosed into the tangle at my feet. I shifted my weight ever so slightly and the eel was gone. One instant it was there; the next it had disappeared in a movement so fast my eye had failed to record it.

For a long time that evening I followed the wandering trail left by a boat that had plowed across the eelgrass beds earlier in the day. It led me above the tan-colored mound of a dead sponge the size of a half-bushel basket, over little openings where the green sea lettuce had collected and above the beautiful *Agardhiella* seaweed, like masses of fine red hair, the favored haunt of the sea horses. My light picked out a spiny crab making its way awkwardly over the bay bottom like something out of *The Wizard of Oz*. A little farther on it revealed the dark shell of an ancient king crab, a foot across and starred with white barnacles. One small opening became an underwater arena where I engaged in a kind of bull fight with a blue crab, heading it off in its rushes, playing a game with it, trying to touch it on the back while it sparred and veered and leaped upward with pincers wide open. A second blue crab, twenty feet away, lay on the bottom completely helpless, its shell split open around the edge. I had found it in the midst of its molt when, soft-bodied, it was emerging from the hard outer skeleton of its previous shell.

But the strangest sight I encountered along this trail through the eelgrass was one I came upon suddenly near its end. A negligent kick with a finned foot had sent me drifting slowly forward when just ahead I saw something round and dark and about the size of an apple perched on top of what looked like a mound of pure white lard. I surfaced for air and descended again. There it was in the beam of my torch, a moonsnail with its great white foot extended. I switched off the light momentarily and the moon of the moonsnail shone eerily in the moonlight of the night. At that moment so strange seemed this world of shallow water from which I had just emerged that it might well have been the setting for the old Norse myth of the fabulous wolf, Fenris, captured at last with the aid of "the breath of fishes, the noise made by a cat's footfall and the roots of stones."

Over much of the bay bottom extended a thin carpet of fine sediment. It rose in a brownish cloud when I walked, veiling the water behind me. From time to time I would see minute spurts of this sediment, as though Lilliputian bombs were bursting, as the glasslike prawns in flickering darts hurled themselves into its protection. More than once that night I came upon imprints in the sediment as though some slender-rayed, many-pointed starfish had rested there. Always these radiating lines extended from a hole in the center of a little mound like an underwater anthill. The source of the marks remained a mystery that evening. But later, exploring this

HIGH TIDE on Monomoy extends long fingers of water among ripples left by wind on the dry sand of the upper beach.

EELGRASS rises in sinuous ribbons through the water. Many marine creatures find protection in its submerged jungles.

hushed world of the eelgrass on a day of brilliant sunshine, I came upon the Alice-in-Wonderland creature that had left this autograph on the floor of the bay.

It was well along in the afternoon and I was leisurely diving again and again, moving through the eelgrass and over little glades in the direction of the lowering sun, enjoying the submerged scene as I saw it then glowing and luminous in the backlighting. Streamers of sunshine slanted downward among the eelgrass and sediment hung in golden motes. Emerging into the beauty of one spotlighted opening I came suddenly on a flower-like fountain of slender, translucent tentacles rising three or four inches above the mud of the bay bottom. Each pale pink tube with the sunshine behind it glowed as though neon-lighted. I reached out my hand toward this glowing apparition. It was still several feet away when the sightless creature sensed its approach. The whole tentacle-fountain whipped out of sight like a sudden indrawn breath. I plunged my fingers into the soft sediment. They grasped only the tough neck of a tissuelike tube anchored a foot or so deep in the sand and mud. For the maker of the radiating lines was one of the solitary sea anemones. Only this once did I see it fully exposed. But several times as I slid down into openings among the eelgrass my eyes caught the swift movement as one of these amazingly sensitive creatures disappeared from sight.

On that day a breeze sprang up, roughening the surface, and the eelgrass of the bay bottom swarmed with running lines of golden light. In an endless parade the mesh of the ripple-reflections ran on and on, over the dark gray of the mud, among the green ribbons of the plants, across the white stretch of half a hundred square feet where I discovered currents had strewn together empty shells of clam and whelk and conch—a reminder that this was Long Island, the Indians' Si-Wan-Aki, "Land of Shells" or "Land of Wampum." For hundreds of years the red men came down the Hudson and from inland to collect the raw material for their wampum here. These cylindrical blue and white beads originally had mainly ornamental and religious significance. It was only after the white settlers, employing lathes, had attained a virtual monopoly on wampum-making that the beads were widely used as money.

One shell, carried by the currents to this underwater wampum-mine, had been almost a rarity a decade before. This was that delicate, ribbed work of art, the shell of the scallop. Its design has been employed in ancient symbolism and modern advertising alike. It is as simple and as beautiful as a Greek column. And no other dweller in the eelgrass forests is more interesting than the creature that inhabits this house of delicate beauty. It is a shellfish that sees with nearly half a hundred eyes. It is a clam that swims swiftly forward or backward. It is a mollusk that can shoot through the water like a flying saucer, jet propelled.

I had hardly left the moon behind and descended among the eelgrass on the very first of my nocturnal dives when my flashlight picked out on the bottom of the bay what looked like a gaping mouth with thick brownish lips and, above and below, rows of shining, blue-green, gemlike eyes. The mouth was the half-open shell of a scallop. The lips were the two mantles formed of innumerable small tentacles just inside the outer edges of the upper and lower halves of the shell. The eyes were round, phosphorescent and functional. Each had a lens, retina and nerve and appeared to be located—as under an eyebrow—beneath one of the projections of the "scalloped" outer edge.

Sometimes these glowing eyes of the mollusks shone out amid the roots of the eelgrass, sometimes they flared into brilliance on the floor of little openings. Once I counted twenty scallops in an open space hardly two yards square. Many of the shellfish were furry above with brownish algae. One had a branching, red *Agardhiella* seaweed, about three inches long, growing upright from its shell. Another, an inch and a half across, carried two limpets, one partly overlapping the other. I was told later of a larger scallop brought up from the bay floor with barnacles, worm-tubes and a hydroid all firmly attached to its shell.

Between the parted lips of the mantles of a number of the scallops my beam illuminated the great central muscle that operates the two halves of the shell. It seemed to form the main contents of the interior, a shining white column like a pillar of alabaster. To the majority of men, this one muscle is all there is of interest to a scallop. It is the only part that is eaten. It forms the popular fried scallops of seafood restaurants. But there is more to scallops than "scallops." In life, the action of this muscle provides the motive power for one of the most unusual of all forms of locomotion. By opening and closing the shell it propels the clam through the water. Each time the shell is opened water rushes in; each time it is closed the fluid is expelled to drive the mollusk ahead.

For a long time I was puzzled as to how, exactly, this took place. I learned by what might be termed research or again might just be called the hard way. Bringing a scallop to the surface I lifted it out of the water. It opened and snapped shut with a sound like a steel trap. I dropped it in surprise. The next scallop managed to close on one of my fingers. It chewed on it rapidly, opening and closing its shell four or five times, before I got it out. After that I was careful where I held a scallop.

That lesson learned, I began to investigate the jets of ejected fluid. Swimming normally a scallop appears to be biting its way through the water. It keeps opening and clapping shut its shell —seems taking gulps of seawater—each time shooting forward with the rounded edge leading and the hinge trailing. Two streams of water, one on either side of the hinge, drive it forward. But exactly where do these twin jets emerge? I assumed they followed channels out the "stirrups" of the hinge. Lifting out one of the shellfish and pushing back my face mask, I peered close. A stream of water shot out and caught me squarely in the right eye. Wiping away the salt water I made mental note that the jet had come, not as expected from the end of the hinge, but from the side of the shell just above the hinge where the two halves bulged slightly apart.

But that is not the only place where a scallop ejects water —as I soon discovered. I was leaning over another, with the hinge and the bulge-openings safely pointed downward, when the mantle parted slightly in the middle and an even more powerful jet squirted its stream into my left eye. I had learned my lesson and the next scallop was held edgewise with the side of its shell toward me. If it shot up or down I would be missed. But it did not do either. It shot through an opening made in the mantle on my side, catching me squarely in the right eye again. That decided me. I knew all I needed to know about how a scallop ejects its jets of water.

These larger streams, fired through openings in the mantle, are used in emergencies. They enable the mollusk to take off in a sudden, hinge-first zoom from the floor of the bay. A single shot from these water guns will sometimes send it scaling ahead for several feet. The jets are also used to flip the shellfish over if it lands wrong side up on the sand and mud. For there is a right side and a wrong side to its shell when it comes to rest. One valve is more curved than the other. By resting on this more rounded side the scallop is lifted slightly above the bottom and so is better able to feed and to take off.

Several times when I headed with an outstretched arm toward a scallop it shot jerkily upward, clapping the two valves of its shell together and leaving a little cloud of sediment rising from the place where it had been. At other times the shellfish made no move even when I extended a hand and picked them up. Until the last moment I thought this was going to be the case when I tried to pick up a scallop where two seemed resting a few inches apart with the hinges toward each other. I had almost touched one when both disappeared in the rush of a toadfish, a rough-bodied, mud-colored creature so perfectly camouflaged that, in the beam of my torch, its body blended exactly with the gray-brown sediment around it. Only its two flat, rounded pectoral fins had caught the eye. And they, in shape and size and pattern and mottled coloring, in ribs and undulating outer edges, were almost perfect imitations of the bay scallops.

A mystery connected with the swimming of the scallop concerns the mass migrations that sometimes have been observed. Great hordes of the young mollusks, all going in the same direction, swim just below the surface of the sea. Why are they moving? Where are they going? Nobody seems to know.

Born early in summer, the baby shellfish soon attach themselves with secreted filaments to ribbons of eelgrass. I found several, half an inch to three-quarters of an inch across, anchored to waving strands about two and a half feet above the bay bottom. They all were attached in the same way, hinges up. Here, in relative safety, the young scallops feed on the minutiae of the sea water and grow rapidly. Before the end of autumn they may be an inch across. Leaving their eelgrass support they begin roaming over the floor of the bay. The plant that thus offers them safety in early months also provides a measure of protection in all the seasons that follow. For unlike many plants the eelgrass remains in dense green patches throughout the winter.

There are times when the whole living world seems a vast chemical engine that is speeded up or slowed down by changes in temperature. Nature advances the throttle in spring, retards it in fall. For the snails and crabs and starfish and scallops and killifishes—for all the cold-blooded creatures of the bay bottom—the chill of autumn, now so close at hand, would bring reduced activity. The history of this time of decreased food and slowed-down growth would be written on the scale rings and shell ridges of fish and shellfish. The changes of fall would run through all this world of shallow bays. The consequences of altered temperature would be apparent among all the interlinking forms of life. But nowhere is the delicate relationship between temperature and growth more dramatically re-vealed than in the activity of the eelgrass itself. It is a classic example of botany.

In his exhaustive monograph, *Morphological and Pheno-logical Notes on Zostera Marina,* published by the University of Chicago, William Albert Setchell gives the story in detail. Throughout winter the eelgrass is in a condition of cold rigor, alive but vegetatively inactive. In spring, as soon as the warming water reaches 50 degrees F., growth begins and seeds germinate. But the mercury has to rise nine more degrees, to 59 degrees, before the underwater flowers bloom. Between 59 and 68 degrees, the flowers are fertilized, seed is set and new rhizomes are produced. Then at the 68-degree mark the plant becomes inactive again, remaining in a condition of heat rigor throughout the hot months of summer. Thus, almost as though controlled by a delicate electric thermostat, its activity during these weeks of growth and reproduction is governed by the position of the mercury. Below 50 degrees the plant is quies-cent; between 50 and 59 it is growing, in its vegetative period; between 59 and 68 it is flowering, in its reproductive period; above 68 it is inactive again. In the autumn the eelgrass slips from heat rigor into cold rigor without a second time of growth. This transition from one period of quiescence into another would be taking place over wide stretches of the bay bottom during the weeks to follow, weeks in which we would be mov-ing westward across the continent-wide sweep of autumn.

Late that night when I switched off my underwater flash-light and removed my face mask and swim-fins and waded ashore, I followed for a time the moonglade that extended in a shining silver path across the water. It was a fitting trail out of these forests of the sea.

THREE

SWALLOW CLOUDS

THE season of summer extends to about September 21 but the summer season ends with Labor Day. Then the newspapers begin referring to summer in the past tense. Vacations are over. Schools commence. To the popular mind, September belongs to autumn as December belongs to winter.

This unofficial beginning of the fall lay behind us as we ran down the New Jersey coast, advancing another 250 miles to Cape May and the drowned river of the Delaware estuary. The air was hazy and heavy under the blaze of the morning sun. We crept through the Long Island suburbs, threaded our way among the sweltering canyons of New York, dipped under the Hudson and emerged amid all the villainous smells of that caldron and retort and crucible of the east, the miles and miles of factories west of the river. Then we were out in open country, on U.S. 1, following the same road that had carried us south, on a February day, to begin our travels with the spring.

Now along that road Queen Anne's lace was going to seed, balling up like fingers closing into a fist. Already a few tupelos had turned a deep and winy red. And out of all the grassclumps arose the steely murmur of the insects, the song of autumn that was to accompany us from coast to coast.

By the time we reached the pine barrens of central New Jersey thunderheads had boiled up around the horizon and vultures pitched and banked in a stormy wind. We passed Forked River and Cedar Run and the purplish, gust-worried water at the mouth of Mullica River under darkening skies. And when, just south of the Mason and Dixon line, we came to old Cape May, the scene of Alexander Wilson's pioneer observations and a mecca for generations of autumn bird watchers, the rain was already a gray curtain over the ocean.

That night the tail end of a hurricane that had headed inland through the Carolinas reached Cape May. We watched the seething white tumult of the surf from an upper room in an old inn facing the sea. All that wild and windy night the rain and spray, the flying foam and driven sand whipped and battered the windowpanes.

We had first looked from those windows nearly fifteen autumns before. Then we were making our initial visit to this far-southern tip of New Jersey, this eighteen-mile point of land thrusting south-southwest with the Atlantic rolling in on one side and the wide Delaware Bay stretching away on the other. Here pirates had once landed to fill their casks with fresh water at Lake Lily. Here, in the heyday of its 150 years as a summer resort, had come Abraham Lincoln and Henry Clay and Horace Greeley and U. S. Grant. Its spacious verandas and lacelike grillwork speak of another age of architecture. Henry Ford, near the turn of the century, had ridden at the wheel of a racing car on the packed sand of its miles of beach. In the swamps of the cape, "cedar mining" had once been a flourishing business with "shingle miners" unearthing blown-down, long buried trees that still contained sound and usable wood. At one time, it is said, Independence Hall in Philadelphia was shingled with cedar mined from the swamps of Cape May.

But to the naturalist Cape May means above all else birds in the autumn. It is one of the great bottlenecks of the Atlantic Coast Flyway. At the tip of the peninsula eleven miles of water extend across Delaware Bay to the high dunes of Cape Henlopen. West across the bay from Cape May Point the distance is twenty miles. To find a crossing of less than eleven miles a bird would have to travel forty miles up the wide Delaware estuary. So, at certain times the migrants, reluctant to venture over the water lest they be driven out to sea by the wind, pile up near the tip of the point in spectacular concentrations. On September 1, 1920, Witmer Stone, author of *Bird Studies at Old Cape May*, counted eighty-six species on a walk along the bay side of the point. Even as late as December 22, the 1935 Christmas census of the Delaware Valley Ornithological Club yielded 111 species. On October 27 of that same year members of a National Audubon Society field trip to the point piled up 123 species. Seventeen years went by before, on September 21, 1952, a party led by Julian K. Potter raised that figure by one to the present record total of 124 species seen in a single day.

While the storm pounded the shingled walls and rattled the windows that night Nellie and I recalled our other visits in the fall to this historic cape. We remembered the time migrating hordes of monarch butterflies embrowned whole branches as they clung to the Spanish oaks within the circle at Cape May Point. We remembered a distant cloud of thousands of sanderlings that appeared and disappeared, flashing like a myriad twinkling lights each time the shorebirds turned and their white underparts caught the sun. We recalled a morning beside Lake Lily when we looked directly up into a revolving wheel of broad-winged hawks, 200 or more circling together, rising higher and higher until the wheel dissolved and all the buteos streamed away toward the distant dunes of Henlopen. We spoke of such things. Recollections of other autumns returned. And as we talked we remembered also a congenial companion on other visits to the cape.

An idea I have encountered from time to time—an idea that no doubt has been carefully nurtured by authors—is the belief that an author is an interesting, exciting person compared to a publisher grubbing among cost sheets, waybills and forms relating to the excess profits tax. The fact is that this companion, Raymond T. Bond, is both a publisher and one of the most complexly interesting men we know. I remember a time when we all started for Cape May late in the afternoon. I had just turned in an index after working night and day and there apparently was some doubt concerning my ability to stay awake at the wheel as we rode hour after hour through the night. But Bondie talked. He talked almost all the way—wonderful recollections so engrossing they kept me wide awake and the car safely on the road.

Who else do we know who ever had a relative who began reading the *Encyclopedia Britannica* from end to end and got through "D" and ever afterwards was amazingly learned in conversation so long as the topics ranged from A to D? Who else ever heard of two unliterary ladies known in their family circle as "The Little-Read Aunts"? Who else ever disconcerted a thug who stepped from behind a tree on a dark street by brushing past with the words: "Sorry, I haven't got a match"? Who else ever had an ancestor who befriended Victor Hugo in exile and was rewarded by appearing in the cast of characters of *Toilers of the Sea?* Or for that matter, being a teetotaler, who else ever had a middle name meaning "Wine Taster"? Certainly no one else ever proved, eruditely and to our satisfaction, that hell is a place where there are no birds by quoting Virgil's famous line from the sixth book of the *Aeneid:* "Easy is the descent to Hell—Facilis descensus Averno." Avernus, Virgil's portal to Hades—a noxious lake in the Italian Campania where fumes were supposed to kill all birds flying overhead—received its name from the Greek *Aornos, a* not, and *ornos* or *ornis,* a bird. So it seemed an eminently logical step to Bond, who has been an avid bird watcher since boyhood, that hell should thus be construed to be a place without birds and a place without birds to be hell.

By morning the storm had largely spent itself. The surf was high but the clouds were breaking. September, a month that along the Middle Atlantic States has fewer days of rain than June, July or August, was reverting to normal. After a quick breakfast in a restaurant where the waitress asked us if we wanted "white or tan bread" we wandered down the side roads of a dripping landscape, into a day of swallow clouds.

By July, each year, the white-breasted tree swallows begin congregating in the coastal marshes of the northeastern states. Their numbers are so great that they sometimes festoon telephone wires, sitting side by side literally for miles on end. Hence a colloquial name: "Wire Birds." Their fall migration, beginning early, is a leisurely drifting down the map. Traveling by day, feeding on the wing, they loiter along the road. If a tree swallow's flight were straightened out it would cover a good many miles in a day. Harold B. Moore, a physician of Harrisburg, Pennsylvania, reported in *The Auk* in the early 1930's that a migrating tree swallow, flying beside his car down a straight road on a windless day, advanced steadily at a speed of twenty-five miles an hour. But most of the time the great flocks of the early swallows pause and advance, move south little by little.

Paradoxically they are one of the first to gather for migration and one of the last to go. In fact some never go. On December 31, the final day of the year, several tree swallows were seen feeding on bayberries and flitting over frozen Lake Lily at Cape May Point. This is the only species of swallow to be reported every week in the year from the New York region. I have sometimes found a hundred or more overwintering among the phragmites and bayberry bushes of the Jones Beach area on the south shore of Long Island.

During late August and early September, especially when the prevailing gentle, southerly breezes are supplemented for a day or so by winds from the northwest, tremendous numbers of tree swallows pile up near the tip of Cape May. This is the first spectacular bird event of fall. Roosting by night among the canebrakes of the phragmites, with as many as four or five swallows clinging to a single reed, and supplementing their insect fare by day with the frosty-gray berries of the wax myrtle or bayberry, they build up the fat that will provide fuel for the later, longer flights of autumn. Not only are birds at their peak in numbers in the fall but they are at their peak in weight. If you could weigh the southbound migrants of an American autumn, you would have more pounds of birds than at any other time of year.

We were heading for the western side of the point—where a concrete ship still lies where it ran aground in World War I and where water-smoothed bits of quartz, "Cape May diamonds," are scattered through the sand—when we came within sight of the first multitude of swallows. Over a wide expanse of open ground they formed a living cloud, acres in extent, continually in motion, continually changing form, swirling this way and that like windblown smoke. The cloud rose and fell. It elongated and contracted. It condensed and grew vaporous. It scudded low across the ground, zoomed as though caught in a violent updraft. Thousands of separate birds were lost in the group movement, lifting, veering, diving, together.

There was something hypnotic, something deeply stirring in the sight. Swarm was the word that came instantly to mind. This teeming cloud of birds not only suggested a swarm of bees but there was something about their wild abandon, their holiday mood, that was akin to the spirit of the honeybees when they leave the hive on the great communal adventure of their lives.

We tried to estimate the number of birds in the moving cloud before us. Perhaps if, like some members of the Linnaean Society in New York, we had trained ourselves by dumping rice grains on a tabletop, estimating the number and then counting them, we might have had better success. As it was we settled for the rather vague term, "many thousands." Without doubt there are oftentimes more than 10,000 white-breasted swallows in one of these Cape May concentrations.

John James Audubon, in the first volume of his *Ornithological Biography*, describes how overwintering tree swallows along the estuaries of the Mississippi in Louisiana flew in dense masses low over the water at dawn. During these flights, he added, numbers of the birds were often killed by canoe men "with the mere aid of their paddles." These beautiful and beneficial swallows at one time were sold for food in the New York market. Alexander Wilson recalls, in his *American Ornithology*, an instance in which a meat-gunner near Cape May fired into a cloud of tree swallows, killing or maiming 102 birds with a single shot. Such slaughter, once familiar to the cape, is now a thing of the past. But even today that ancient, and currently self-righteous, enmity of the human predator for the avian predator persists and every Cape May autumn is still tainted with the senseless slaughter of hawks for sport and so-called food.

The cloud of the swallows drifted away. Later we saw this same concentration again and, driving northward up the cape, at least two other swallow-swarms—one over pastureland, the other above a wide salt meadow where a river entered the sea. All the evolutions on this day were comparatively low in the sky but sometimes a cloud of swallows will ascend up and up until the individual birds are nearly lost to sight. Several times, here and there, we came upon small groups resting and feeding on the bayberry bushes. So voracious are these autumn swallows for the gray, waxy fruit that as many as forty-one bayberries have been found in the digestive system of a single bird.

There were, that day, various other early migrants—redstarts, veeries, sharp-shinned hawks, red-breasted nuthatches. We saw them among the bushes and trees along the roads, near the seventy-foot Cape May Lighthouse and amid the sorry wreckage of the Witmer Stone Wildlife Sanctuary, blighted by chemical dust from the high chimneys of the neighboring magnesite plant. But this was our tree-swallow day. Above all else it was the swallow clouds, the thousands upon thousands of white-breasted, dark-winged birds swirling and scudding in unison, that made this particular one of the traditional "thirty golden days of September" so memorable. The swallows of Cape May formed our outstanding recollection of the Atlantic Coast Flyway, that first of the four great paths of migration down the North American continent.

While we would be working west toward and across the other three, the flood of migrant birds would mount at Old Cape May. Some, like the knots, would follow a narrow lane close to the edge of the sea; others, like the thrushes and kinglets and warblers, would be moving south on a wide advancing front. It is these latter birds that are swept into the long pocket of the cape by northwest winds in the night. Many of them are carried out to sea and lost. Others, when dawn breaks, find themselves still within sight of land and are able to come ashore. I remember one morning when a steady parade of sharp-shinned hawks, hours long, came in from the sea. So numerous were they that we sometimes had half a hundred within sight at the same time.

On another occasion, when a great wind from the northwest was booming over the boardwalk at Cape May on a September night, I came upon a little kinglet fluttering against a lighted window of the Municipal Pier. I caught it, holding it loosely in my hand, and felt the violent pounding of its tiny heart. Suddenly it fluttered; the wind tore it from my grasp; it disappeared in an instant, whirled away across the white surf, out over the tumultuous sea, a small, doomed bird in the midst of a night of terror. In that moment I remembered the many times during these autumn expeditions when I had wished for a wind from the northwest to concentrate birds at Cape May. And I regretted every wish. At such times we see only the survivors. We miss the many small migrants that, helpless in the wind and dark, are carried to death at sea.

Although we found no "Cape May diamonds" along the sandy western shore of the point, that day, we did glimpse something far more precious, an avian jewel once given up for lost, a bird that was listed half a century ago as totally extirpated in the state, a snowy egret passing overhead in buoyant flight. Another persecuted species at one time familiar here but now long gone is the whooping crane. With hardly more than a score of individuals in the world today, it is making a final stand at the Aransas Wildlife Refuge in southern Texas. Yet hardly more than a hundred years ago it sailed on seven-and-a-half-foot, white, black-tipped wings above this very shore. It fed among the sea meadows and marshes near by. Sometimes it even overwintered in the swamps of the Cape May region.

We wondered if any of these stately birds had been on the shore that late April day in 1808 when the dismasted, storm-battered *Halcyon*, bound from Liverpool to Philadelphia, dragged itself past the cape into the estuary of the Delaware. At the rail was a young ex-apprentice printer and amateur naturalist, Thomas Nuttall, come "to explore the natural history of the United States." Nearly thirty-five years later he recalled that moment: "The beautiful robing of forest scenery, now bursting into vernal life, was exchanged for the monotony of the dreary ocean, and the sad sickness of the sea. As we sailed up the Delaware my eyes were riveted on the landscape with intense admiration. All was new! The life, like that of the season, was then full of hope and enthusiasm."

Fatherless at twelve, apprenticed to a printer-uncle at fourteen, Nuttall was twenty-two at the time he passed between "the capes of the Delaware" and entered the New World. A self-taught naturalist, he knew so little of American plants that when, on his first walk, he encountered the common smilax, or greenbriar, he exclaimed: "Egad, a passion flower!" Yet within less than a quarter of a century Nuttall was curator of the Botanic Garden at Harvard University, a Fellow of the

Linnaean Society of London and author of the celebrated *A Manual of the Ornithology of the United States and Canada*, a book not only filled with original observations but still enjoyed for the charm of its style. "None," John James Audubon declared, "can describe the songs of our different species like Nuttall." The oldest bird club in America, the Nuttall Ornithological Club of Cambridge, Massachusetts, bears his name. His writings in the field of botany are basic and, as a plant explorer, he added more new species to the lists of science than any other man in America.

In 1810, two Aprils after he first saw the wooded shores of Delaware Bay, he set off alone for the interior. Ignorant of woodcraft, unable to shoot or even swim, robbed by Indians, racked by ague, once so bitten by mosquitoes he was thought to have smallpox and was turned away from every door, Nuttall wandered for a year and a half along the Great Lakes, up the Missouri and down the Mississippi. Like some scientific Adam he collected new, unknown plants in the botanical Eden of the wilderness.

Eight years later he roamed through the wild Arkansas country where no scientific man had ever been before, traveling 5,000 miles in sixteen months and returning laden with rich stores of specimens. Then in 1834 with the young ornithologist, John K. Townsend, he accompanied the expedition of Captain Nathaniel Wyeth over the Rockies to the mouth of the Columbia, sailed for Hawaii and, later, returned to Boston on the same ship that brought Richard Henry Dana home after his two years before the mast.

Dana's fellow sailors nicknamed Nuttall "Old Curious." His appearance was striking. Of medium height, slightly stooped, he had a noticeably large head. He was completely bald and his gray eyes looked out from beneath overhanging brows. Naturally economical, he paid scant attention to dress. He never married and was excessively shy. At the Harvard Botanic Garden he cut a trapdoor in the ceiling of his study so he could

, COOT, moving south with the autumn, often spend the winter feeding amid the great spatter-dock leaves in southern swamps.

MOODS of autumn are reflected in the morning mist, previous
two pages; and, above, heavy dew, fallen leaves, frost and ice.

climb a ladder to his bedroom without entering the hall outside. His meals were served on a tray pushed beneath a flap,
hinged at the top and with buttons at the bottom, that was
installed on his door. When absorbed in his studies, these
meals were often ignored. Everything else was forgotten. Once
when the Wyeth expedition was in hostile Indian country and
a band of braves appeared and all members of the party prepared to defend themselves, it was discovered that Nuttall's
gun was useless. The muzzle was packed with hardened mud.
He had been using the barrel for digging plants.

When Nuttall was 56, his printer-uncle died without immediate heirs and willed Nutgrove, his country place in Lan-
cashire, to the naturalist with the proviso that he live there
nine months of every year. Reluctantly, accepting mainly for
the benefit of his sisters, he returned to England writing sadly
at the time: "I must now bid a long adieu to the New World,
its sylvan scenes, its mountains, wilds and plains, and hence-
forth, in the evening of my career, I return, almost an exile, to
the land of my nativity." His far, adventurous wanderings were
over; as a small landed proprietor he spent the last seventeen
uneventful years of his life.

The trail of this remarkable man—which we thus first encountered at Cape May—was one that we were to cross many
times in our travels with the fall, at the western end of Lake
Erie, by the Fox River in Wisconsin, up the Missouri, along
the Columbia, in the highlands of the continent. During weeks
to come we would remember Thomas Nuttall many times, in
many places.

It was late that afternoon when, north of Great Egg Harbor,
with swallow clouds left behind, we swung to the west, across
the pine barrens, through a great gossamer shower where
George Washington had crossed the Delaware, over the rolling land of eastern Pennsylvania with hills starred in the sunset
by drifting thistledown. We were leaving the coast now, traveling toward the interior, as in ages past evolving life had crept

from the waves and moved onto the land. The sea and the smell of the sea were behind us. We would encounter them again only on the far side of the continent, at a tide-line we had never seen before, thousands of wandering miles away.

FOUR

THE LONG VALLEY

STANDING in the autumn sunshine amid the lichen-spattered jumble of Tuscarora sandstone at the top of Hawk Mountain, in eastern Pennsylvania, we had watched in other years a parade of soaring migrants. On set wings the hawks had drifted or scudded by. They rode as on an invisible tide that swept them down the long ridge in a great curve toward the south. The trail they followed was the same autumn pathway their ancestors had used long before the *Santa Maria* crossed from the Old World to the New. It was a trail that, all down the Endless Mountain, provided supporting updrafts that enabled southbound hawks to cover hundreds of miles with scarcely a wingbeat.

As the migrants had grown small in the distance we had followed them in imagination. We had pictured the invisible sheets and columns of rising air on which they soared. We had felt, in fancy, the thrust of the updrafts against outspread wings. We had debated how they steered their course, choosing the aerial path best suited to their needs. We had conjured up the scene that unrolled beneath them as they sailed on and on down the length of the Great Valley, through five states, keeping to their ancient pathway through the autumn skies.

These things we had imagined. Now imagining was past. Now the ridge curved away—green below, blue in the distance—beneath our wings. Now we experienced at intervals the hard updrive of the invisible air currents. Now we were seeing, as the hawks saw, the forested wall of rock, the patchwork of valley fields moving past below us. That morning we had taken off in a light plane from the Harrisburg airport. We were following, for a hundred miles and more, the aerial road of the hawks.

The night before we had stayed at Camp Hill across the Susquehanna from Harrisburg. Through the years a good many friends I have never met, those who have read my books and written to me afterward, have invited me to visit them. I remember one year calculating that the mileage involved in such invitations, impossible to accept, was almost as much as the diameter of the earth. One of the longest standing of these friends-by-letter was William T. Clapp, of Camp Hill. We had accepted his suggestion that we stay overnight with him and his wife, Marion, on our way west. The evening had passed in pleasant recollections of things seen in the woods and in watching remarkable motion pictures of pileated woodpeckers taken by William Rhein. It was close to midnight when we went to bed. But we were out early, keyed up for the hawkway adventure that lay ahead.

By ten o'clock we were airborne. In a long curving climb Johnny Abiuso's green-bodied, silver-winged Beechcraft Bonanza carried us up to 3,000 feet. Beyond the left wing—with "N8568N" painted in black on silver—I could see the shining serpentine of the Susquehanna flowing down its corridor through the ridges. Smoking factory chimneys, rows of red- and green-roofed houses, the sooty spider web of a railroad yard steadily grew smaller below us. Like an expanding ring on water the horizon pushed back as we climbed.

At two miles a minute we headed north. Looking like some Roman aqueduct in the distance, the longest stone arch span in America, the railroad bridge over the Susquehanna at Harrisburg, drifted away behind us. Ahead, out of the hazy distance, the curving green waves of parallel ridges a thousand feet high dragged their immense lengths across the landscape—Blue Mountain, Second Mountain, Peters Mountain—with the titanic furrows of the valleys between. We crossed over the first ridge. High above it the plane lifted and dropped on swells of bumpy air, disturbed by the updrafts.

This easternmost of the ridges—the Endless Mountain or Kittatinny Ridge of the Indians, now officially called Blue Mountain—swings in an arc from east central to south central Pennsylvania. It is the most eastern of the Appalachian chain. Its towering wall of sandstone forms the escarpment of the folded Appalachian mountains. Under various names, bordering the Great Valley, it extends almost without a break from New York's Shawangunk Mountain, on the north, to Mt. Oglethorpe, in Georgia, on the south. Down the Pennsylvania length of the ridge, in former times, ran the Tuscarora Path of the Shawnee Indians. Today, the most famous of modern footpaths, the Appalachian Trail, follows its crest. And in the air—unmarked and trackless, far older than the Tuscarora Path or the Appalachian Trail—the road of the hawks parallels the ridge.

"When the wind is strong," Abiuso told us, "especially when it blows from the northwest, it is really rugged up here." At such times the same winds that fill the pocket of Cape May strike the Kittatinny Ridge at right angles and shoot upward in a powerful ascending flow. The greatest hawk flights occur on such days between late August and mid-November. Then, Abiuso says, he flies high not only to be above the turbulent air but also to avoid hitting the hawks. The weight of a golden eagle or one of the larger hawks would be sufficient to damage a wing or shatter a windshield. Mostly the hawks fly low. But once, when mist hid the ground, he came abreast of a large flock of Canada geese winging south at an altitude of more than 4,500 feet.

As the warmth of the morning increased the sky over the valley was sown with small cumulus clouds. To escape the bumps of the heated rising columns that formed them, we climbed to 5,000 feet. There we rode in a tranquil sky. We flew north, curving toward the east as the ridges curved. Across the valley below, where the cloud-shadows moved, the fields of the farms varied endlessly in shape and size and color. They seemed, viewed from the air, laid out haphazardly without rhyme or reason. Yet behind each boundary line lay the logic of topography, the weight of legal decision, the chance of inheritance, the story of expanding success or contracting misfortune.

The forested ridges were green now with only here and there an isolated splash of color. But all down their lengths, a few weeks hence, they would be gaudy with the vivid, lavish hues of autumn foliage. Far below us, along the skirts of the Kittatinny Ridge, we caught glimpses of lonely little farms snipped from the forest. At long intervals the path of a power line ran in a narrow, cleared band up and over the top. And, as the summit of this Endless Mountain moved past below our right wing, curious openings began appearing in the forest. They were sometimes square, sometimes rectangular, sometimes curving. Sometimes they turned back upon themselves. They looked like hieroglyphics or Mayan ruins on the ridgetop. They puzzled us at the time. Abiuso said he had begun to notice them only a few years before. Later I learned their meaning. The clearings were made by the Pennsylvania Game Commission to provide feeding areas along the top of the ridge for deer, wild turkeys and other forms of wildlife.

We passed Indiantown Gap and the dark Swatara River, Pine Grove and Summit Station. Hamburg and the gray line of U.S. Highway 22 lay to the southeast as we passed over the nestling village of Drehersville and crossed the coal-laden Little Schuylkill River. Then suddenly the white, tumbled sandstone of the Hawk Mountain lookout burst into view. A dozen persons stood among the rocks. Their binoculars swung in our direction. This was Hawk Mountain as tens of thousands of migrating hawks had seen it.

We cut in above the ridge and curved back, skimming out over the lip of the 1,000-foot drop. Three times we circled the promontory. Many a hawk, I remembered, had seen that rocky height we looked down upon as its last sight on earth. Within the space of this tight circle of our plane, passing hawks had been blinded, blown to pieces, maimed, or with a shattered wing had fallen through space in days when the Tuscarora slabs bristled with shotguns. Here, at this world-famous sanctuary, hawk-watchers have replaced hawk-gunners. But this promontory is but one of eleven points along the Kittatinny Ridge where the passing migrants were shot for sport. And only here has the killing stopped. The shooting still continues at all the other ten. A succession of sanctuaries, a chain of Hawk Mountains running the Pennsylvania length of the ridge, is needed to halt this autumn slaughter.

As we curved away, straightening out for the return flight, we waved to the hawk-watchers.

"If they don't see any hawks today," Nellie said, "they can put down two migrating Teales."

As a matter of fact, Maurice Broun, curator at Hawk Mountain since it was established, told us later that on that September day, eighty-three hawks passed the lookout. Forty-nine were broadwings, six sharpshins, two redtails, four marsh hawks, three ospreys and seventeen sparrowhawks. Represented by single individuals were the bald eagle and the peregrine falcon.

Flying south, down the path of the migrants, we studied the air currents. We cruised along the summit and at either side. We vaulted back and forth over the top, first from one direction then from the other. Abiuso, long experienced with the air currents of the hawk ridges, showed us where the upthrust was strongest. This came not at the exact summit but a little back of it. When a northwest wind strikes the wall of the ridge it shoots up and over in a vaulting arc. The current thus deflected sometimes rises into the sky as much as four times the height of the ridge. Beyond its high point this comber of the air drops in a swift descent. A lightplane pilot, inexperienced in the region, may narrowly escape crashing into the tree tops when caught in the grip of this powerful downdraft.

On this day the breeze was light and mainly from the north. We passed—and saw in fleeting glimpses—hawks soaring down the ridges. On such days of little wind the birds tend to follow a path farther out over the valley where the thermal currents rising from the sun-heated fields give them added lift. But whether a hawk is riding on thermals or slope-winds it is always gliding downward. The spiraling bird that mounts on set wings up and up into the sky is really descending all the time through the air. It is circling on a downward cork-screw path within a column of air that rises faster than it descends. It is like a man walking slowly down the steps of a rapidly rising escalator.

In the fall of 1942, Maurice Broun and Ben V. Goodwin timed the speed of passing hawks over a two-thirds-of-a-mile course at Hawk Mountain. Fourteen species and 152 individuals were clocked by the two men. Their soaring speed ranged from sixteen to eighty miles an hour. The average rate of speed for all the hawks was thirty miles an hour. The holder of the top record was an osprey. It was soaring south in a particularly powerful updraft. Without losing altitude the bird was, in reality, diving steeply all the way.

Most of the time the hawks avoid the more violent, turbulent updrafts. In their long slide down the ridge that stretched away before us, I suspect that they set their course through rising air that will enable them to glide at normal cruising speed, so to speak, without losing altitude. Always nosing down, always using the motive power of gravity, they adjust their soaring speed by the steepness of their glide. I have watched red-tailed hawks cross the slight gap before Hawk Mountain and then, as they reached the stronger updrafts of the ridgeside, tilt slightly downward and increase their speed without loss of height. By employing the air currents that will carry them upward at the same rate that they descend the migrating hawks ride for hundreds of miles down the valley with altitude unchanged.

The wing-loading of hawks, the relation of weight to wing surface, is a factor in their speed and in the strength of the updrafts needed to support them. Among these birds this element varies considerably. When Earl L. Poole, some years ago, published in *The Auk* the weights and wing areas of various American birds, his figures showed that a goshawk may have a wing-loading nearly twice that of a sparrowhawk and a peregrine falcon three times that of a marsh hawk. Oftentimes on days of strong winds—when the birds fly lower and closer to the ridge—the migrants pass Hawk Mountain soaring with wings partially closed, adjusting their surface and wing-loading to the conditions of the time.

Out over the valley, when we were halfway down the ridge, we saw one of the most lightly loaded of all the soaring birds, a turkey vulture. It rocked and turned among the thermals a full 1,500 feet above the ground. Even feeble updrafts will carry these broad-winged birds aloft. From one rising current to another they make long, shallow glides across the sky. But on days of heavy winds these lightly loaded birds are at a disadvantage. They lack the weight to give them ballast and stability.

A bird in the wind—that, to the average person, is one of the most confusing aspects of avian flight. "It is a well-known fact," a reader wrote in the correspondence column of *The New York Herald Tribune* in the summer of 1955, "that birds rest, when possible, by letting the winds carry them along." And in a U.S. Department of Agriculture bulletin, published in 1935, there occurs the sentence: "Even strong winds that blow in the direction of aerial travel are unfavorable for the birds, as they interfere with their balance and disarrange their feathers." Both these statements are based on a fundamental misconception of the relationship of the bird and the wind. They are derived from the viewpoint of the ground rather than from the bird's viewpoint in the air.

A bird does not drift through the sky like a thistle seed, or a gust-blown piece of paper. It does not float on the wind as a chip drifts downstream on water. It does not rest on the air: it flies by moving through it. It must maintain a certain minimum speed to support it. This it achieves either by the muscular effort of moving wings or by using the power of gravity in gliding—which becomes soaring when the air around the gliding bird is moving upward as fast as or faster than the bird moves down. Only during the comparatively infrequent instances of hovering and when fluttering down to a landing does the bird drop below this minimum forward speed. It maintains it whether flying with or against the wind. And in either case its speed *through the air* is the same.

For a bird in the wind is like a man in the coach of a speeding express train. The car may be rushing over the rails a mile a minute. Yet as the man looks about him within the coach everything is standing still. He and the coach are moving at the same speed. So it is with the bird in the wind except that the bird cannot, like the man, sit down or remain passive. It has to maintain its minimum speed for normal flight. But this it can do moving in any direction. It advances as though in a calm, as though it were in fact flying this way and that within the moving railway coach. There is no more pressure on it when it moves in one direction than when it heads in another. When flying in and out of winds the bird feels the changing pressures. But when it is in the heart of the moving air it has no more sensation of meeting the force of the gale when it flies in the direction from which it blows than a man has of feeling the weight of the train pushing against him when he walks back along the aisle. The bird can no more be struck by the wind than the man can be struck by the train on which he is riding. The moving mass of air in a wind carries the bird with it. It may sweep it far off its course. But it does not push against the bird. There is no pressure on it when it is riding with the moving air. It is being transported by the wind as the car transports its passengers. For the bird in the wind the whole sky is moving and it is moving with it and it flies as in air that is calm.

Looking down at the ridge below our Beechcraft Bonanza, winging its way back to Harrisburg, we saw the steady slide of the trees slipping to the rear. The rate of their movement, our speed over the ground, was an entirely different matter from our speed through the air. In ground speed—both for us and for the bird—the direction and force of the wind do play an important part.

If we may return for one last time to our old friend, the man on the mile-a-minute express: Sitting still he is moving over the ground at sixty miles an hour. If he leaves his seat and walks ahead along the aisle at five miles an hour he is moving over the ground that much faster, or sixty-five miles an hour. If he turns and walks back along the aisle at the same pace he subtracts five miles from his speed over the ground, reducing it to fifty-five miles an hour. All the while the man himself in the coach is moving only five miles an hour. Similarly the bird advances at its own speed within the "coach" of the moving wind. But its rate of progress *over the ground*—as opposed to its speed through the air—leaps ahead or lags behind according to the direction of its flight and the movement of the wind.

Twenty miles from Harrisburg we crossed the ridge for a final time and curved out over the far-famed fertile fields of the Lebanon Valley. Our shadow trailed across patches of tasseled corn that looked like shaggy rugs cut into squares and rectangles; over orchards with little rows of round twig masses seen in two dimensions; down the length of a pasture where a flock of crows, no larger than flakes of soot, trailed down to land among toy cattle, red and white and black. Once, far below us, we sighted a green field strewn with a multitude of minute, white, elongated objects like kernels of rice. Only after we had flown past and looked back at an oblique angle did we see that the kernels were flocks of white hens feeding at a poultry farm.

Then the Roman aqueduct of the railroad bridge drew near, the red- and green-roofed houses spread out below us, the dark flow of the Susquehanna passed beneath our wings and, with idling engine, we soared on and on to touch at last the long black strip of the runway. I looked back at the curve of the Endless Mountain. We had seen it from the viewpoint of the airborne hawk. Now its 1,000-foot wall reared against the sky—its normal aspect for human eyes. Later that same afternoon we were to see it from still a third point of view. On the Pennsylvania Turnpike, heading west toward the Ohio line, we watched the ridge expand upward into the air ahead of us. We saw it tower directly above us. Then in a rush its exterior disappeared to be supplanted by the mole's-eye view of a tunnel that burrowed through the solid rock of its base. When we emerged on the other side and sped on, the ancient pathway of the hawks, the Kittatinny Ridge, also lay behind us.

FIVE

THE AUTUMN STARS

DOWN the long, gradual decline of the Appalachian Plateau, far into Ohio, we rode next day. America is the Land of the Turning Wheel—a myriad wheels turning in factories, millions of wheels turning on the highways. Here in the Middle West, with its Akrons and Detroits, we were riding through one of the strongholds of the wheel. But here also we noted another side of America. That undercurrent of poetic feeling that runs through the great mass of men was revealing itself everywhere on place-signs and on rural mailboxes. Here, as all across the land, it was finding expression in the names bestowed by farmers on their homesteads: The Seven Pines, Hidden Acres, Long Furrow Farm, Willow Bend, Green Pastures, Killdee Farm, Far Hills, Hickory Stick Farm, The Windy Oaks, Meadow Lane Farm.

That morning we had started early. We met—as we were to meet in so many other dawns—the same sequence: the milkman, the bakeryman, the cats sitting beside doors; then the workmen waiting for busses, schoolchildren with books and lunches, and finally businessmen and salesmen on the road. The signs of autumn were all around us in this land of buckeyes and shagbark hickories. Teasels stood dry in the sunshine. Every larger pond held a coot or two, birds we could visualize among the great spatter-dock leaves of lower Florida where many spend their winter months. Everywhere across the open fields, browning the weed tops, ran the rust of autumn. Cut-

ting down the length of Ohio from east to west, we were cross
ing the path of monarch butterflies moving south. Once again
the coming of fall was ushering in one of the great insect migrations of the world.

This was September. This was the first of the "ber" months
of fall. Name aloud the twelve months of the year and you
will find that the four that comprise autumn, the only months
that end in "ber," have the most round and melodious sounds
of all—September, October, November, December. And three
of the four, appropriately for a time when the fires of the year
are dying down, end in "ember."

On this day we noticed many things. We saw a robin shoot
up and over a speeding automobile and speculated on how
many birds are saved from death by the streamlining of the
modern car. We observed how television antennas provide a
new kind of signpost—pointing ahead as we approached big
cities, pointing back after we had passed them by. About noon
we stopped at a filling station for gasoline. On the grass near
by lay a spotted dog sound asleep. The dog wore sunglasses.

"That," the attendant told us, "is the laziest dog in the
world. He sleeps all day long. Two hours ago I put those glasses
on him as a joke, and he doesn't even know they are there yet!"

Not long after we passed Broken Sword Creek, near Oceola,
we noticed a kind of toning to the woodlot trees. The creeping
hues of autumn had run along the edges while the inner trees
were green. This perhaps was due to the stronger winds at the
woodland's edge—for one scientist found that in the interior of
an Ohio woods the wind had been slowed down to one tenth
its velocity at the border—or it may have been the consequence of some local condition, some thermal belt or topographical effect such as we were to encounter all across the
autumn. There are always these little seasons within the seasons, little retreats and advances within the great retreats and
advances.

In the twilight that evening, just before we settled down for the night, we passed a vaguely seen bird in a dead treetop.

"A sparrow hawk," I said. "Or was it a flicker? It could have been a crow."

And we both laughed, recalling that favorite passage in the *Journal* of Henry Thoreau:

"November 1, 1853. Saw three of those birds . . . They must be either sandpipers, telltales . . . or plovers (?) Or may they be the turnstone?"

The next morning we rode the Lincoln Highway into Delphos. Less than thirty miles from the Indiana line, this Ohio town with its population of 6,000 lies on the old Miami and Erie Canal. At one time it was surrounded by extensive fields of clover and was known as The Honey Center of the World. Today its fame rests less on honey than on comets. For Delphos is the home of the noted comet collector Leslie C. Peltier. Searching the night sky from his cornfield and backyard observatories, he has discovered eleven comets, a record unequaled by any other amateur astronomer in America.

I found Peltier, near the western edge of Delphos, cutting his grass with a power mower. A slender man with graying hair and a quiet and engaging sincerity of manner, he was in his early fifties. He has been fascinated by the night sky since he was sixteen. That year he bought his first telescope, a thirty-power glass advertised in *The American Boy*. It cost eighteen dollars. We found ourselves on a common ground of experience when he recalled how he had earned those dollars. Long ago, as a small boy in the sandhill country of northern Indiana, I picked something like 20,000 strawberries, at two cents a quart, to earn my first camera. Peltier, too, had picked strawberries, at the same rate of pay, to earn his first telescope.

He brought it from the house, a spyglass with sliding tubes made by the A. S. Aloe Company, of St. Louis. It had arrived in July, right after the strawberry picking season had ended. I squinted into the eyepiece, looking at distant trees and a faraway passing plane. With the brass tubes fully extended, it gave a magnification of thirty diameters; with an auxiliary lens in place, the magnification was boosted to eighty diameters. This is the only telescope Peltier has ever owned. The two instruments he has used subsequently in his comet hunting were loaned him by Eastern universities. The first of these, a four-inch glass, was forwarded by Harvard University. The second, which he has used since 1923, is a six-inch telescope sent on loan by Princeton.

During the months that followed the arrival of the original spyglass, the sixteen-year-old farm boy contented himself with looking at the Milky Way and the rings of Saturn and the craters of the moon. No one else in all that region had any special interest in astronomy. Two years later one of his presents at Christmas was William Tyler Olcott's *Field Book of the Stars*. It was a footnote in this book that turned him to a serious study of the sky. It asked all readers interested in undertaking definite projects in star-watching to write to the author. Peltier did. As a result, at the age of eighteen, he began studying those pinpoints of brilliance that wax and wane in brightness—the variable or "flare" stars. He sent in his first variable-star report in March 1918 and he has not missed a month in all the years that have followed. This record of more than 400 months without a break is another distinction of his that is unapproached by any other amateur.

In 1925, two years after the Princeton telescope arrived, Peltier discovered his first comet. In the middle of the strawberry patch, which by then had become a cornfield, he had constructed, with his father's help, a nine-foot observatory with a revolving dome of galvanized sheet metal. We drove four miles east of Delphos that afternoon to see the discarded dome, which still lay like an immense white mushroom behind a red barn on the farm where Peltier spent his boyhood. He pointed out an old black-walnut tree that stood at the edge of the cornfield. Long ago, from the top of that tree, he had snapped a bird's-eye view of his observatory with a folding Kodak. It was

GOLDEN flowers are numerous in September. They include the black-eyed Susan, a native of the prairies, now widespread.

COMET HUNTER, Leslie Peltier, in his back-yard observatory.
Below, a male Kirtland's warbler bringing food to the nest.

from this observatory, on the night of November 13, 1925, that he saw the first of his eleven comets.

He had swung his telescope toward the constellation Hercules. Each pinpoint of brightness in that part of the sky was as familiar to him as the lights of the neighboring farmhouses. Instantly he noticed a spot of brilliance where no light had been on the night before. He studied it minute after minute for nearly an hour until there was no possibility of doubt. The far-away light was that great prize, dreamed of by every amateur astronomer, a new comet.

Peltier leaped on his bicycle and began pedaling four miles through the dark to Delphos. The official discoverer of a comet in America is the first to get word to the Harvard Observatory at Cambridge, Massachusetts. The telegraph office, when he reached it, was dark and deserted. He raced toward the signal tower of the Pennsylvania Railroad. There emergency telegrams could be dispatched at night. It was a little after midnight when breathlessly he reached the top of the stairs. A few minutes later his message was on the way. A Russian astronomer independently discovered the same comet. But that was four days later. Peltier's cornfield telescope was the first in the world to be trained on this speeding visitor in outer space.

"That was on Friday the thirteenth," he told me. "I'm not superstitious but I notice that on every Friday the thirteenth in November I look over the sky with special care."

For no reason that he can suggest, he has made more discoveries in February than in any other month of the year. So far he has never discovered a comet in December.

"Someday," he said, "I hope to get one in December as a special kind of Christmas present."

The reason he has found more new comets than any other amateur is, he believes, simple. No one else has spent so many hours hunting in the night skies. He has averaged more than an hour at his telescope for every clear night in the past thirty-six years. Even on nights of intermittent clouds he studies the heavens in the open spaces. On bright moonlit nights, when observation is impossible, he often gets up at two or three o'clock in the morning, after the moon has set, to spend an hour or two in comet hunting and variable-star watching, before going back to bed. We calculated the total time he has spent at the eyepiece of his telescope and found it came to more than 225 continuous days and nights of concentrated observation.

Because comets are brightest when nearest the sun, a favorite hunting ground for these heavenly bodies is the eastern sky just before dawn and the western sky just after sunset. Most comets are reported from these portions of the firmament. Peltier, however, spends little time searching there. All around the world observers have their telescopes trained on these spots. So he hunts elsewhere. As a consequence his finds are less likely to be anticipated by others. It was while thus engaged, searching the northern heavens near the Pole Star on the night of May 15, 1936, that he made his greatest discovery, a comet so brilliant that by July of that year it could be seen with the naked eye. In honor of the farm-boy astronomer it was named the Comet Peltier.

After he left the farm and moved to Delphos, where he is designer for a furniture factory, Peltier built his second observatory in his back yard. It is even smaller and more economical than the first. We walked out to it, a simple white box about six feet square, resting on a concrete foundation at the edge of a dahlia garden next to a patch of late sweet corn. The sheet metal of its flat roof was below the level of my eyes. This observatory, in which Peltier has discovered five of his comets, was made mainly from odds and ends. Its total cost was fifteen dollars—less than the amount paid for the original spyglass telescope.

He swung open the door. On hot summer nights it is held ajar by the pressure of a down-bent portion of the edge of the metal roof; in winter weather it is kept shut by means of a simple hook and eye. Everything about the observatory is unpretentious, often improvised. The "dew shield" at the end of the telescope is merely a sheet of corrugated cardboard held loosely around the barrel by a strand of wire. It can be slipped forward to protect the lens or pushed back along the barrel out of the way when the telescope is lowered into the box observatory and the opening in the roof is closed to make the interior watertight.

I peered inside. Just within the door one half of the front seat of a junkyard automobile had been mounted behind the eyepiece of the telescope. I eased myself into this seat and looked around the crowded interior. The counterweights on the telescope were pieces of lead from a discarded battery. Just in front of my knees there rose a steering wheel salvaged from another junked automobile. I turned it and the whole box of the observatory began rotating on small flanged wheels that followed the circle of a single rail mounted on the concrete foundation. Above my right hand a disk of wood carried a knob at its edge. Winding this disk elevated or depressed the end of the telescope. Elbow-high on my right, a shelf held a loose-leaf book of star maps and jottings on the backs of envelopes beneath a ten-watt photographic safelight in a crook-necked lamp. This faint illumination is all that is needed for making notes, and it does not affect Peltier's eyes sufficiently to upset his judgment of the comparative brilliance of distant stars. Thrust forward under the telescope, my feet rested on the bars of a shallow cage. It contained an old electric hot plate—a foot warmer for winter nights. Peltier, not infrequently, maintains his lonely vigil in zero weather and on at least one occasion he followed his hunting across the skies on a night when the thermometers stood at twenty degrees below zero.

I slid out of the seat and we walked back toward the house. That evening, as soon as it became dark, we planned to return to this telescope that had brought first intelligence to the world of the existence of nearly a dozen comets. Through it we would watch the autumn stars.

Amid the Everglades of Florida, at the start of our trip north with the spring, Nellie and I had seen the arc of the sun steadily mounting the sky. Now, in these latter months of the year, the movement was reversed. Day by day the course of the sun was descending, sinking steadily, if almost imperceptibly, into the south. Shadows at noon were growing longer. The astronomy of fall was ushering in the fall.

This third season, according to Greek mythology, was born of the Silver Age. First came the Golden Age when all the year was spring. Then, a step downward, followed the Silver Age. Spring shrank to a single season, and summer, autumn and winter came into being. Thus the ancients accounted for the four seasons of the year. Now we know that their source is rather the position of the tilted earth on its journey around the sun. At night, we see our shifting relationship to the center of our universe reflected in the course of the stars. Our fate, so far as it is affected by the seasons, is written in the sky. During these initial days of our travels westward, the movement of heavenly bodies—without haste, without pause—was bringing to the Northern Hemisphere the earliest of all the multiform changes of autumn.

The night before, we had watched the constellations stretching across a clear and brilliant firmament above the level darkness of an Ohio countryside. We had seen the "evening star" of this autumn sky, the planet Venus, hanging low in the west, just above the ebbing colors of the sunset, when twilight came. The nearest of all the planets, almost a twin of the earth in size, Venus is surrounded by a heavy blanket of silvery vapor. It is this vapor, reflecting the rays of the sun, that makes it the brightest planet in our sky—the "Splendor of Heaven" as the Arabs called it. Although the maximum light it reflects to earth is only about $\frac{1}{1,000}$ that of the full moon, it is concentrated into one small spot in the heavens. Venus as the "evening star" is a feature of the autumn sky of only certain years. But the rising of Orion, the brightest of the constellations, ascending higher and higher in the eastern sky each night, is a feature of every fall. The annual bluish swarm of meteors, the November Leonids, is another. But the greatest, the most far-reaching, event in the firmament during this season of the year is the apparent southward journey of the sun.

This illusion is owing to the fact that the axis of the earth, on which the globe spins, is tilted 23½ degrees away from vertical to the plane of the earth's orbit around the sun and always points in the same direction. In consequence, the Northern Hemisphere is inclined toward the sun in summer and away from it in winter. This fact, in combination with the curvature of the earth's surface, results in uneven heating at the same moment at various latitudes. The more vertical the rays, the more heat they bring to the surface of the planet. This is both because they travel through less heat-absorbing atmosphere and because they are spread over less area than are slanting rays striking the curved surface of the globe.

During autumn, the Northern Hemisphere progressively tilts more and more away from the sun. In spring, of course, the reverse takes place. Only twice a year—at the time of the spring and the autumnal equinox—do the rays of the sun fall vertically on the equator. The word equinox, coming from the Latin, means "equal night." On these two occasions only are day and night of approximately equal length all over the earth except near the poles. Autumn, incidentally, is warmer than spring. In fall, the hemisphere is slowly cooling off; in spring, it is slowly warming up. And there is a lag in both of these seasonal changes.

As we waited for evening to come to Delphos, that afternoon, the astronomy of the season was working toward an event 9,000 miles away above far-off Molucca Strait, near the island of Celebes, in the Dutch East Indies. There, 123 degrees, 21 minutes, 54 seconds longitude east of Greenwich, England, at 9:24 P.M., Eastern Standard Time, on a day not far distant now, the sun would reach the Celestial Equator. It would shine straight down on the lonely sea that forms this portion of the earth's equator. And for all the Northern Hemisphere, at that precise moment, autumn officially would begin.

At Delphos the evening came at last. And while the twilight deepened into darkness we lingered over the chicken, the hot biscuits, the muskmelons, the peach cobbler, the long train of dishes of a midwestern feast Mrs. Peltier had prepared. We listened to recollections of a time when Peltier, just married, made a living collecting rocks in the Southwest for the Ward's Natural History Establishment, of Rochester, N.Y. It was after eight o'clock when we finally started for the observatory. At that moment the great disappointment of the trip enveloped us. Ever since the storm at Cape May the skies had been clear. For half a month afterwards the nights were cloudless and brilliant with stars. On this one evening of all those many evenings, dense overcast had swiftly spread across the sky, sheeting it from horizon to horizon, making invisible every planet, blanketing every star.

It was a long time before I could accept the reality of this fact. Endlessly I turned the steering wheel that revolved the observatory. Endlessly I wound the wooden disk that raised and lowered the telescope. I was like a pilot caught above fog, seeking a hole through which to escape. Everything was one uniform blankness. Only once the telescope recorded light— a sudden glow of brilliant red like some rare heavenly body. It was the ruby warning lamp at the top of a radio tower.

At length I gave up. The looked-forward-to experience was not for us. We had, however, met a man of lasting interest and that was worth traveling far to find; we had made friends in Delphos. But the stars and planets still moved invisible behind their veil of overcast when we bade the Peltiers good-by that night. Yet, seen or unseen, by night and by day, we knew, the movement of these heavenly bodies across the firmament was foreshadowing all the impending changes of fall. The flow of the seasons already had altered its direction; we would feel its current quicken during the weeks ahead. For autumn advances like the rising tide. It has its warmer days and its days of increasing chill. Its waves move forward, then retreat. But all the while its average progress—like that of ocean water rising to the flood—is set in one direction.

SIX

BUTTERFLIES IN THE WIND

I F, on any map of Lake Erie, you run your finger eastward from below Detroit along the northern shore, you will come to a narrow wedge of land, thrusting nine miles out into the shallow waters. This is Point Pelee, the southernmost tip of the mainland of Canada. Its extremity is farther south than part or all of seventeen of the forty-eight states in the Union. Now a Canadian national park, Point Pelee has been famed for more than half a century as a kind of inland Cape May, a pocket into which countless migrants funnel during the autumn flight.

We came to the curved spit that forms its outer end early on a Monday morning. Behind us lay a wandering course from Delphos. We had crossed into Indiana to see, in a Fort Wayne yard, a descendant of one of the original Johnny Appleseed trees. We had followed the Maumee River northward through country where thornapple branches were red with autumn fruit and fox squirrels leaped, in glistening fur, from limb to limb. On Sunday evening we stopped at a small town just south of Detroit. The only restaurant open had the improbable name of The Sweetie Pie Diner. And the sole available item on its menu was the even more improbable dish of hamburger sandwiches dipped in chili con carne. A restless night followed and we were early on the road—early diving under the Detroit River, early popping up in Windsor, early crossing the Canadian countryside with its corn already in shocks.

A little after nine o'clock we stood alone on Point Pelee's tip where a sand and gravel spit trails off in a gentle curve toward the west. For a hundred yards its outer end was white with resting herring and ring-billed gulls. They rose in a fluttering cloud and moved away over the water into a wind that blew steadily from the south. Running down the sides of the spit two shining lines of white joined at the tip. Each line was a windrow of gull feathers pushed up on the sand by the waves.

As autumn approaches each year, the main molt of birds takes place. The breeding season is over. Plumage frayed while feeding and caring for the nestlings is replaced. All the migrants of fall ride south on fresh and unworn pinions. Birds that remain in the north develop not only new feathers but more feathers than they possessed in summer. All of the white flotsam here on the sand, these feathers of varied shapes and sizes, had fallen free in the process of molting. Some had been shed as the birds preened themselves at the edge of the sand; others had ridden the waves in from the open lake. During these September days, all across the land, how many tons of feathers were dropping silently onto land and water in a wide-scattered, unappreciated descent!

We followed one of these converging lines, stooping from time to time to pick up long primaries, stiff and strong; downy contour feathers; short wing coverts. They all represented one of the great turning points in evolution. It was when feathers developed from scales that birds departed from reptilian life. Feathers enabled them to become warm-blooded, providing an insulating layer that prevented body heat from dissipating, a thing that scales could never do. Being warm-blooded, they could remain active in cold weather when reptiles, of necessity, become dormant. They could spread into new regions, survive in greater numbers. The lightness and strength of the feather opened the way to the highest perfection of flight. It gave the evolving bird vastly increased mobility and freedom of movement. It permitted a rapid change of feeding grounds. It made possible the long and swift movements of migration. Thinking of the innumerable consequences of this turning point in evolution, I remembered J.B.S. Haldane's logical solution of the old conundrum: "Which came first, the bird or the egg?" The answer is the egg. Birds evolved from reptiles that laid eggs so the first bird must have hatched from an egg that came before it.

The last remnants of the prefeathered, prehistoric condition of birds is seen in the scaled legs of many species. Among feathers, the simplest and most primitive is the down that covers nestlings. It is formed by fingerlike projections that extend beyond the skin and split into filaments that move apart and harden. The thickest covering of such feathers occurs among birds like ducks and sandpipers in which the young leave the nest almost as soon as hatched. It is entirely absent in woodpeckers and hummingbirds. In at least one instance, that of the Australian bush turkey, the downy stage is passed through before the bird breaks from the shell. It is found only within the egg.

Each of the feathers in the white line stretching down the sand before us had begun with the growth of special cells in the epidermis of the bird's skin. As a nestling develops, a circle of cells around the base of each downfeather becomes active. These cells elongate. They form a column. They push the downfeather out of its socket and carry it farther and farther out from the skin at the end of the lengthening column. Eventually the downfeather is broken off and the column, the pinfeather, remains within its thin, horny sheath. As long as it is growing, a feather is connected with the blood supply of the bird. But when its growth is completed, the feather "sets." It becomes dry and hard; it is cut off from the circulation of blood; it is lifeless like a hair or a fingernail. As it grows dry the pinfeather bursts its sheath and spreads out to assume the beauty, strength, resiliency and utility of the fully developed feather. Thus the plumage of every bird comes into being.

The quill, the two rows of barbs that bear the smaller barbules that carry, in turn, the innumerable barbicels—those tiny hooklets that interlock zipper-fashion to hold the vanes together—all these are formed of strong-walled hollow cells. William Beebe once found about 600 barbs to the row on either side of a six-inch pigeon feather, a total of about 1,200 barbs. And each barb contained something like 275 barbules, some 330,000 for the two sides of the feather. The number of microscopic hooked barbicels, other counts have shown, may attain the astronomical total of 30,000,000—all in a single feather from a bird's plumage. In its complicated perfection, the feather is one of the most amazingly effective of nature's inventions.

Probably the strongest of all feathers are the wing primaries of the falcons and eagles. The middle pair of feathers in woodpecker tails are specially stiffened and pointed to act as braces. A friend of mine once tested the strength of such a feather from the tail of a flicker. He found that two-thirds of the way from the base to the tip it is capable of supporting three times the weight of the entire bird. The longest functional feathers of any bird are said to be the two central pairs of tail feathers of the Reeves's pheasant, a dweller in the remote mountain passes of western China. Like the long steering oar of a whale boat, they permit sudden changes in direction during the meteoric flight of these birds over the jungles in deep ravines. Incidentally, the fan of the peacock is not a tail at all. It is formed of the enlarged upper tail coverts.

Because it lacks life, a feather has no power of growth. It cannot repair or renew itself. If it becomes worn, frayed or broken it must be shed and replaced entirely. This is the function of molting time. All birds molt at least once a year, a few three times a year and most twice a year. The loss of a feather, it has been noticed, seems to stimulate the growth of a new one. On German farms where tame geese were plucked repeatedly it was found that the birds produced as many as five crops of feathers in the course of the year. Each new feather, replacing an old one, pushes out as a pinfeather encased within its sheath. Then, extending beyond the end of the sheath, it expands much in the manner of an unfolding butterfly's wings. In the case of land birds that need to fly in order to find their food or escape their enemies, the vital wing feathers are replaced two at a time, one from one wing and the corresponding feather from the opposite wing. Not until these replacements are almost full grown is the next pair of feathers shed. At the other extreme is the case of the flightless penguins. They shed their relatively unimportant wing feathers in bunches. They shrivel up, turn brown, and fall away like patches of skin on a lizard.

It was the brilliant whiteness of the feather-flotsam on the sand of Point Pelee that first attracted our attention to it. The discarded plumage shone like the whitest of foam on a seashore. And, in fact, feathers and foam gleam in the same immaculate hue for the identical reason. There is no white pigment in the feathers of a gull as there is black pigment in the feathers of a crow. Pound a crow feather, crush it up, and all the fragments still are black. Pigment colors them down to the tiniest particle. Smash, similarly, the chromatically brilliant feather of a hummingbird or parrot and its metallic hues disappear entirely. They are the product not of pigment but of tiny grooves or striations set at such an angle that they reflect to our eyes only the wave lengths of light that represent the colors we see. The whiteness of the gull feather, however, derives from still another source. Neither pigment nor striation explains it. It is due to the infinite number of minute air spaces within the hollow, horny cells. Acting like the bubbles in masses of foam, these air spaces bend and reflect the light rays to create the effect of immaculate whiteness that we see.

In the sunshine of Point Pelee, that morning, we remained for a long time absorbed with these white lines of molted

feathers. They were the first thing we saw. The second was the
parade of the sharpshins. The third was the host of the passing
butterflies.

Charles Darwin, when he reached the illimitable pampas of
Argentina during the voyage of the *Beagle*, noted that the average man rarely looks more than fifteen degrees above the
horizon. The events of the sky above him occur, in the main,
without his being aware of them. Once, west of Lake Okeechobee in lower Florida I talked to an elderly man who had spent
most of his days in the open. He was then earning his living
trailing and capturing diamondback rattlesnakes.

"I pay no mind to what is overhead," he assured me ear-
nestly, "but I know everything that goes on on the ground."

We, that morning, commenced to "pay mind" to what was
overhead when the shadows of hawks, one after the other,
drifted along the sand where the feathers lay. The flight of the
sharpshins had begun.

During September—with the migration waves reaching
their peak in the middle of the month—these hawks pour
down from hundreds of thousands of square miles to the north
and pile up near the tip of this nine-mile arrowhead of sand.
When in 1882 W. E. Saunders, an ornithologist of London,
Ontario, first reported the autumn hawk flight at Point Pelee,
he was hardly believed. The number of migrants shot there—
in days when the hostility toward these swift accipiters was
untempered by any understanding of their role in the balance
of nature—gives an indication of the extent of this annual
movement. One farmer sat in his front yard and shot 56 sharpshins without getting out of his chair. In the 1880's, two men
stood thirty paces apart with double-barreled, breech-loading
shotguns firing at the hawks as they flew overhead. The birds
streamed by faster than the men could reload. In thirty minutes, on a September day about the turn of the century, P. A.
Taverner and B. H. Swales counted 113 sharpshins passing
over the tip of this jumping-off place on the northern shore of

the lake. Such flights first brought scientists to the area.

Sometimes the hawks we saw came low over the trees, bursting out upon us suddenly. At other times they soared down the point so far overhead they were only sparrow-sized in the sky. The lower migrants circled uncertainly when they reached the spit of sand with its edging of slaty-blue waves tinged with yellow from the mud of the shallow bottom. They mounted in an ascending spiral, beating their wings and gliding, then beating their wings and gliding again. High above us they straightened out at last and headed away across the water. Watching the "blue darters" thus, with hawk after hawk passing by, we noticed how endlessly varied in shading they were. Some appeared extremely light, others abnormally dark. How many hawks we saw that day I do not know. But hour after hour the parade continued.

Other birds also were piling up near the end of the point. We saw bluejays and goldfinches, black-throated green warblers and black-and-white warblers, martins and barn swallows, crows and flickers, a varied assemblage. The smaller birds clung to the thickets or flew low among the bushes, seeking the greatest protection from the passing hawks. Here a woodpecker was once seen hopping adroitly around the trunk of a tree, avoiding time after time the bullet rushes of a hawk. And here a bluejay, safe in the heart of some thicket, taunts in a screaming crescendo each sharpshin that skims or circles over the tangle that protects it.

Occasionally one of the sharpshins becomes the attacked instead of the attacker. In 1905, Taverner and Swales received a bedraggled hawk that some fishermen had picked from the lake close to the end of the point. They had seen herring gulls surround it, buffet it, and knock it down into the water near their boat. Along the Atlantic coast I have run into several similar instances of these gulls attacking smaller birds and hurling them into the sea. A friend of mine, fishing from a boat several miles off the south shore of Long Island, once watched gulls attacking exhausted warblers that had been blown off their course and were circling about the craft. They seemed to pick the most spent of the migrants, the ones barely able to keep in the air. After knocking them down the gulls alighted and apparently fed on the drowned birds. In other cases, tree swallows, a dovekie that had just been released after it drifted ashore in an oil slick, and even a barn owl that had been chased out over the water by crows, were attacked and knocked down by herring gulls.

On this sunny September morning, under the migrating sharpshins another migration was taking place. It was, in retrospect, the most dramatic event of the day. Whenever we think of Point Pelee we will always think of butterflies in the wind.

We first saw evidence of this migratory movement of insects among the stranded feathers of the spit. At intervals we came upon the black and orange of drowned monarchs. They, too, had been washed ashore—butterfly-flotsam among the feather-flotsam. Farther up on the sand the wings of monarchs drifted about like windblown leaves. This was the wreckage of a great mass movement that was continuing all around us.

As the day advanced the monarchs increased in number. They came drifting along the shore or emerging from among the bushes. Occasionally they paused on some flower or bush to feed or bask in the sunshine. But always they took up once more their interrupted journey, pointing south, winging their way along a path of migration that is one of the most puzzling features of the American fall.

As they left the shelter of the woods and came out above the exposed sand at the farthest tip of Point Pelee a few of the butterflies landed on the beach, spreading their wings in the sun. But most of them flew straight on, without a pause, down the length of the spit and out over the open, windblown water. This ancient highway of the birds was an ancient highway of the autumn monarchs as well.

The wind that day was fresh and steady. It swept across the

lake from the south or slightly east of south. As nearly as I could judge, its speed was between fifteen and twenty miles an hour. All the passing monarchs headed directly into the wind. They beat their wings steadily. Here was no flap and glide, no skater's veering from side to side in the manner of the monarch's leisurely progress on a still summer day. This was serious business.

Some of the journeying butterflies flew low over the waters. Others rose higher and higher as though seeking some lighter headwind. At times the insects seemed standing still. Only gradually—from our viewpoint on the ground—did they forge ahead into the teeth of the wind. We followed one monarch with our field glasses for more than five minutes. At times it veered widely to this side and then to that like a kite in a shifting breeze. For a while it flew low, almost touching the waves. Then it rose up and up until it was at least half a hundred feet in the air. Once a ring-billed gull soared on a long downcurve beneath it. Gradually the monarch grew smaller. Its beating wings carried it always in the same direction —into the wind, toward the south. And thus, so small, so frail, so undeviating, the butterfly disappeared over the wide plain of the lake. In spite of the wind, it was launching out across thirty-five miles of rolling water, heading directly toward an unseen shore.

Another monarch that followed it remained low, just above the wave tops, as far as our eyes could follow. Each time a wave went under it, the pushing wall of water created a lifting updraft that caught the lightly loaded insect and tossed it in the air. Thus we saw it riding a kind of endless roller coaster on its low flight above the wind-formed ridges of the lake. We watched it breast the wind, move out beyond the rip-currents, watched it swallowed up in space, watched it all with that sense of wonder and mystification that comes so often in the fall when we observe these small migrants charting their course without a landmark, guiding themselves instinctively

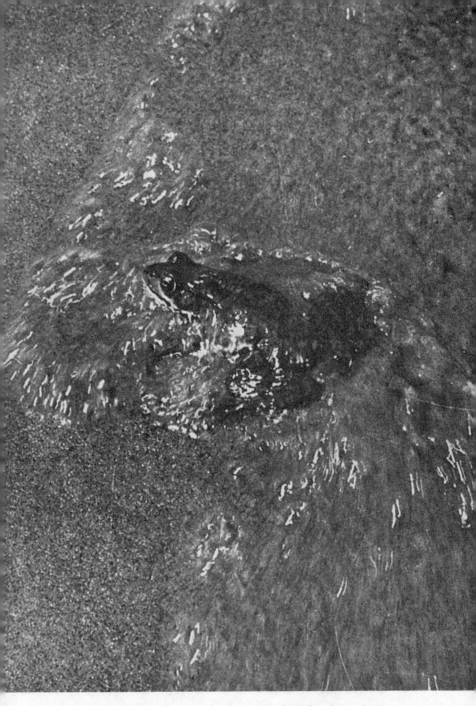

FROG bathed by a wave on the sand of a lake shore. Being
cold-blooded, frogs remain dormant from fall until spring.

SUNFLOWERS are many flowers massed together in one head.
On this and the next page, at the top, the four photographs

show the opening of a sunflower. Below, across both pages, progressive blooming of florets; close-up of florets, seeds.

BEGINNING in this woodland brook flowing from Lake Itasca the Mississippi starts its 2,552-mile journey to the Gulf.

in a manner that we can still but dimly understand.

We sat down on the sand, absorbed by these butterflies in the wind. They came in a steady parade, an unending stream of insects that continued for hours. They, like the birds, had funneled from a vast area to the north into the narrowing confines of Point Pelee. We counted the migrants as they fluttered by. At the end of fifteen minutes, twenty-four monarchs had flown along the spit and headed away across the lake. At the end of half an hour, the count had risen to sixty-four. During that thirty minutes, the butterflies had been passing by at the average rate of one every twenty-eight seconds. And this long procession of insect migrants flowed on and on.

The monarchs almost always appeared singly; rarely two at a time. Lone fliers, rather than members of a flock, they were depending individually on instinct to guide them. As we sat there, shadow-butterflies—as well as shadow-sharpshins—from time to time trailed across the sand around us. Amid the movement of the monarchs we began to notice also a surprising number of other insects.

Red admirals, small brown skippers, sulphurs, even white cabbage butterflies pressed forward over the sand and out across the water. Each determined insect was beating its wings rapidly, forging slowly ahead into the wind. None we saw returned. Several wasps, some *Polistes*, followed the spit to its end and then headed away over the lake along the same path the monarchs were taking. Both the spicebush swallowtail and the giant swallowtail have been reported leaving Point Pelee along this same migration trail. The most surprising butterfly I saw that day heading south toward the far-off Ohio shore was the mourning cloak. This species hibernates in hollow trees and under debris to appear—"the thaw butterfly"—during the milder days of winter. Yet here it was, starting like a monarch across the thirty-five miles of open water in a definite southward movement.

I have come to believe that these butterflies may move about in fall more than is realized. On a more recent September day, I drove the fifteen miles between Jones Beach and Captree along the ocean front on the south shore of Long Island. In that fifteen miles I encountered twenty-five mourning cloaks. They were all flying in the same direction, southwest, along the same path being taken by the migrating monarchs. All were heading in a straight line, all were flying steadily, all were maintaining a speed of about fifteen miles an hour. It may be that such autumn movements of mourning cloaks are a kind of partial migration, a pilgrimage to more favorable hibernating areas.

That afternoon, when we walked back along the tip of Point Pelee, we talked of the formidable and hazardous journey that lay ahead of these butterflies in the wind. How long would it take them to fight their way to the other shore, overcoming the handicap of a wind that carried them back almost as fast as they moved forward? How many, we wondered, would reach it; how many would fall exhausted, overcome by fatigue, to be washed eventually to some distant point on the rim of the lake?

It was nearing evening when we bobbed up once more at the Detroit end of the tunnel and began working our way out of the city. In days that followed we roamed northward through a country of inland lakes and bogs and tamarack trees. We crossed Looking Glass River. We passed Blue Gill Lake. We ran, mile on mile, never out of the sight of goldenrod and with the universal singing of the crickets in our ears. North of Clare, in Michigan's lower peninsula, the character of the country suddenly altered. Farms dropped away. Leathery sweet fern and everlasting dominated in the poorer soil. Bracken was brown and dead, already killed by heavy frosts. Here we had leaped ahead in autumn. Then in the cool of a northern evening, with the smell of aspens strong in the air, we came to Roscommon.

SEVEN

WARBLER RIVER

SOME time after four o'clock the next morning we awoke in the darkness of our cabin. A clattering roar was mounting in volume outside. I looked from the window just as a stubby locomotive, belching black smoke, its headlight probing far down the single track, rushed by, dragging two dimly lit coaches behind it. Gaining momentum after a stop at Roscommon, the morning train was going north. Only two trains a day, one going north, one going south, halt at Roscommon. The southbound train arrives at midnight, the northbound at four o'clock in the morning.

We listened while the roar and clatter diminished and grew small in the night. Half a century before, standing on the platform of the Roscommon station, another man had listened to that same sound coming down the single track as that same train puffed away into the north. The man was Norman A. Wood. An enthusiastic amateur naturalist and curator-to-be of the ornithological collection at the University of Michigan, in Ann Arbor, Wood had reached Roscommon in the early dawn of the long last day of June, in the year 1903, on a singular mission.

Some fifty years before, on May 13, 1851, a small bird with striped blue-gray back and yellow underparts had been shot in a tree top on the western outskirts of Cleveland, Ohio. It was new to the leading naturalist of the region, Jared P. Kirtland, Cleveland physician, friend of Agassiz, author of valuable scientific papers and compiler of the first catalogue of Ohio birds. In honor of Kirtland, Spencer F. Baird of the Smithsonian Institution in Washington called the new bird *Sylvicola kirtlandii*, a name that has since been changed to *Dendroica kirtlandii*. This same Ohio physician is honored in the names of a mollusk, a water snake, a cherry tree, a fossil plant, a bird club and an Ohio township. Moreover, Kirtland Hall at Yale University and Kirtland, Ohio, a community east of Cleveland, derive their names from the same source as the Kirtland's warbler.

About a decade after this first specimen was collected a second was obtained—also at Cleveland and also during migration. Then in the year the Civil War ended, 1865, Baird made an astonishing discovery. In checking over specimens collected by Samuel Cabot, Jr., on a voyage to Yucatán, he came upon a perfect skin of a Kirtland's warbler. The bird had been shot at sea, near the island of Abaco in the Bahamas, in October 1841. This was almost a full ten years before the type specimen was collected in the Cleveland tree top. For a quarter of a century the warbler had gone unnoticed among the many specimens brought back by Cabot. Thus a clue to the wintering ground of the warbler was obtained decades before its northern home and breeding area were discovered. That clue was given complete substantiation when, in 1879, Charles B. Cory collected a Kirtland's warbler on Andros Island in the Bahamas.

So matters stood for the rest of the nineteenth century. At rare intervals single specimens of the migrant warblers were obtained in Ohio, in Illinois, in southern Michigan, in South Carolina. In winter they were seen on several islands of the Bahamas. But during the rest of the year the warbler disappeared. Ornithologists speculated on the mystery of its breeding range. Some thought it nested in Alaska, others picked Labrador, still others maintained it bred on the tundras of northern Canada. As late as the fall of 1898, Frank M. Chapman was writing in *The Auk* that he believed the warbler nested in the region of Hudson Bay. "Owing to its rarity and the remoteness of its probable breeding range," he added, "its nest and eggs will doubtless long remain unknown."

That prediction, however, soon went awry. By 1903, nest, eggs, breeding place all were known. And as he stood in the darkness on the Roscommon station platform that June day, Norman A. Wood was drawing near to the solution of this ornithological mystery. A friend, returning from a fishing trip on the Au Sable River, had showed him a small bird shot near a bridge in the jack-pine wilderness of Oscoda County. Wood recognized it as a Kirtland's warbler. Without delay he headed north on the Toledo, Ann Arbor and Northern Railroad for Roscommon, the nearest point by rail to the bridge where the bird had been seen. When—after a sleepless night and two changes along the way—he was set down on the deserted platform of the little lumber town, Wood was thirty-five miles overland and sixty miles by water from his destination. As soon as the sun rose and people were astir, he rented a rowboat. By seven he was afloat on the south branch of the Au Sable River, beginning a downstream ride through sixty miles of wilderness.

"This country," he later wrote, "is wild and very interesting and the songs of many birds cheered me as, with notebook in hand, I floated along."

Bird voices, no longer singing the songs of spring, were awakening in the woods around us when, a little before seven, we stowed away our knapsacks in a canoe and—half a century after Norman A. Wood's historic journey—started down this same wild water trail he had followed into the country of the Kirtland's warbler. Dawn mist curled from the water. In nearly complete silence we stole along the winding, narrow, shadow-filled ravine down which the south branch begins its flow from Roscommon. Oscoda, Crawford and Roscommon counties all are located on the high tableland of the Lower Peninsula, 1,200 to 1,400 feet above sea level. From this plateau rivers flow east and rivers flow west, east to Lake Huron and west to Lake Michigan. The Au Sable, dropping 609 feet during its 300-mile course from Roscommon to Lake Huron, is one of the swiftest rivers of the region.

In recalling his journey down this watercourse Wood remembered how great blue herons flew downstream and landed ahead of him over and over again. Cedar waxwings were numerous all along the banks. Once he overtook a family of hooded mergansers. And another time, swinging around a sharp turn, he suddenly came upon two bald eagles fishing. By the end of the first day he had listed forty different species of birds.

We too, after a lapse of half a century, found birds everywhere along the way—phoebes and brown thrashers and white-breasted nuthatches and spotted sandpipers and myrtle warblers and robins and ruffed grouse and red-tailed hawks. For the first mile or so, six mallards kept us company, taking off with a great skittering and quacking ahead of us as we rounded each successive turn. In a quiet stretch where a floating log had stranded among waterweeds, we came upon a spotted sandpiper sound asleep. We drifted by with paddles trailing. Just as we came abreast, the bird's eyes popped open. It was wide awake instantly. Before long the ravine widened out, the banks shallowed, the river grew lighter and the day life of the woods began.

The trilling of the waxwings accompanied us as it had accompanied Wood. Great blue herons took off and landed downstream as they had before his drifting rowboat. Instead of eagles we had kingfishers plunging into the stream before us as we rounded almost every curve. There is one turn of the river's winding course that we will always remember as Chickadee Bend. The trees were alive with darting, calling black-capped chickadees. Fully half a hundred swarmed among the branches of a large white pine. Later in the day, as we rounded a curve, we met a solitary sandpiper flying low over the water directly toward us. Apparently blinded by the sun, it saw us only at the last moment, after Nellie, in the bow, had already ducked her head. The bird veered wildly away, the black and white ladder markings on its tail brilliant in the sunshine. Of all the birds we saw the most numerous, I think, were the flickers. We met wave after wave of the migrating wood-peckers. For several days they had been moving through, moving south, upstream along the northward-flowing river.

After the first two or three miles the riverside cabins disappeared. We were in canoe wilderness. For fully seventeen of the twenty-five miles we paddled that day we seemed cut off from the present, on a stretch of river hardly changed since Wood saw it. Mink and muskrat and otter tracks led along the mud of the stream's edge. Beaver had been at work among the aspens. Ruffed grouse shot away with a windy roaring and once three climbed steeply above the water and alighted in an overhanging tree, peering down at us with alert, round eyes as we drifted underneath. Deer drank in the shallows of many reaches. Once we came upon eight does and fawns drinking together. They stood immobile, heads lifted, water dripping from their muzzles. Then with a great splashing of mud and shooting sheets of spray they whirled in a snorting stampede for the cover of the trees. Many a deer that we failed to see, no doubt saw us as we passed by. I remember once looking to the left as we rode with rhythmic paddle strokes down a long straight stretch of the river. Behind the barricade of a fallen tree a doe peered out at us between two barkless branches—a wild cow gazing through the bars of a wild pasture gate.

Ours was a leisurely progress. Our day was as wide as the sky. We would paddle for a while with long, free-swinging strokes, then drift or swing to the bank to listen to the music of the wind in the pines or to see the kitchen middens of cone fragments left by squirrels on a mossy log or enjoy the brilliance of cardinal flowers rising from the moldering ruins of stranded driftwood. Then for long stretches we would ride the current, the sandy, gravelly bottom slipping by with every water-smoothed pebble visible below us. Sometimes where the current rippled over shallows we would run the chutes with the canoe bottom barely afloat. Then we would drift the length of some deep pool where trout—brown or brook or rainbow—shot away as the bulk of our canoe loomed over them.

In such places, Wood recalled, he would let his boat drift while he got out his fishing tackle. "As I glided along," he wrote, "I threw a cast of flies—'red ibis,' 'dark coachman' and 'white miller'—and took 'here and there a lusty trout and here and there a grayling.' "

When he pulled into his rowboat "here and there a grayling" he was catching some of the last of these great gamefish on the Michigan peninsula. Today, nowhere along the full length of the Au Sable is there a single survivor of the hosts of the grayling, the fish that first made the river famous. They have disappeared from these waters as completely as the passenger pigeons—whose migrating autumn flocks were once mirrored in the river pools—have disappeared from the skies. The cause of the decline and disappearance of the grayling was, like the nesting ground of the Kirtland's warbler, long debated by naturalists. Apparently a number of factors contributed to the disaster.

Milton B. Trautman, now of the Ohio State Museum and formerly assistant director of the Institute for Fisheries Research of Michigan, once reviewed these factors for me. The grayling was easily caught. The growing pressure of angling simply "fished out" sections of the stream. About 1850 brook trout and brown trout and rainbow trout were introduced into the river where they had not lived before. The grayling was unable to withstand the competition, especially that offered by the brook trout. Again the cutting of cedar swamps let more sunshine reach portions of the river, warming the water beyond the tolerance of the grayling eggs. But another byproduct of lumbering was even more disastrous. The spawn was laid in the gravel early in spring. These eggs were delicate and easily damaged. Year after year they were destroyed by the log runs that followed. Moreover the great runs of the 'eighties scoured the river bottom, destroying many of the natural spawning grounds. Although the grayling still lives in a few streams in western Montana, this famous gamefish—placed by scientists between the trout and the salmon—is found nowhere in Michigan waters and, except in Montana, nowhere else in America. It is commemorated on the banks of the Au Sable by the town of Grayling.

Wood found that at many places along the banks where cedars overhung the river, the trees had been undercut and had settled into the water where they formed "sweepers" which he had to avoid carefully lest they overturn his boat. We saw hundreds of such trees, tilted outward or toppled into the stream. In passing cedar swamps we sometimes wound among a dozen or more "sweepers," many stretching half across the river. Some were ancient and weathered to shining silver; others were still alive, with tips upturned. These northern white cedars—in reality arbor vitae trees—are durable, free from insect pests, long lived. The span of their years may extend over two or even three centuries. If any of the ancient, silvered, spidery sweepers we passed that day had escaped the decades of lumbering they may well have been older than the United States. From the leaves of these trees, now known to contain vitamin C, the pioneers brewed a remedy for scurvy. From the wood—the lightest in the region, weighing only nineteen pounds to the cubic foot dry weight—the Indians formed the frameworks of their birch bark canoes.

A little after noon we pulled up on a shelving bank beneath a high bluff to eat our lunch of ham sandwiches and tomatoes. Monarch butterflies passed us—all flying upstream. Like the flickers they were following this river road south across the tableland. Deer trails ascended the side of the bluff and fanned out over the top among the sweet fern and birch clumps. In a moist spot beside one of these trails we came upon a plant with slender stems rising nearly a foot above leathery, rich-green, heart-shaped leaves. Crowning each stem was the cream-colored saucer of a five-petaled flower, each rounded petal delicately veined with lines of green. We were seeing at last the grass-of-Parnassus in bloom.

This was a great event for Nellie. Years before she had seen a picture of this plant—which, of course, is no grass at all but a member of the saxifrage family—in a botanical book. One of her ambitions was to see the herb in bloom in the wild. So long ago, the ancient Greek naturalist, Dioscorides, had named the plant after Mt. Parnassus, sacred to Apollo and the Muses. There are certain common names on the lists of botany, such names as enchanter's nightshade, viper's bugloss, tick trefoil, Venus's looking-glass, nodding pogonia, wild comfrey and pale corydalis, that have the light of another time around them. And of such is the grass-of-Parnassus. The flowers, their ovaries fertilized, would produce single-celled capsules about half an inch long and filled with small winged seeds. But now they were full blown, almost an inch across, even in the shade shining out against the green of the leaves below. Well deserved is another name for these flowers: the bog stars.

A winding road and a winding stream have special appeal. Something new, something interesting, lies around every bend. That afternoon as we drifted with the current downstream, the interest that lay around successive curves sometimes proved to be wildlife, sometimes autumn foliage. On this northern highland frosts occur every month of the year and summer may contain as few as seventy growing days between killing freezes. Here a birch and there a maple had already turned to gold or crimson. I remember one half-submerged granite rock, black and wet, mottled with brilliant splashes of yellow where the currents had plastered birch leaves all over its upstream surface. Already canoes had been reserved for a little later in the season when the autumn foliage would be at its height. "Color tours" are now a feature of the fall in many parts of the country, by stream, by road, even by air. On this day we were paddling through merely the fringes of the great autumn rainbow that we were to see in its full glory farther west and farther north, in the hardwood forests of Minnesota.

Bridges are the milestones along the Au Sable and in the course of time we reached the third bridge that was our destination, the place where we and our canoe would be picked up and taken back to Roscommon. Wood had passed this place on the first day and had traveled on to the evening of the second day when he had reached his goal, a steel bridge not far from the present village of Red Oak. There he began seven days of searching that ended on July 8, 1903 with the discovery of the first Kirtland's warbler nest and eggs and the solution of a tantalizing riddle of American ornithology.

The bridge that formed Wood's landmark in 1903 still stands. We could visualize it in our mind's eye. For, a few years before, we had driven 2,000 miles to visit the jack-pine plains of the Lower Peninsula during the breeding season of this rare and restricted warbler. Now, sitting beside the river that had carried Norman A. Wood to the heart of the warbler's secret, we recalled the events of that trip. We remembered the wonderful days with the booming of the nighthawks at dusk and the sweet crepuscular song of the wood peewee in the half light before dawn.

Oscoda County is still the most sparsely populated county in Michigan. No railroad runs through it. Until World War II it had no bus line, no dentist, no doctor. Its few scattered communities all originated as lumber camps. Over the pale-gray dirt roads that cut the endless jack-pine plains into one-mile squares, we wandered for two days, listening for the singing of an unfamiliar warbler. At the end we were pouncing on snatches of familiar songs, even slamming on the brakes at unusual squeakings of the car. That evening, frustrated, we came to Mio. As I was signing up for a cabin at a tourist camp just north of town, the manager noticed my field glasses.

"A lot of people here are interested in birds," he volunteered. "We've got a couple of bird doctors in camp right now. They come up every June."

The "bird doctors," to our great delight, turned out to be Josselyn Van Tyne, ornithologist of the University of Michigan, and Harold Mayfield, for years secretary of the American Ornithologists' Union. Van Tyne—who, like Norman A. Wood, is curator of the university's ornithological collection —has spent more time in intensive study of the Kirtland's warbler than any other scientist in the world. During many seasons he has devoted at least twenty days of every June to observing the nesting warblers, often remaining in a blind from five in the morning until six at night. For nearly a dozen years Mayfield has assisted him in his work.

At four o'clock the next morning we were sharing a breakfast of doughnuts and coffee and bread and orange juice and canned peaches and grapefruit slices with the two bird doctors. Thus fortified with vitamins we started out with Mayfield to investigate a new area that had just been reported while Van Tyne retired to his blind for another day of concentrated observation.

Normally the breeding season of the Kirtland's warbler extends from mid-May to the last of June. The birds return from the south, both males and females together, some time between the tenth and the fifteenth of May. In its yearly cycle, the warbler spends only about four of the twelve months among the jack pines of north central Michigan. But here alone—and nowhere else on earth—it nests. In half a century no nest has ever been found more than sixty miles from the spot where Wood made his initial discovery. The three counties of Oscoda, Crawford and Iosco embrace almost its whole breeding range, with a few scattered records from adjoining counties. This area, largely drained by the Au Sable, is about 60 miles wide and 100 miles long. In this relatively small spot on the face of the earth every Kirtland's warbler is born. Not only does the bird breed in no other place but even here it nests only in special spots, only in areas where new-growth pines have sprung up in the wake of a forest fire and the trees have not yet reached a height of eighteen feet. As soon as the pines attain that height the warblers desert the area. Thus this curious little bird—known to scientists around the world because of its strangely restricted breeding ground—depends, literally, upon forest fires for its nesting sites.

Most warblers are shy and elusive, appearing and disappearing to the frustration and bafflement of the bird watcher. But not so the Kirtland's. When one of the scattered colonies is discovered, the song of this warbler becomes the dominant voice of the jack pines. As we drove west that morning we heard the trill of the pine warbler, the up-scale "zee-zee-zee" of the prairie warbler and the curious drawling, insect-like "buzz-buzz-buzz, buzz, buzz" of the clay-colored sparrow. We were not prepared, when we reached the nesting site of a pair of Kirtland's, for the ringing, far-carrying song of the male. I heard it a fifth of a mile away with the breeze blowing in the wrong direction. It is the ear that first detects the site of the nesting warblers.

Repeated every ten seconds or so for minutes at a time, the song is short, lasting, as Mayfield pointed out, about as long as it takes to say: "Chattanooga choo-choo"—two seconds or less. Starting low, it progresses with an ascending "che-che-che," almost like a stammer, before suddenly bursting out in a loud and ringing "wee-wee." The song grows louder and faster as it advances until the final notes come out with an explosive rush. The final "wee-wee," heard near at hand, actually hurt our ears.

When it sings, the male appears to be in a kind of spasm. It vibrates, jerks, bobs, seems to jump up and down with the violence of its efforts. On a mild morning in June a male will sing at the rate of from five to nine songs a minute. It is rarely silent for as long as thirty minutes. Each pair of Kirtland's warblers has its own area, from one to four acres in extent, and the singing of another male in the distance seems to stimulate the male at the nesting site to greater effort. In one experiment, a recording of the song was played in the field. A male came close and appeared to sing in competition. We saw males sing, not only when perching, but also in flight. Several times we observed a male arriving at the nest with its bill crammed with small caterpillars. In spite of this impediment to song, it would pause on a branch, lift its head, and utter its notes as loudly and clearly as ever.

Sitting in the grass beside our drawn-up canoe, we recalled the appearance of the Kirtland's warbler—as arresting as its song. Conspicuous black streaks mark the bluish-gray back of the male. Its breast is lemon yellow with bold markings of black along the side. A large warbler, it measures five and three-quarter inches from bill to tail. The male has a distinctive black mask running back along the sides of its face. The female, lacking this mask, is clad in duller, grayer plumage. Both male and female have the same habit of jerking or bobbing their tails.

Another trait of this jack-pine warbler, we recalled, is its surprising fearlessness. Individuals vary but, on the whole, the Kirtland's warbler is noted for its lack of fear. One male, singing in the top of a small pine, let me take a position directly beneath him. He merely cocked his head on one side to look down at me and then took up his singing again. Even when I shook the tree he flitted only half a dozen feet away to the top of a neighboring pine. Later in the day when I had my camera set up on a tripod not far from a nest, the female perched on the extended bellows even while I was in the act of focusing and the male made a dash between the legs of the tripod in driving away a trespassing chipping sparrow.

Not far apart that day, Mayfield found two nests. Both were hidden amid sweet ferns and blueberries and dry wiry grass, little cups in the ground lined with fine grass, bark and deer hair. One nest had been deserted. We dug it up carefully later on and it now rests in the collection of bird nests at the American Museum of Natural History. The other contained four fledglings in pinfeathers. They had hatched from small white eggs speckled with brown after an incubation period of about two weeks. Ten days after hatching, these baby warblers are ready to leave the nest. When we saw them they were nearing the end of this period of rapid growth. They were ravenously hungry and the day was one long meal.

We watched the parents come and go. Hour after hour they combed the lower branches of the surrounding pines for forest caterpillars. Occasionally one of the adults would gobble down a caterpillar before it began gathering food for the nestlings. It always followed the same procedure. It cocked its head, snapped up the worm, gulped it down rapidly, then hastily wiped both sides of its bill on a twig as though whetting a knife, jerking and wagging its tail all the while.

Invariably the baby birds were fed from the same side of the nest. A little tunnel or pathway led into the bower of overarching grass beneath which the nest was located. The bird bringing the food always landed at the entrance of the tunnel and disappeared within. When it emerged it always gave a little fluttering bound, about six or eight inches high, as it flew away. Most of the food brought to the growing warblers is formed of small caterpillars. But, as we watched that day, we saw this fare varied with an occasional adult ant-lion. Once the male came in with the gauzy wings of one of these insects extending out on either side of its bill like a long mustache. Another time the female fluttered aloft like a flycatcher to pick a passing ant-lion from the air. A curious thing about the feeding habits of the Kirtland's warbler has been noticed by Van Tyne and Mayfield. They have never seen one of these birds take a drink of water. Perhaps they obtain ample moisture from the heavy dews that are characteristic of the region or, it may be, the larvae they consume provide sufficient fluid for their needs.

In 1953, in the January issue of *The Auk*, Mayfield reported the results of the first comprehensive census of these warblers ever made. With the aid of thirty-two field observers, he surveyed all known breeding sites. The figures show that the total number of Kirtland's warblers in the world is, in all probability, less than 1,000. This census, incidentally, appears to have been the first attempt ever made anywhere in the world to count all the members of an entire species of song birds.

On this September day of turning foliage and monarchs moving south, we had seen no bird along the way that resembled this warbler of the jack pines. For already the birds had left their curiously restricted breeding area. By the middle of September, each year, all are gone. On this day, as we drifted down the stream that had carried Norman A. Wood to the solution of an ornithological riddle, the stream so long associated with the lives of these mysterious warblers, the stream that drains the land where every one of them first sees the light of day, the birds themselves had been far to the south Already they were well on their way, moving in migration to ward the far-off islands of their winter home.

EIGHT

DUSTY AUTUMN

FOR 200 miles the next day we rode south with the long chain of the Michigan dunes on our right. The arid yellow of their tops, in an undulating horizon line, rose against the cloudless blue of the sky. Killdeers called from every plowed field and pastureland. Overcome by autumn wanderlust, woolly bear caterpillars humped across the concrete of the highway. And all down the eastern shore of Lake Michigan monarch butterflies drifted southward over the hayfields and orchards and fallow land now splotched with goldenrod and painted wine red by the tinted stems of frost-touched grasses.

Beside the road black walnut trees, almost bare of leaves, were decorated from top to bottom with the green globes of their wild harvest. Green, too, was the duckweed on black swamp water but its autumn migration down to the muddy bottom was only weeks away. Everywhere around us, from the dry fields, came the universal simmering sound of the insects, the most characteristic music of fall.

This was fruit country, orchard and vineyard land. Roadside stands were laden. Vines were redolent with their blue burden and apple trees bent low with the weight of the autumn harvest. Mile after mile we rode among gray-barked peach trees where fallen fruit on the ground below outlined the form of the trees like shadows at noontime. All through this fruit belt of western Michigan this was harvest time, payoff time, the season of profit and plenty.

The cool air of the warbler river now lay far behind us. Even before we crossed the Indiana line we were plunged into a midwestern September heat wave such as we remembered from childhood. The mercury was close to ninety-five degrees when we rolled through Michigan City and into the dune country beyond. One vivid memory remains of passing through the city. A small boy, five or six at most, had picked up a dead monarch butterfly from a pile of litter beside the street. He was standing entranced, bending forward, oblivious to all around him. It seemed as though I were looking at myself when young. A door was opening for him, a door beyond which lay all the beauty and mystery of nature. I wondered who he was and what his future would be and—like the small boy I once heard whistling to himself in the Virginia dusk, imitating all the bird calls of the region—I wished him well.

The next day, in ninety-six degree heat, I rode the interurban to Chicago to have a balky camera shutter repaired. White and brown and red and gray, the steelmill smoke at Gary poured toward the sky. Sulphuric acid polluted the stagnant air. Overwhelmed by the heat, I stared with almost unseeing eyes at the passing miles of sunflowers along the right-of-way. Returning in the afternoon, I was depressed, deadened, left limp and half-conscious by the great city. At sunset we drove down a dusty back road and I suddenly came alive. For there, with the sundown light upon it, still green all along its upper half, was the spire of the old cedar tree that still stood where once my grandfather's gate had led to Lone Oak Farm. And in the darkening bushes all around the calling of the katydids linked the present with those summer nights long ago.

Down katydid roads, after dark, we drove to Chesterton. There I found Jim Fuller, who had worked as a young man at Lone Oak. And there, as we talked that evening, I solved at last the mystery of the lost woods. That lonely tract, seen once with my grandfather when I was very young and it was winter, had been sought in vain in later years. I could find no place that looked like it. No one recognized it from my description. It remained in my mind a mysterious, elusive, dreamwoods, never forgotten, never seen again. From it came the title of one of my books, *The Lost Woods*. But Jim Fuller remembered it well. All the trees had been felled in the winter of 1911. He had helped cut them. He had helped haul the logs on sleds to Furnessville where they started for their destination, the Benton Harbor Box Company, in Michigan. There they became barrels and crates and strawberry boxes, some of which—by a kind of "rivers return unto the sea" sequence—may well have held the berries I picked during succeeding Junes at Lone Oak.

Seventy miles away, under a hazy prairie sky, the next day we followed U.S. 6—now a thousand miles west of its Cape Cod beginning—into Joliet, Illinois. Fallen thornapples scalloped the edges of the highway with partial disks of brilliant red. Hazel nuts were plump in the dusty thickets, fox grapes were turning and hips sprinkled the wild roses. Seeds of a thousand shapes were drying on the roadside plants and the sweet smell of distant leaf fires scented the air. Autumn change was everywhere.

Beside Hickory Creek, that rocky stream on whose western bank I was born, we neared the city. Each turn recalled some thing of the past, memories of swimming holes and sunfish and hellgrammites under stones in the riffles, memories of butternut and walnut and hickory trees, memories of lowland stretches yellow with marsh marigolds in the wake of the melting snow, of Davison's Woods carpeted with spring beauties in the time of returning warblers.

We turned off on the side of the road and I walked back along the edge of this same woods, along the same Michigan Central Railroad tracks that once had provided a kind of highway into wildness, a cinder-coated path leading east from the city's edge into a realm of herons and muskrats and thornapple feasts in autumn. A railroad right-of-way, to a returning native, is one of the most permanent of landmarks. A street or stream changes more. When John Burroughs revisited Polo, Illinois, a generation after he had taught school there one winter in his youth, he noted in his journal that all was so changed only one thing seemed the same, the land along the railroad. As I walked east this autumn day the tracks and their surroundings seemed hardly touched by time.

Here were the wild strawberries growing close to the cinders just as I had remembered them. Here was the hillside dropping down in tangles of wild grapes, false buckwheat, sumac and asters. Here was the hobo jungle where tramps camped all summer long. Here were the elderberry bushes laden with fruit and filled with the quick, dashing motion of feeding birds. And here, below the right-of-way, giant ragweed rose shoulder to shoulder in rank stands eight and even ten feet high.

To those who suffer from hayfever in the fall, the ragweed is a botanical villain. To those like Nellie and myself who are fortunately immune to the effects of its pollen, it is an interesting plant of remarkable characteristics. The giant ragweed, *Ambrosia trifida*, is the tallest of all the composite group. One plant was once found to measure eighteen feet, four inches, in height. Known variously as bitterweed, richweed, horse cane, buffalo weed and wild hemp, the giant ragweed usually occupies lower land and moister areas than the smaller common ragweed, the Roman wormwood of early settlers, *Ambrosia artemisiaefolia*. It was Roman wormwood that Henry Thoreau battled with his hoe along the rows of his bean patch at Walden. For the ragweed is a plant pioneer. Wherever land is cleared, wherever roadsides are graded, wherever city buildings are torn down and lots left vacant, wherever the earth is stripped and left bare, there the ragweed springs up in profusion.

The minute seeds possess amazing longevity. When buried too deeply in the ground they remain dormant for years—in one case for forty years. Then when the soil is disturbed and the seeds are brought close to the surface the plants spring up as though from a magician's hat. Oren C. Durham, of North Chicago, once counted 240 ragweed seedlings in a single square foot of fallow stubbleland. Such seedlings develop into the swiftly growing plants that flower and produce their copious pollen in the shortening days of late summer and early fall. Like the chrysanthemums and asters, ragweeds are plants that grow vegetatively during the long days of summer and only produce their flowers, in response to the decreasing hours of sunlight, as autumn approaches. Because it is the length of day that governs the blooming of the ragweed, the appearance of the flowers can be predicted almost exactly for any given latitude.

A few years ago, in the course of tobacco researches in the south, scientists made an odd discovery about ragweed, revealing the hitherto unsuspected importance of this despised plant. The exact relationship is still a mystery but the research workers found that good tobacco crops depend upon a preconditioning of the soil by ragweed.

From the massed blooms of the ragweed beside the railroad track that September day tens of thousands of minute, buoyant pollen grains were riding off on the breeze. Like the grasses, ragweeds are wind pollinated. In such a hit-or-miss broadcasting of pollen grains the supply must be immense. Scientists estimate that more than three-quarters of a million tons of ragweed pollen drift through the air above the United States each year. This living dust is carried miles upward into the sky. It is said to travel as far as 1,000 miles from the plant that produces it. Researches have shown that, during the height of the ragweed season, more than a hundred pounds of pollen falls on every square mile of New York City. Even more drifts in the atmosphere overhead. At Indianapolis, Indiana, during the latter days of one summer, samples taken by scientists indicated that 827 pounds of this buoyant pollen floated in the air above each square mile of the city.

I tapped one of the ragweeds sharply with my hand. A cloud of pollen, like a puff of smoke, shot into the air. Each of the tiny pollen grains descends through perfectly still air at the rate of about ten feet a minute. It is roughly spherical, suggesting at first glance, when seen through a microscope, a battered golf ball. Small spines thrust outward from the surface or, as Nehemiah Grew expressed it when describing a somewhat similar pollen in his *The Anatomy of Plants,* in 1682, they are "beset round about with little thorns." Because goldenrod happens to bloom at the same time ragweed does, it was originally considered the cause of hayfever and the affliction was first termed "goldenrod fever." However the pollen grains of the goldenrod are heavy and sticky and do not—like those of ragweed—float on air. Wherever airborne pollen grains have been studied in America those of the ragweed have usually been found to be more abundant than those of all other kinds put together.

About pollen we know today a great deal more than did the men of the Renaissance who believed the floral dust was given off by plants to purify their sap. We know, among other things, how amazingly durable is the sculptured outer coating that protects the speck of protoplasm within. Buried in peat bogs these fragile-looking shells have endured for thousands of years. Fossil pollen, laid down in successive strata, provides scientists with glimpses into the distant past, revealing facts about weather conditions and plant abundance even in prehistoric times.

I tried to imagine all the infinite multitude of invisible living specks riding in the blue expanse of the sky above me. Their ballooning flight requires a time of dryness. Every hayfever sufferer has experienced the feeling of increased discomfort when rain has begun, bringing down greater concentrations of pollen and then the sudden later relief as the downpour cleanses the air. Sometimes the pollen is so thick it

colors the falling water and produces the yellow rain of the so-
called "sulphur showers." But always, before it can soar away
on the upcurrents the dust of the flowers must be thoroughly
dry. It rides the air most buoyantly in times of low humidity.
Thus autumn aids its travels. For autumn is the season of increasing dryness.

Every tree and bush and plant is, large or small, a kind of
invisible fountain. Moisture rises from its leaves, given off by
the vital processes of plant life. As the leaves slow down their
activity at the end of summer, as they begin to lose their hold
and drop to the ground, these fountains dry up. This is one of
the reasons why autumn tends to be a time of dryness and dust.

Wherever we drove that day the dryness of the season was
accentuated by the heat wave. Dust lay over the leaves of the
old box elder trees in front of the house where I lived as a
child. It swept across the playground at Woodland School.
And all along the edges of Brown's Pond the weeds were gray
with dust, autumn dust, the dust of dusty autumn.

Brown's Pond, as I remembered it from childhood, was a
realm of muskrats and bullheads and cattails and willows and
the singing of redwings. In the intervening quarter of a century the cattails had pushed out from shore and the willows
had followed. The trash of the years, dumped from the banks,
had formed shoals and bars, shallowing the bottom. In that
endless seesaw of land and water, the land had encroached
on the pond, pinching and contracting it until its dimensions
were less than half those I recalled. Dotting its unwholesome
surface were floating beer cans and whisky bottles and half-
submerged auto tires. This city-edge stretch of water, that I
remembered from a better time, seemed nearing the end of a
long, inglorious decline.

Saddened by the sight I drove on a quarter of a mile and
pulled up beside the wasteland of a long-abandoned gravel
pit. It, too, I remembered well for it was the nearest wildness
I knew as a boy. It had stretched away for hundreds of acres

across the street from the house where I had lived. There I had found parts of fossil plants and thought them Indian beads. There, in the limestone quarries beyond I had combed the chipping piles for fragments of prehistoric ferns. The old expanse, wasteland then, was wasteland now, hardly altered by the decades. Here was the gravel, here were the enduring stones, here the remnants of the glaciers and here were the memories of boyhood.

I smiled a little ruefully at the recollection of one of my first discoveries in natural history made here in the fall. I was, at the time, in second grade. The teacher asked us to bring in brilliant autumn leaves and I found the most brilliant of all on a slope of the gravel pit. I knew my moment of triumph when I handed the large bouquet to the teacher. But it was short-lived. A few days later I was not at school. Neither was the teacher. For the bright-colored leaves were the autumn foliage of the poison ivy.

For more than an hour I wandered over this remembered gravel land, noting the narrow-leaved cattails that had obtained a foothold in the damp depressions and the dragonflies that skimmed and whirled about them. Thistledown drifted past and grasshoppers rattled away on sounding wings and crickets sang among all the low vegetation and I found myself repeating a line from a half-forgotten poem: "Oh to be a cricket in a dusty thistle thicket!"

And all the thistle thickets *were* dusty that day. Here, too, the gray autumn dust had settled. It coated my shoes. It surrounded my feet in a moving cloud when I strode through the dry vegetation. Dust—the bane of the immaculate housewife, the cause of choking and sneezing, the reducer of industrial efficiency—dust to a naturalist represents one of the great, essential ingredients in the beauty of the world.

If it were possible to banish dust from the earth, the vote probably would be overwhelmingly in favor of it. Yet subtract dust from the 5,633,000,000,000,000-ton atmosphere that sur-

BADLANDS scenery is created by erosion. At times, carved
hillsides, such as seen here, resemble vast amphitheaters.

TUMBLEWEEDS growing in western sand and, below, an autumn chipmunk not long before going into winter hibernation.

rounds the globe and you would subtract infinitely more. You would drain blue from the sky and the lake. For fine dust, as well as the molecules of vapor and the air itself, scatters the blue rays and contributes color to the heavens above and reflected color to the waters below. You would eliminate the beauty of the autumn mist and the summer cloud. For every minute droplet of moisture in fog and cloud forms about a nucleus of dust. You would halt the rain and never know the whiteness of drifted snow. For raindrops and snowflakes and hailstones also come into being about a center of airborne dust. You would remove the glory of the sunrise from the world and wipe all the flaming beauty of the sunset from the sky. For sunrise and sunset, as we know them, are the consequence of the rays passing through the hazy, dusty air near the surface of the earth where the blue rays are filtered out and the red and orange rays pass through.

For this reason forest fires, filling the air with fine particles of smoke and ash, turn the sun red at noonday and when, in 1883, the explosion of the South Pacific volcano, Krakatoa, hurled a cubic mile of fine ash high into the atmosphere, one result was abnormally brilliant sunsets observed all around the world for two years afterward. The everyday sources of atmospheric dust are infinite in number. Soil is carried aloft on updrafts. Smokestacks belch soot into the air. Bacteria and the spores of mold and the skeletons of diatoms all ride through the sky. With every puff of a cigarette, one scientist reports, a smoker sends something like four billion microscopic particles into the air around him.

Almost all the airborne motes are infinitesimal in size, bits of solid matter so minute that they are supported by the atmosphere after they have been carried upward by rising currents. They are, of course, always descending but their rate of fall is so gradual that they are continually being carried aloft again by fresh updrafts. This process in the far-distant sky is the creator of much of the beauty we know. Close at hand, in our eyes and noses, dust is an abomination. But distant dust lends enchantment to the view.

Nearly as much as the scent of leaf fires in the dusk, the smell of dusty autumn weedlots is part of early memories of the fall. During our westward travels with the season I asked many people what scent first came to mind at the mention of autumn. To some it was the fragrance of ripe grapes, to others the kitchen smells of canning and jelly-making, to others the aroma of the apple harvest; to most, I think, it was the scent of burning leaves, but to more than I expected it was the mingled odor of the weedlot, the smell of ragweed and sunflower and sweet clover and dust, the very breath of autumn's dryness.

That was the smell that was all around me as I climbed the slope of a gravelly ridge. Like the heavy odor of hot tar under the August sun, the scent of woodsmoke on the winter air, this was a nostalgic smell with roots that extended far back into childhood. On the low ridge side I stopped beneath a scraggly tree to fill my pockets with red thornapples and again beside a dusty elderberry bush to taste the autumn tonic of its dark, clustered fruit. High above the ridge three dead cottonwoods lifted barkless and silvery branches. They brought to mind another natural-history discovery made here when I was seven or so, the discovery that thick and heavy cottonwood bark is no substitute for white birch bark in making an Indian canoe.

Beyond the ridge killdeers were calling. And from toward the horizon, mellowed by distance, came that plaintive, lonesome, far-carrying sound, the sustained whistle of a locomotive. As a child I had whistles to wonder at, whistles to dream about. For a prairie boy, there is magic in the lonely, lovely music of a train whistle far off in the night.

I topped the ridge and saw spread out before me a sudden scene of strange, wild beauty. Years before, the land to the east of the ridge beyond an ancient spur of the E J & E Railroad, was an extensive expanse of low-lying peat bog. Perhaps the water level of the area sank slightly when I was nine or ten, for about that time fires broke out in the peat. Burning slowly they ate out pits and spreading troughs in the bog. By night these hollows shone red like volcano craters and the heavy, choking smoke they gave off settled over the town. Repeated efforts failed to extinguish the slowly spreading fire. It burned on and on until almost the whole area was consumed. Now in a hollow at one end of this blighted, blackened stretch, a little lake had formed. A few cattails grew there, muskrats had built their houses along the edge and the green of duckweed ran across the surface. Here, in this miniature wilderness flanked on the north by wallpaper mills and on the east by the remote houses of Logan Avenue, here nearly thirty killdeers had congregated.

I sat down and for a long time watched the coming and going of the plovers. Every muskrat house had a killdeer perching on it. Soon a sparrowhawk dropped down on the stub of a long-dead tree near the cattails. The killdeers paid no attention to this smallest of the falcons. They circled over it, swept beside it, alighted beneath it. Wherever I looked along the shore the "noisy plovers" were in motion, running, stopping, alighting, taking to the air. Their flashing wings gave vibrant life to this scene of desolation. The clamor of their calls intermingled into wild and deeply stirring music.

Sitting there, I shared for a time the autumn excitement of these beautiful birds of passage. Perhaps it was a plaintive recurring note in the killdeer's call. Perhaps it was the smell of the dusty weeds, associated in my mind with a return to city and school, with the end of summer freedom at Lone Oak. Perhaps it was the faraway, lonely, nostalgic sound of the train whistle. Perhaps it was the singing of the September insects, that dry orchestral music that carries like an overtone the thought of swiftly passing life. Perhaps it was compounded of all of them—this wave of autumn sadness that enveloped me.

In a day, a week, a month at most, the plovers would move

on. All this intensity of living would leave the blighted pond. And nature—absorbed with species and averages, not with individuals—cares but little whether *these* birds return again. All the insects singing in the grass, all the leaves still spread to the sunshine, all the dusty annuals and the waning flowers— they all were living their last days and the end was moving swiftly toward them. Life would come again in the spring— but not *this* life, not to *these* flowers, not to *these* leaves, not to *these* crickets and grasshoppers.

All the multitudinous life that passes in the fall contributed to my somber mood. "Give me," Thomas Hardy wrote in a similar moment, "the roughest of spring days rather than the loveliest of autumn days for there is death in the air." This, too, is an aspect of autumn we must face and accept, an aspect that cannot be parried aside. But only here during all our travels with the fall did it intrude itself with so heavy a weight upon my mind.

I walked slowly back over the ridge. Descending the farther side my foot scuffed in the gravel. A pebble rolled away down the incline before me. What vast stretches of history were encompassed by the span of that pebble! Lying there since glacial times it had been warmed by the springs and cooled by the autumns of aeons of time. How much of human life and plover life and grasshopper life had passed away while its insensate existence had gone on and on. Yet, surely, better a single moment of awareness to enjoy the glory of the senses, a moment of knowing, of feeling, of living intensely, a moment to appreciate the sunshine and the dry smell of autumn and the dust-born clouds above—better a thousand times even a swiftly fading, ephemeral moment of life than the epoch-long unconsciousness of the stone.

So, cheered somewhat by so simple a thing as the roll of a pebble, I regained the car. We drove away, south and west, across the rich cornlands of Illinois toward the Great River, that age-old flyway of the autumn birds, the Mississippi.

NINE

THE GREAT FLYWAY

ALL during my boyhood the Mississippi was a kind of unseen presence, aloof, almost legendary, lying off to the
west, beyond the city, beyond the Illinois farmland that spread
away to the horizon, beyond the horizon itself. I never saw it,
never visited it, although it was only 120 miles away. Yet, during those years, I was always conscious of it, always aware that
off there, behind the western skyline, there flowed the Father
of Waters.

On the day we reached the river we started early. We rode
south on highways ribbed with sunshine and shadow. High
cornstalks pressed close to the road and the rising sun threw
the slender lines of their black shadows across the pavement.
Behind us lay Starved Rock, that sandstone island in the
prairie sky, the home of "trapped plants" isolated by the retreat of the glaciers. Behind us also were the nuts tasseling the
tree branches, the rank stands of the roadside weeds. Here,
all across this wide, level land, the trees had been felled, the
roadsides sheared, the rich soil devoted to corn and corn
alone. Small islands of shade trees, remote from each other,
marked the location of the farmhouses. And on all the fences
metal signs proclaimed the type of hybrid corn growing in the
fields beyond. Gaping husks revealed the kernels of immense
yellow ears. This was autumn, seedtime, the practical, far-
seeing season of the year. In a few days the harvest would begin. In a few days these high stalks, running like an unending

picket fence beside the road, would come down and their shadows across the pavement would be gone.

Thus began our four-state day. First the cardinal, then the goldfinch, then the bluebird, then the robin were the state birds of the land through which we traveled. By 9:01 that morning we were rolling over the bridge to Keokuk, crossing the river from Illinois to the second state, Iowa.

On this day, as on every day, the stupendous flood of the Mississippi moved toward the sea laden with silt. It was brown with the topsoil of tens of thousands of farms. Flying over the mouth of the river in the spring of another year, I had seen the silt-formed delta extending for hundreds of square miles out into the Gulf of Mexico. As much as five centuries go into nature's slow production of a single inch of topsoil. And agricultural scientists calculate that the equivalent of 125,000 160-acre farms move down the rivers of America every twelve months. There was a flow of farms as well as of water under the bridge to Keokuk.

At a street sign, so sheathed in autumn gossamer it looked like a grasshopper encased in silk in a spiderweb, we turned south. For miles we ran with the river on our left. We crossed the line into Missouri, riding all the way with migrating monarch butterflies. For the valley of the Mississippi is the great central flyway not only for birds but for butterflies as well. We turned around and, now with the river on our right, started the long run north.

All the countryside of Missouri and Iowa that day was brilliant with the gold of sunflowers. They extended away over the fallow fields and up the hillsides and along the fence rows. The sight brought back memories of another autumn, more than twenty years before, when Nellie and I had ridden west toward Wichita across the rolling miles of Kansas. Then all the roadsides and the open fields had been resplendent as far as we could see with one unending galaxy of sunflowers.

The most striking feature of the early prairie fall, *Helianthus* blooms in a rising tide of color. It ranges across the Great Plains and southward from Canada to Mexico. It is both tolerant of drought and immune to early frosts. To the pioneers—and before the pioneers to the Indians—it was a plant of many uses. Its seeds produced oil. Its leaves formed fodder. Its flowers provided yellow dye. Its stalks yielded textile fibers. Gerard, of the famous *Herball*, speaking of "The Greater Sun-Floure or The Marigold of Peru," notes: "We have found by triall, that the buds, before they be floured, boiled and eaten with butter, vinegar, and pepper, after the manner of artichokes, are exceedingly pleasant meat." Mush-and-milk and sunflower seeds were two of the staple foods of early settlers on the plains. Roasted and salted the seeds were eaten like peanuts. Roasted and ground they formed a pioneer substitute for coffee. The seeds, at one time, were considered a cure for rheumatism and an early belief that was widely held maintained that sunflowers planted around a cabin provided protection from malaria. Even today sunflower seeds are dispensed by pushcart vendors in New York City, and on northern farms, where the short season and early frost prevent the growing of corn, the leaves are used for ensilage.

During the first hours of the morning all the sunflowers we saw were pointing toward the river, toward the east, toward the sun. Botanists explain the turning of the sunflower to follow the course of the sun across the sky as an example of phototropism. Hydraulic pressure, water gorging the cells on the shaded side of the stem, advances the flower with slow, steady change through the arc of its daily movement. The same force turns it back toward the east at dawn.

One of the legends of the plains Indians accounts for the origin of the plant in the story of a Sioux youth so bewitched by the brilliant disk of the sun that he spent all his days standing on a hillside following it with his eyes. In time, blinded by the glare, his body grown thin like the stalk of a plant, he was transformed into the rooted sunflower that proverbially turns

its face toward the light. Ever since Greek mythology with
its tale of the water nymph, Clytie, and her love for Apollo the
sunflower has been a symbol of constancy.

"Do not the flowers of August and September," Henry
Thoreau wrote in his journal, "generally resemble suns and
stars—sunflowers and asters and the single flowers of the goldenrod?" If you examine closely the face of *Helianthus* you see
that it forms a whole floral galaxy. The great sun of its central
disk is made up of scores, sometimes hundreds, of five-pointed
florets that sweep toward the center in curving lines like the
arms of a spiral nebula. Each golden star is a separate flower.
A sunflower is not one flower but a community of flowers. It
represents one of nature's last and most successful inventions
in the floral line. It belongs to the *Compositae,* the largest
group of flowering plants, comprising some 13,000 species. It is
as though, on some day of inspiration, Nature watched a bee
flying from one single flower to another single flower and suddenly the thought occurred: Why not have a score or a hundred flowers growing together in one head? Then a visiting
insect would pollenize many blooms at once. That is the essential idea of the *Compositae.* At one stroke, the clustering of
many flowers together increases the chances of the blooms being fertilized and thus increases the number of seeds to spread
the species.

As the day advanced, and we ran north, the road carried us
past pumpkins piled high at roadside stands, past corn-harvest-
ing machinery trundling along the edge of the pavement, past
the solid green balls of the Osage oranges, and always past the
red and purple and russet and yellow of the autumn grasses.
From crests of rises we sometimes saw far-off Iowa grain elevators shining white in the sun. The farther north we drove the
more golden grew the cottonwoods. The increasing yellow in
their leaves represented a kind of yardstick measuring our
movement up the map.

All the rivers we crossed—the Skunk, the Flint, the Iowa, the

Wapsipinicon, the Maquoketa—flowed in the same direction, east to join the mightier stream. Once, late that morning, we stopped beside a bridge where a cloud of redwings had settled near by, blackening the riverbottom cottonwoods and filling the air with the storm of their calling. Giant ragweed rose in dense canebrakes from the rich mud of the stream edge. And, thrown high by the waters of some past flood, tangles of drift-wood slowly decayed with shelf fungus thrusting out and shining white against the dark silt-water below. Here, as amid the rotting leaves and flood debris of ravines and weed-choked banks of tributaries all along the upper Mississippi, lay hidden small, white, elongated eggs, the eggs of the floodwater mos-quitoes. Unseen they would wait, perhaps for years, to hatch in another time of high water.

The story of those eggs, only recently fully understood, rep-resents one of the most remarkable of the long-range provisions for the perpetuation of a species. The female mosquito always deposits them "between the tides," so to speak. She selects a place on the stream bank well above the normal water level but below the high-water mark of the flood stages. Here they lie dormant in debris until the crest of the rising water of some subsequent flood reaches them. What then occurs is the most remarkable part of the story. It was first revealed in 1953 by the work of William R. Horsfall and Alfred F. Borg at the University of Illinois.

A hen sits on an egg to hatch it. A reptile relies on the warmth of the sun. But the floodwater mosquito depends upon bacteria for the incubation of its eggs. When, in the laboratory, these minute organisms were removed from the outside of the mosquito eggs nothing would make the eggs hatch. Under normal conditions, the Illinois scientists found, as soon as flood waters inundate the eggs the bacteria multiply and the eggs produce mosquitoes. This occurs only at times of high water. No flood, no floodwater mosquitoes. It is this chain of cause and effect that explains the hordes of ravenous insects that appear at certain times. On those years high water and bacteria have done their work.

As we drove on we passed, from time to time, cornshocks running in lines across the fields. We talked of the mice already installed within these snug castles of plenty. There they would spend weeks in early autumn protected from the wind and surrounded by food. But sure to come was a day of dispossession. Husking time, in the mouse world, we decided, must rank with such catastrophes as the eruption of Vesuvius in human history. In a sudden overwhelming disaster their shocks would disappear and their world of abundance would collapse.

By early afternoon we were at Muscatine, walking along a levee where rotting burlap sacks spoke mutely of battles with flood crests of the past. In the sunshine we watched for a long time the lazy slide of the brown water drifting past, without haste, without pause, languid swirls turning here and there on the wide slow sweep of the river. Cicadas shrilled in the warmth of the day with a rising and falling din like the sound of many knives being sharpened on small, lop-sided grindstones. Over us towered a dead cottonwood with thirteen dark disks on the polished silver of its trunk and limbs, each the round entrance of a woodpecker hole.

We were walking back along the levee when a scattered band of tree swallows swirled around us and then drifted away downstream. It was hard to realize that this random passage of birds was part of the prelude to the vast autumn movement of the Mississippi flyway. The warm weather of recent days had extended far to the north. It had brought migration to a virtual standstill. But the days were growing shorter. Lessening sunlight was stimulating the urge to migrate. A sharp drop in temperature, a cold wind from the north, and the hosts of many migrants would be pouring down from Canada, funneling into the flyway of the Great River. During the next few weeks, by night and by day, they would stream southward, millions strong, past the very levee on which we now stood.

Barn swallows from the Yukon would go by on their way to a second summer in Argentina. Palm warblers from the shores of the Great Slave Lake would pass en route to Cuba. Mallard and pintail and canvasback ducks, Canada geese and blue geese from above the Arctic Circle, would descend the river skyway in skeins and wedges, draining away the summer wild-fowl population of the north. Some of the migrants, like the kingbirds and nighthawks, would be flying only with their own species. Others, like the wood warblers and sparrows, would be winging their way south in mixed companies. Often-times young birds would be migrating in advance of their parents. And all the birds passing by, from swans to kinglets, would be plump with layers of fat deposited beneath the skin to provide the energy needed for their long flight south.

If you could behold, by some magic gift of perception, all the multitudinous migrants moving down the map of North America—or if each flying bird left a trail in the air as a rabbit does in snow—you would see a kind of spreading tree or vine implanted on the continent. The main trunk would be the Mississippi. The branches would be the tributary flyways that descend through Canada from Baffin Land on the east to Alaska on the west. The Mississippi not only represents the continent's greatest river; it also represents North America's greatest roadway of migration.

There is, of course, a general southern seepage of migrants all across the map. But it is down the four great avian rivers that the mass of migration is channeled—down the Atlantic coast, the Mississippi, the Rockies and the Pacific seaboard. Of the four, the most important is the flyway of the Mississippi. "It is followed by such vast numbers of ducks, geese, shore birds, blackbirds, sparrows, warblers and thrushes," writes Frederick C. Lincoln, of the U.S. Fish and Wildlife Service, "that observers stationed at favorable points in the Mississippi Valley during the height of migration can see a greater number of species and individuals than can be noted anywhere else in the world." But this great spectacle of autumn was one we were to miss. Its vanguard had been held back by the unseasonable warmth; its main flow would not come until later.

From migration on this colossal and continental scale we descended that afternoon to autumn movements of Lilliputian dimensions. The winged flood of the Mississippi migrants was lost to us. But a humble form of seasonal travel began to absorb our attention as we drove north. We saw, as we had seen for days, wandering woolly bear caterpillars crossing the pavement. Some were going from left to right and some from right to left. One had just reached the center stripe when the whirlwind of two passing cars sent it spinning around and around. Frequently we saw other woolly bears rolled sidewise for a dozen feet or more by the hurricane gale of a speeding car. Always these travelers righted themselves and continued their crawling, a prey to autumn wanderlust.

I have long since learned in my travels that the best way to save the life of a turtle crawling across a highway is to put it on the side toward which it is heading. Its mind is made up. Putting it back on the side from which it has come merely postpones its danger. Within the sluggish-seeming turtle brain there is a sense of orientation that seems nearly infallible. How about woolly bears? Do they have the turtle's sense of direction? Do the spinning, rolling caterpillars right themselves and resume marching in the same direction?

This autumn travel of theirs, a feature of completed growth, is in its way a definite migration. It is a movement to winter hibernating quarters. Before entering the long months of immobility the caterpillars set out to see the world. Each woolly bear, for a time, becomes an insect Ulysses. Its autumn days are spent adventuring far and, about highways, daring much. As we zigzagged now and then to miss these wanderers in their perilous travels, we began speculating on the answers they would give us if we questioned them in what the French scientist, J. Henri Fabre, called "the language of experiment."

We became more and more engrossed in our woolly bear questions and planned to begin querying the caterpillars the next day. As it turned out, events had other plans for us. But later on, in the northwest and back home along the Atlantic coast, over several thousand miles of roads, a hundred times and more, we stopped to cross-question with experiments the journeying woolly bears.

I picked them up and set them down facing in the opposite direction. They reversed themselves and started off across the concrete of the highway in the same direction as before. I watched them regain their feet, without any loss of sense of direction, after being bowled over by the wind of a passing car. I whirled them around and around in my hand and set them down. They headed away as before. I shook them up in a brown paper bag and dumped them out. The result was the same. I picked up one woolly bear going in one direction and another going in the opposite direction and put them down, curled up into round pincushions, on the center stripe of the highway. They waited a minute or two, then uncurled and began walking away from each other, each stubbornly holding to its original direction of movement. Over and over again, I picked up woolly bears, drove from two to a dozen miles, stopped and put them down on the pavement. They seemed only momentarily confused before they headed off toward the same side of the highway they had been trying to reach miles away. Except for a negligible number of exceptions, the woolly bears all returned to their original course, they all retained their turtle-like sense of direction.

At first we thought they might be heading for landmarks, masses of dark and light formed by trees and open spaces beyond the wide, level plain of the concrete highway. A mathematical friend figured out the distance to the horizon line on level concrete as seen by eyes only half an inch above the ground. It was not, as I had imagined, but a few inches distant.

Assuming the caterpillar was far-sighted enough—and the concrete was perfectly level—it would be a full quarter of a mile away. However, proof that landmarks offered no explanation of the woolly bear's feats of orientation was easy to obtain. I picked up a caterpillar walking toward trees and set it down, a mile away, facing open pastureland. All its former landmarks were gone. Yet it started off at once toward the same side of the road it had been trying to attain before.

It happened that our earliest experiments were made on north-and-south roads where the sun shone either from one side or the other. Were the woolly bears simply walking toward or away from the sun? Again refutation was easy. The journeying caterpillars crossed just as readily when the sun shone lengthwise of the pavement on east-and-west roads and when it shone from all angles on winding stretches of highway. Moreover, where the road wound about and we set a woolly bear down at different points, in crossing toward the same side as before it often moved in a totally different direction in relation to the sun and, not infrequently, in the diametrically opposite direction so far as the compass was concerned. Whatever the explanation of their ability, these humble wanderers—on the move that day all up the Mississippi Valley —have within their pinhead brains or primitive nervous systems a sense of orientation that enables them to hold to their course once they start to cross the road.

Toward sunset, as we neared Dubuque, a river of redwings flowed across our path, draining eastward toward great roosting grounds along the Mississippi. Beyond them a dusky cloud rose and fell and wheeled continually. Starling flocks in mass evolutions are a regular feature of the late hours of autumn afternoons. Without a captain, without signals or orders, so far as we can see, a thousand birds act as one bird, turning and wheeling with all the precision of drill troops on parade. The starlings had landed and the sun had set beyond a long band of salmon-colored clouds when we crossed the bridge into Wisconsin and in this fourth state of the day found a cabin for the night.

I awoke the next morning feeling listless, feverish, coughing a great deal. During that panting day in Chicago, I had had my hair cut in a barbershop near the La Salle Street Station. Between snips of his shears the barber had gone into paroxysms of coughing. A huge electric fan at the back of the room drove a gale of wind directly on him and me. I asked him why he did not shift chairs and get out of the wind. He was a little vague but I came to understand that his was the Number One chair. It was the place of honor. It apparently meant more to him than health or life itself. Whatever he had, I had caught. Hoping to leave it behind, hoping that if I paid no attention to it it might go away, I drove north.

Out of that fevered day little glimpses of autumn come back to me—redwings among corn tassels; asters tumbling down a railroad embankment like a purple waterfall; fluff from thistles forming little lakes or pools of silver in the grass; autumn foliage along the Fox River down which Thomas Nuttall had paddled so long before; fifty green-winged teal rising from a pond near John Muir's Wisconsin homestead. That double parade of fall, monarch butterflies above and woolly bear caterpillars below, continued all across this rolling land. Purple asters were at their peak but most of the roadside plants had reached their seedtime. The beauty of the summer flower had become the utility of the autumn seed.

When we settled down at dusk near the Wisconsin Dells, I was running a fever of 102 and coughing continually. Thoughts of a long delay, of mountain snow, of the trip coming to an end before we reached even Minnesota plagued my troubled sleep. I determined to get across the Minnesota line before I gave up. So we started out, Nellie driving, at dawn.

Most of that day I lay with my head on the back of the seat, opening my eyes from time to time to see the Mississippi, to catch glimpses of wild, dark forest bogs, to view the beautiful bluffs that extended like great waves along the distant farther bank of the river. I remember watching a flock of feral pigeons feeding along a railroad track on grain spilled from boxcars. I recall my disappointment when we passed the gate leading to the home of Emil Liers, The Otter Man, whom I had long wanted to meet. But everything that day was clouded by the wavering mist of a 103-degree fever.

As we neared Red Wing, the massive bulk of Barn Bluff, or Mt. LaGrange, reared up at the river's edge, 450 feet high and half a mile long. I saw it through sick eyes just as, nearly a century before, Henry Thoreau had seen it when, stricken with tuberculosis, he had traveled to Minnesota for his health. At the modern clinic in Red Wing I saw a doctor and received a prescription for a virus-fighting wonder drug. Then on the edge of town, in the snug nest of the Hultquist Motel, I stretched out at last—the naturalist laid low.

There I remained quiescent until the second day, opening my eyes only at long intervals to enjoy the blending grays and greens and reds of curtains at the windows where the back lighting produced an effect of stained glass. Each morning the kindly proprietor would look in at the door, find me stretched out supine, sniffling and coughing and croaking when I spoke, filled with antibiotics and aspirin and cough syrup (red, cherry flavored), and each morning he would shake his head sadly and give voice to the same observation:

"I be sixty years old. I never wear gloves in winter. I never have even a cold. You yust live right and everything is all right!"

By the midmorning of the second day I had lived right long enough for my temperature to be back to normal. Appetite returned. Ambition returned. We could go on with the trip!

Toward afternoon I began to wonder if, by climbing slowly and resting often, I could not reach the top of Barn Bluff. There, on a June day in 1861, with the immense reach of the river view spread out below him, Henry Thoreau had read

MOUNTAINEER birds, like this Clark's nutcracker, frequently migrate downhill into the valleys when the autumn comes.

ROCK RABBITS live in a labyrinth of tunnels in the jumble
above. Below, overflow from a hot spring steams in the dawn.

letters from home, from his sister, Sophia, and his Concord neighbor, Frank B. Sanborn. In the intervening years the local Kiwanis Club had collected contributions from citizens—ten dollars a step, each step to bear the name of the donor—and had built a concrete stairway zigzagging up the side of the promontory. About three o'clock in the afternoon, under a brilliant, windy sky, we began mounting these stairs.

Around us as we ascended slowly grew sumac and boneset and goldenrod, woodbine with blue berries and red leaves, burdocks bearing clusters of dry, brown burs, old man's beard like dusty miller with finer fringing. When we reached the third step from the top we found it bore the name of the estimable Hultquist. Russet, the wild, healthy hue of autumn, formed the predominant color of the bluff top. All across the headland we found small bumblebees already bedded down for the night, anchored in the purple flowers of the blazing stars.

Around the edges of the bluff top ran a straggling line of cottonwoods, with yellowing leaves, and a scattering of bur oaks, solid, densely covered, deeply green. Flickers swarmed everywhere, flashing their white rump patches, calling stridently, leaping up from their ant-hunting among the grasses, as many as ten pouring from a single tree as we approached. They reminded us that here, too, we were on the main sky highways of the northern birds, that over this russet-clad eminence, as over the sandy levee at Muscatine, the migrant hosts would pour in ensuing weeks.

Looking off to the far horizon, seeing the land as the daybirds would see it, we had within our eye-reach immense stretches of river and forest and farm, all brilliant in sunshine and dappled with cloud-shadows. Except for the more numerous farms and the concrete highway and the railroad paralleling the river, the scene spread out around us was much the same that Thoreau saw, the same that, in 1805, greeted Colonel Zebulon M. Pike—the Pike of Pike's Peak—when, as the first recorded white man to climb the bluff, he reached its summit.

Upstream the great river flowed toward us with the molten-silver brilliance of reflected sunshine. Opposite us it widened into the lagoon-like upper end of that remarkable body of water the Indians called Lake of the Mountain, the Franciscan fathers knew as Lake of Tears, and that now bears the more prosaic name of Lake Pepin. Among the 10,000 lakes of Minnesota its origin is virtually unique. If you double the speed of water flowing in a stream you multiply by 64 the weight of the particles it can carry. Each time the water speed is doubled its carrying power is increased 64 times. This explains how, in the Rocky Mountains, spring torrents sometimes roll along boulders weighing ten tons. It also explains the origin of Lake Pepin. Rushing down from the high tablelands of western Wisconsin, some 30 miles south of the bluff on which we stood, the swift-flowing Chippewa empties into the Mississippi. There it deposits its heavy load of sand and gravel on the bed of the slower-moving stream. This debris forms a natural dam, a barrier that is continually being rebuilt and that backs up the water into thirty-four-mile-long Lake Pepin.

Rafts of waterfowl floated on its calm waters and in the shallows our glasses revealed great blue herons fishing. Standing motionless among them were eleven large, snow-white birds—American egrets. In 1932, when Thomas S. Roberts published his *Birds of Minnesota*, he described this species as having "formerly occurred as a straggler from the South." For decades, following the ravages of the plume hunters in southern swamps, the egret population was reduced and no birds wandered to the upper Mississippi. Then, in the summer of 1934, two appeared at Heron Lake. Others were sighted in succeeding years. Now, below our Barn Bluff eyrie, there were eleven in one flock. The return of this beautiful bird provides an encouraging and dramatic footnote in the story of American wildlife.

Elated by what we had seen, invigorated by the sun and air, rejoicing at the prospect of going on, we lightheartedly descended the stairs. I was tired. But I was no longer sickly tired. That evening while I pored over maps beneath a lamp and Nellie, with guidebooks and a pocket magnifying glass, sought the identity of an unknown plant from the bluff top, the dusk became windless. The thermometer dropped. The stars shone with a steely glitter and lonely train whistles carried far through the frosty air. And, moment by moment, this sudden cold at the end of the day was working in the darkness, splashing new, intense and flaming colors across the already painted forests of the north.

TEN

PAINTED FORESTS

CROW WING LAKE and Red Eye River, Hay Creek and Mantrap Valley. Chilled birds warming themselves in the sun. Snow fences rolled up at the roadside. Corn shocks extending up and over a hilltop like the last tepees of this Indian land. A farmer's wife, her shawl flapping, cleaning a stovepipe in the yard. Such things we saw as we rode north from Red Wing in the morning.

Our way threaded among swales and bogs. We were in a land of little lakes, each with a grebe or two floating on it. The monarchs lay behind us, but all that day we ran through mourning-dove and robin flocks. For more than 200 miles we followed the winding course of the Mississippi northward. That night we slept in a cabin beside Fish Hook Lake. And the next morning, not long after dawn, in the stillness of the forest, we came to the shore of Lake Itasca, to the very beginning rill of the mighty Mississippi.

All around us we saw, as Thomas Hood so long before had seen in England, "old Autumn in the misty morn standing shadowless like silence listening to silence." This was one of the perfect moments of our trip. We seemed, in the hush of that silvered hour, very close to some inscrutable secret of the noiseless wood. Then the sun rose above the treetops, tourists arrived, cries and exclamations succeeded the silence of the dawn. People from fifteen states came that autumn day to see the wonder of Old Man River as an infant.

Twenty-five hundred and fifty-two miles from the Gulf, 1,475 feet above the level of the sea, water was overflowing from the northern tip of three-pronged Lake Itasca and gurgling away in a shallow flow among granite boulders. This was the beginning of the Mississippi. Stepping from stone to stone, we crossed it in four strides. Beyond the water-smoothed rocks the current slowed as the bed beneath it deepened suddenly into a narrow, ditchlike channel winding away amid alders and red osiers.

I stood for a long time on this first crossing of the great river. Looking down at the clear, swirling water beneath me, I reflected on the adventures that lay before those transparent drops streaming by. Some would be sucked through the gills of fish, some evaporated into the air to float as clouds, some drift downstream frozen in ice cakes. They would slide along wharves and swirl among the roots of undercut trees and rush over dams and slow down in eddies. On that long flow toward the sea they would pass towns and factories and farms and the mouths of innumerable tributaries. How many drops of this clear flow now gurgling among these granite stepping-stones, I wondered, would ever reach the salt of the sea?

My reverie was interrupted by an elderly heel-and-toe walker who came marching down the path, resolutely stepped from rock to rock in a two-way passage, observed over his shoulder, "Now I've crossed the Mississippi!" and rapidly disappeared marching back up the trail again. All day long people cross these stepping-stones or stand in the middle of this first of the innumerable crossings spanning the great river to have their pictures taken.

One woman stared around her in bewilderment.

"What's everyone coming here for?" she demanded of a companion. "There's nothing to see here but a swamp!"

It has long been my contention that there is no place on earth where there is *more* to see than in a swamp—with its immense fertility and its teeming life. But I am sure the

lady would not have understood what I was talking about if
I had told her so. Nellie and I wandered away along the bank
of the infant river.

In my mind's eye I could see the final miles of the Mississippi as I had seen them on a spring day, flying high above
the delta, watching the river's titanic flow crawling away to
the sea between restraining levees. Here it was hardly wider
than a beaver canal. It meandered through boggy ground thick
with sphagnum moss and pitcher plants and Labrador tea.
A frog leaped into the water—the first frog of the Mississippi.
Whirligig beetles spun in the shelter of a tiny nook—the
earliest bay of the river. A dark swamp sparrow darted from
red osier dogwoods and disappeared around a turn—the initial
curve in the long course of the stream. Everything here was
a first—first frog, first bay, first curve. Here, in these initial
wanderings, minor events were taking place that were des-
tined to be repeated innumerable times along the 2,552-mile
course of the Father of Waters.

We returned to the shore of the lake. All along the shallows, where the wild rice grew, thousands of slender stems
were mirrored on the glassy stillness of tinted water. They
seemed growing in the midst of the bluest of skies, rising
with snow-white clouds drifting among them. This was the
season of the wild-rice harvest, in Indian days a time of feasting and thanksgiving. The pale yellow-green of the seed heads
had turned a delicate purple. Within, the kernels of the ripened grain were cylindrical in shape, olive green to purplish-
black in color, about half an inch in length. To the Algonquin
and Chippewa, they formed the staple grain of the land. Explorers, trappers and pioneers knew them by many names:
Indian oats, wild oats, water oats, mad oats, Canadian rice,
black rice, marsh rice, squaw rice. Linnaeus, in 1752, named
the plant *Zizania aquatica*. Peter Kalm tried unsuccessfully to
introduce it into Europe. The grain is, in truth, a rice and
not an oat. It is a wild, New World relative of the plant so

widely cultivated as a main source of food in the Orient.

Nearly 300 years ago Father Marquette noted in his journal that the finest of all Indian dishes was wild rice mixed with buffalo fat. No other grain I have ever tasted had a flavor so deliciously delicate. Its only rival among the taste sensations of our trip west with the fall was the wild and haunting flavor of pinyon nuts in the Far West. Not only did the rice nourish Indians and pioneers; it also fed and fattened the myriad waterfowl that, around the headwaters of the Mississippi, added to the overflowing abundance of autumn. Even today the wild grain is gathered by Chippewas on Minnesota lakes. Its past importance in the economy of earlier times is reflected in the fact that the names of fully ninety lakes and streams and communities, in this single state, are derived in one way or another from wild rice.

That night we slept by another forest lake. With the sinking of the sun the mercury dropped swiftly. The sturdy north-country owner of the camp observed:

"It's getting pretty chilly these nights."

"If you think this is chilly," I said, "what do you do when winter comes?"

"I go to Florida."

After an early breakfast next morning, a breakfast we will especially remember because of a sampling of another glorious food of fall—pumpkin pie—we rode once more in the dawn light down the winding roads of the 32,000-acre Itasca State Park. Itasca is not, as many persons have assumed, an Indian word. Its origin is erudite. It is formed of parts of two Latin words, the last of *veritas*, meaning truth, and the first of *caput*, meaning head or source. The man who coined this word in celebration of his discovery of the true source of the Mississippi was the remarkable Henry Rowe Schoolcraft. Geologist, Indian agent, naturalist, poet, friend and helper of Audubon, discoverer of the evening grosbeak, author of a monumental six-volume work on the aboriginal tribes of America, Schoolcraft had been sent into the region by President Andrew Jackson. His mission was to bring peace between the Sioux and the Chippewas. As a side activity he discovered the headwaters of the Mississippi.

One hundred and fifty-nine years after Father Marquette first sighted the river, on July 13, 1832, Schoolcraft reached the modest woodland brook that carries away the overflow from Lake Itasca. His guide was the Chippewa chief Yellow Head. After heating pitch to repair the birch-bark canoes that had been portaged over ridges, across matted tangles and through primeval forests gray with lichens, Schoolcraft and his small band of men began the descent of those first miles of the Mississippi in which it traces a giant question mark on the map before straightening out into its southward flow. Once on the way downstream they saw overhead a bird no man now sees in Minnesota, that most graceful and beautiful of all the hawks, the swallow-tailed kite. Confined at present almost entirely to the river swamps of the Southeast, this persecuted species once ranged widely, even nested in Minnesota.

Schoolcraft enjoyed the bird's superlatively graceful flight—something we could not experience. But all around us lay superlative beauty of another kind—beauty Schoolcraft did not see during that long ago visit in July. Then it was summer and the forests were green. Now it was autumn and, surrounding the lake, running down the banks of the beginning Mississippi, extending away over the ridges were the colored leaves, the tinted trees, the painted forests of the fall.

All across the country behind us—the realm of the round-headed hardwoods, the oaks and beeches and maples—autumn's annual chromatic show was rising to its peak. Nowhere in the world are the hues more rich and varied than in the climax woodlands of the eastern United States. We could visualize the colors now, or soon to be, on plant and bush and tree all along the path we had followed: The purplish

GOLDEN aspens run in clouds of autumn foliage among the
dark evergreens of the Uinta Mountains of northern Utah.

BEAR RIVER and its delta are seen above. Below, midges in a smokelike cloud, left, and on threads of gossamer, right.

red of the Cape Cod cranberry bogs, the scarlet sheets and clouds of New England's sugar maples, the wine hue of the Cape May tupelos, the tapestry of many colors clothing the Kittitinny Ridge, the old gold of sycamores along Ohio streams, the waves of crimson running down the swamp maples beside the warbler river, the golden mittens of the sassafras in the dune country of northern Indiana. Everywhere the leaves of the third season of the year were bringing the growth of spring and summer to a dramatic rainbow end. These were the days when the flames of autumn burned most brightly in a fleeting but memorable show.

Even overnight, it seemed, new richness had been added to the colors around us as we stood once more in the dawn light beside the bridge of stepping-stones. Every twig of birch and aspen was clothed in gold. Deep purple-red sheeted all the clumps of viburnum. And above our heads, stretching out over the flow of the beginning Mississippi, the branch of a maple tree extended, against the blue of the autumn sky, foliage in which scarlet and gold and orange intermingled. Not only around Lake Itasca but wherever we wandered those days through the wonderful Minnesota autumn, we were in a world of color, color subtly commingling, infinitely varied. Everywhere the life of the leaves was nearing its end. Yet there is no sadness of farewell in the foliage of autumn; all flags are flying at journey's end.

Looking about us, where the mirror of the water reflected sky and clouds and autumn leaves, we speculated on how far the stirring colors of fall go in stimulating our minds. The clear, bracing air of this third season, with its lowered humidity and its touch of chill, is given credit for the alertness and sense of well-being that characterizes our autumn mood. But is there not a corresponding lift to the mind in this riot of color, exciting and exhilarating? In the forest, fall is the season of light. The aureate leaves, the golden carpet of fallen foliage reflecting rays upward from the ground, these fill the deciduous woodlands with a luminous radiance unknown at other seasons of the year. Henri Amiel noted in his *Journal Intime:* "The scarlet autumn stands for vigorous activity; the gray autumn for meditative feeling." Later in the season there would come slaty skies, brown leaves, gray autumn. But now we wandered in the multicolored early days of fall, the time of vigor and elation.

A universal excitement runs through the land when the autumn foliage arrives. Newspapers headline it. People talk about it. Visitors come to see it. In New Hampshire half a hundred spotters, scattered over the state, send in reports on the progress of the autumn colors: "Just beginning"—"Almost at height"—"At height"—"Still colorful"—"Gone by." This state also pioneered in putting out special autumn-foliage bulletins. Every year an increasing number of New England communities hold Fall Foliage Festivals. In New York City, papers print almost daily reports on the condition of the fall colors and several states now feature "Color Tours" that carry visitors through the most beautiful displays of tinted leaves. The third season's greatest show—an American superlative—has become an expanding autumn business in many areas of the North and East.

To the red man all these tintings of fall were of miraculous origin. They came, grew in brilliance, tarnished and faded away. It has taken the researches of a host of modern scientists to decipher the story of the painted leaves. And even so this narrative of autumn change contains a number of pages that still are blurred or partly blank.

The simplest of the autumn colors to explain is yellow, the gold of the aspen and the hickory and the birch. Carotene, the pigment found so abundantly in carrots, and xanthophyll, the coloring matter found in egg yolks and the feathers of the canary, are present in these leaves all summer long. In fact there is a greater quantity of these two pigments in the green leaves of midsummer than in the yellow leaves of fall. But then they are masked by the outer layers of chlorophyll.

During the warm months the tree produces and uses chloro-phyll continually, with production and use balanced. Then comes the chill of autumn. It retards the production of chlorophyll more rapidly than it does its consumption. In a bleaching process that is only partly understood, the chloro-phyll breaks down into colorless compounds. The green disappears from the leaf and the yellow pigments are no longer masked. Each year we see this sudden shift of autumn on elm and birch and tulip tree, the change from the green of summer to the gold of fall. The new tints we see are not new at all. They are colors that have been there all the time.

Of the two pigments, carotene and xanthophyll, autumn gold is chiefly composed of the latter. In laboratory experiments this pigment was found to be twice as abundant as carotene in yellow autumn leaves. Both together, however, represent but an infinitesimal part of the total weight of the leaf. All the sheets of golden foliage that clothe autumn boughs are the product of such small amounts of these two pigments that they have a combined weight that is only one half of 1 per cent that of the leaves they glorify.

The yellows of autumn thus are produced by subtraction, the subtraction of chlorophyll. The reds of autumn are produced by addition, the addition of something that was not present in the leaf before.

From flaming scarlet to deepest purple, the most brilliant hues of the autumn woods are the products of coloring materials known as anthocyanins. They are the "cell-sap pigments." While the green of chlorophyll and the yellows of xanthophyll and carotene are contained in the protoplasm of the cell, the anthocyanins are carried in solution in the sap. Thus all the infinitely varied shades of red, the most striking feature of autumn's greatest show, are the products of tinted sap within the leaves.

Around the world and all through the vegetable kingdom the anthocyanins are distributed. They are responsible, in stem and bud and leaf and flower, for magentas and blues as well as reds and purples. They contribute the red to red bananas in the tropics and the red to red cabbage in northern fields. The cranberry and the poppy, the grape and the violet, the radish and the poinsettia all get their colors from anthocyanins. If the cell sap is acid the plant tends to produce bright reds. If it is alkaline it tends to produce blues and purples. How intense the colors of some of these cell-sap pigments are is demonstrated by the red cabbage. All its color comes from one layer of cells within the leaves.

The production of anthocyanins is an inherited ability possessed by many plants and trees. Some, like the purple beech, possess it so abundantly that the pigment produced masks the chlorophyll even in the summer leaves. Others, like the hickories, possess it not at all and their leaves always turn to yellow. Still others, like one isolated aspen we came upon as we drove south from Lake Itasca, produce slight amounts that impart to the outer leaves a faint rose tinting. They are the leaves that receive the greatest amount of sunshine. For anthocyanins are "sun pigments" as well as "cell-sap pigments."

With very few exceptions—notably the garden beet, which produces its bright-red root underground—the coloring material develops only where sunshine strikes. Thus the stem end of a red apple is usually more brightly colored than the flower end which hangs down away from the sun. In experiments, opaque letters have been attached to the side of such an apple before it ripened and letters or words in green have been produced on its red surface where the skin, shielded from the sunshine, developed no anthocyanin pigment in its cells. Scientists have even printed simple photographs on apples, in varying shades of green and red, by attaching negatives to their sides during the period when the fruit was ripening.

There are, of course, apple trees such as the greenings that never develop anthocyanins and never have red fruit.

Occasionally as we wandered through the fall we came upon a tree that was red-tinged on the outside and yellow within. The shaded leaves had failed to produce anthocyanins in sufficient quantity to make the red pigment noticeable. White oaks sometimes exhibit leaves in autumn that are reddish on top, where they have been struck by the sunshine, but whitish beneath. A breeze among such foliage produces the striking effect of an ever-shifting pattern of red and white. Again, it has been noticed that the flaming colors of the sugar maple are usually brightest at the ends of the branches, where they receive the maximum amount of sunshine.

There appears to be another reason why the red of the sugar maple is the most brilliant of all. The presence of sugar in the sap is conducive to the formation of this color. When a research worker tested bright-red leaves from a Virginia creeper, he found they contained more sugar than green leaves from the same vine collected at the same time. The leaf containing the greatest amount of sugar is believed to turn the brightest red. But all summer long there is sugar in and sunshine on the leaves of the sugar maples. Yet they remain green. Why? Another factor is missing. That is cold.

When the temperature drops to forty-five degrees F., or below, it interferes with the removal of sugars and other substances from the leaves and this favors the accumulation of the pigments in the sap of the cells. A sudden drop just after the sun has set—such as occurred that last evening at Red Wing—is especially productive of brilliant autumn leaves. So are crisp, sunny days. The high, clear skies and sparkling weather that usually mark the third season in the New World have much to do with the many-colored splendor of the forest trees. England's autumn, with mild and cloudy weather, produces duller foliage, mainly yellows and browns. Alice in Wonderland, judging by the somber groves and copses of the English fall, remarked that she always thought a wood in autumn looked sleepy.

At one time it was believed that the frost painted the autumn leaves. Now it is known that, with or without frost, lowered temperature achieves this end. In fact a hard frost or freeze early in the fall tends to destroy the yellow pigments and prevent the formation of anthocyanins. In such seasons the trees merely turn brownish without developing the reds and yellows and the infinitely varied combinations of the two. And, as every autumn progresses, even the most colorful of the painted leaves, even those of the maples that unite the ultimate brilliance of scarlet and gold and orange, they all—clinging to the tree or on the ground where they have fallen—tarnish and fade and lose their glory. Where do the pigments go?

Already some of the fallen leaves were brown along the paths we followed through the Minnesota woods. Others lay among them still tinted but with their colors slowly ebbing through oxidation. All the leaf pigments are unstable. Chlorophyll is the least stable of all. Next come the yellow pigments. Finally, most stable, are the anthocyanins. But even they oxidize in time, turning brown much in the manner of a slice of apple that is white when cut but takes on a brownish cast if subjected to prolonged exposure to the air.

The exact process by which the tide of autumn colors recede and browns of varying shades take their place is still imperfectly understood. Tannins, always present in the changing leaves, are believed to play a leading role. Throughout the whole chromatic parade of the fall foliage, all the tints and hues and combinations and shadings are the work of various pigments. But the universal brown that envelops the autumn leaves at last is rather the product of gradual decomposition, of chemical changes taking place little by little.

These changes—the long, slow ebbing of this forest splendor—had barely begun when we drove south again, this time through western Minnesota. Everywhere the flaming pageant was at its peak. It moved behind meadowlarks singing on a hundred fenceposts; it circled ponds where muskrat houses had been newly reënforced against the chilly nights; it trooped into the outskirts of farming towns where all along main streets the lamp posts were decorated with cornstalks; it stood in the background behind a curious stretch of rolling plowed fields where every rise was topped with silvery soil so that the farms all seemed dappled with sunshine and shadow. And so we came to the North Dakota line and Fargo and the Red River Valley. So we left one of the states we wanted least to leave—Minnesota. Before us lay the prairie; behind us stretched the thousand miles of the eastern hardwoods, now all clad in their coat of many colors. We had, in Minnesota, seen their chromatic splendor at its height, and we had, in Minnesota, come to the western border of their range.

ELEVEN

MYSTERY SLEEP

AN unpaved road led north a hundred miles to a pile of
stones in an open field that marked the exact geographical
center of the North American continent. A branching highway
angled away to reach, after many a zigzag, the Souris River
marshes where all five species of American grebes nest together. A side road swung to our right in the direction of the
village of Eldridge. For miles along the way we had read signs:
"Poor Little Me-Eldridge." Among the bustling, booster towns
of the North Dakota prairie, "Poor Little Me"—with its
population of 76—was doing its best to attract attention.

We wished we could turn off to Eldridge. We wished we
could stand at the exact center of the continent. We wished we
could visit the wild, marshy home of the grebes. But we had
other appointments with autumn farther to the west. A bless-
ing of Old India—"May you live for a hundred autumns in
this world"—came to mind and it occurred to us that we would
need a hundred autumns to see one American autumn in its
entirety.

We had left behind the Red River Valley with the vivid
green of its sprouted winter wheat and the honey-colored miles
of its cut-over grainfields. We had penetrated into a wide and
lonely land. Tremendously long trains of empty boxcars rolled
behind puffing engines and, on distant dirt roads, automobiles
crept along the skyline like insects moving down the edge of
a leaf. Each far-spaced house rose behind its windbreak of

willows and box elders and Russian olives planted to the west and north, pointing out like vanes the direction of the prevailing winter storms. Western meadowlarks, grayer than the eastern birds, with a sweeter, more warbling whistle—the state bird not only of North Dakota but of Nebraska, Kansas, Wyoming, Montana and Oregon as well—were gathering in flocks, ready for migration. And beside the road ring-necked pheasants stalked in metallic grandeur or scaled away on down-bent wings. They were at peace now but soon they would be hunted by the thousands of gunners who, in a single autumn season, kill as many as 3,000,000 pheasants in the two Dakotas.

Wildflowers were brown and dry. The grain harvest, long in, overflowed the elevators. At Spiritwood great mountains of the surplus wheat, weathered a deep rich gold, rose in a range of peaks beside the railroad tracks. All down the slopes of this cordillera of wheat ran little pits and pockets eaten out by English sparrows—an opulent flock of bird-millionaires feasting on a Thanksgiving dinner each day of the autumn. That night, far out on the plains, we saw the wide glitter of the northern stars and the next morning, when we pulled out onto the road and toward the west again, white rime silvered the prairies.

Our road, that day, carried us through wonderful country, rolling land where, mile after mile, we rode the great swells—literally ground swells—that lifted us up and tobogganed us down again into the trough beyond. And at the bottom of every trough we came to a marshy place, a pothole or slough. Two weeks, three weeks, and all this land of little marshes would be teeming with migrating waterfowl. But not as in former days. For too many years now a migration of another kind had coincided with it. Hunters from as far away as Missouri and Tennessee and Indiana had converged on the sloughs to prey on the alighting birds. We talked to one old-timer who had pulled off the road to look over a pothole two or three acres in extent.

"The ducks just don't come this way like they used to," he

told us. "I remember when all these slews were solid with ducks and geese every fall. Now the birds must go south some other way."

That explanation for the depleted ranks of waterfowl was one we heard all across the country. Wherever we were, the birds were going south a different way.

Twenty or thirty miles east of Bismarck we spent the latter part of the morning beside one wide and shallow slough where varied migrants had collected. Least sandpipers, those mice of the mudflats, fed along the edges. Dowitchers, hundreds huddling together, covered a projecting bar from end to end as though with dense brown moss. Coot and teal and mallard and shoveller floated on the water. Once when an airliner droned high overhead a shoveller tilted its great bill first to one side and then to the other as it peered aloft with each eye in turn. But the birds that first caught our attention were the brilliant black-and-white avocets. On slender legs, a flock of more than a hundred worked across the shallows swinging their long, upcurved bills in the water. They advanced like mowers wielding scythes in a hayfield. Then, all of a sudden, they all ceased feeding and lifted into the air. Facing the wind they sailed low over the highway, luminous birds with the sun behind them, while the multitude of their shadows—black shadows cast by black-and-white wings—trailed over and around us as they passed.

We had been standing for some time overlooking this slough when we became aware of a dry, sliding sound among the dead weeds of the embankment. Tracing the sound to its source we caught the movement of a glistening green body blotched with black. Slowly, laboriously, working upward through the weeds on its four short and stubby legs, one of those primitive creatures, a salamander, was ascending the embankment. It reached the top and, without a pause, plodded steadily across the concrete to disappear at the other side. A little later we saw another and then a third. All were about eight inches long.

All were dark green with markings of black. All were tiger salamanders, probably the Devil's Lake tiger salamander of eastern North Dakota. And all were moving in the same direction. Later that morning, as we drove on, we encountered salamanders crossing the highway from other sloughs. We journeyed for a dozen miles that day in the midst of one of autumn's most rarely noticed movements, a migration of tiger salamanders.

There is about the salamander a primordial strangeness. Scientists, who long have known that different species of tiger salamanders have different rates of heart beat, have more recently discovered that the heart of one species transplanted into the body of another species will continue to pulsate at its old rate in this new environment. Twice every year these strange, secretive creatures take part in a seasonal movement. In the early spring they sometimes travel across snow to reach the breeding area of a melted pond. In the fall, reversing all their normal habits and coming forth in the full glare of the day, they migrate toward their winter hibernating quarters. This is the most daring and dangerous time of their lives. Autumn restlessness grips them as it does the traveling woolly bears. And the movement of both leads to the protection of some cranny where they will drop into the long oblivion of their winter sleep.

That sleep, the deathlike torpor of hibernation, was drawing near for a host of other creatures. Already most of the Richardson's ground squirrels, those widespread rodents that are the source of North Dakota's nickname, The Flickertail State, were drowsing in their burrows. We saw only a few, at rare intervals, sitting upright like tent pegs beside the road. Somewhere west of the Red River Valley, as we had moved out across the prairie, we had passed through the vague, shadowy western borderline of the woodchuck's range. Behind it, all the way from Maine to Minnesota, these pastureland marmots were sleek and fat, curling up in their underground rooms, closing their eyes, breathing ever more slowly, their heart beats separated by greater and greater intervals. Undisturbed by wind or sleet or blizzard, unaware of cold or scarcity of food, the woodchuck and its fellow sleepers would spend the winter wrapped in the profoundest of slumbers.

This dropping into a sleep that seems so close to death is one of the strangest adventures of the animal world. The flame of life, for months on end, sinks so low it almost—but not quite—goes out.

During the summer a woodchuck breathes between twenty-five and thirty times a minute, reaching a hundred times a minute when excited. Yet, during hibernation, it may breathe only once in five minutes. Normally its heart throbs about eighty times a minute. In emergencies it may jump to two hundred times a minute. During the long sleep of hibernation, however, its pulse may slow down to four or five beats a minute, just sufficient to keep its thickened and sluggish blood in motion. Its limbs grow rigid. Even though, like all hibernating animals, it rolls itself into a ball to conserve heat, its temperature drops as low as thirty-seven degrees F., only five degrees above freezing. Thus for months on end—for as much as five months and sometimes more—the hibernating woodchuck skirts the fine line that divides the living and the dead.

At the same time millions of other creatures—frogs buried in the mud of pond bottoms, bats hanging upsidedown in caverns, chipmunks rolled into striped balls of fur, bears hidden in dark and silent dens—would be lost in the depths of their winter sleep. Reptiles that would twine themselves into masses to reduce the evaporation of their moisture were already moving toward crevices in the various Rattlesnake Buttes of the Dakotas. To infusoria, to land snails, to bumblebees, to toads, to alligators, to grizzly bears the coming of fall brings the drowsiness and torpor of what the Indians called The Long Sleep. Even a bird, the desert poorwill, has been found hibernating in the southwest, its temperature down to sixty-four degrees F. For all these infinitely varied creatures their ability to hibernate turns the winter into one long night of slumber.

The depth of that slumber varies greatly. Some animals, like the chipmunk and the red squirrel, are light sleepers. They awake from time to time, feed, then drowse again. Others, like the woodchuck and the ground squirrels, are deep sleepers. They can be rolled across the floor like a ball without awakening them. So can the dormouse of Europe, familiar to all readers of *Alice in Wonderland*. The Richardson's ground squirrel, spending the winter well below the frost line, sometimes sleeps curled up vertically like a wheel resting on its rim. It is so lost to the world that it can be tossed high in the air and caught repeatedly while it slumbers on.

In one instance a research scientist amputated the limb of a ground squirrel while it remained apparently insensible to pain under the anesthetic of its hibernation sleep. Moreover only a few drops of thickened blood oozed slowly out. In many animals circulation to the extremities almost ceases in hibernation. A laboratory worker once injected bright blue dye into a vein in the leg of a hibernating groundhog. It was not until the woodchuck awoke in the spring that the dye reached the rest of its body. But when the scientist repeated the experiment in midsummer the swift flow of the bloodstream carried the color to all parts of the animal's body, even temporarily tinting its eyeballs, within the space of a few minutes.

Deadly poisons often have no effect upon an animal during hibernation. And at the University of Chicago, in 1953, Kenneth P. DuBois and his associates discovered that irradiation sickness, the dreaded by-product of atomic warfare, was held in abeyance by hibernation. When active, nonhibernating gophers were exposed to doses of 800 roentgens of X-rays they died within fifteen days. Hibernating gophers, given the same deadly dosage, were alive at the end of a month. But once they were aroused from their slumber they, too, died within fifteen days. Hibernation had merely slowed down the progress of the sickness. With its sluggish circulation, its low body temperature and reduced metabolism, the sleeping animal exists in a state approaching suspended animation.

This condition makes it immune to many dangers. Paradoxically its nearness to death saves its life. A sleeping hedgehog has been thrust underwater twenty times in succession without drowning it and a hibernating bat was left submerged in a pail of water for an hour and then pulled out little the worse for its ordeal. In one laboratory scientists sealed a woodchuck in an airtight jar filled with carbon dioxide gas. After more than an hour in this lethal chamber the animal was examined and found to be apparently unharmed. Infinitesimal amounts of oxygen sustain an animal during hibernation. In the course of a single summer day a woodchuck takes in as much oxygen as it requires for the whole of its winter inactivity.

Although scientists have been studying the mystery sleep of the hibernating animal for hundreds of years it is still largely a puzzle unsolved. Like the riddle of migration among birds, its effect is obvious; but its hidden causes and its exact manner of functioning are relatively unknown. Both migration and hibernation enable creatures to live winterless lives, to escape the effects of cold and scarcity of food. Both are nature's schemes for keeping alive, in a given area, more creatures than there is food to feed the year around.

What induces hibernation? What trigger sets it off? It is not always cold although cold is usually a factor. Most of the long sleepers have disappeared by the time the mercury falls to fifty degrees F. But woodchucks frequently den up while it is still comparatively warm and some ground squirrels commence their hibernation as early as midsummer—beginning a sleep that may last for thirty-three of the fifty-two weeks of the year. Moreover daily readings of a thermometer placed in a woodchuck burrow revealed that the lowest temperatures came late in winter at a time when the animal was waking up.

Nor is the main cause scarcity of food. Animals in captivity often drowse off into their winter slumber with ample food beside them. Nor is the single explanation the lessening light of the shortening days. For hibernators nod and fall asleep in well-lighted, well-ventilated laboratories. Under wild conditions cold, hunger, darkness, quiet all seem important to hibernation. But there is no one cause known. Moreover, just as only certain birds have the instinctive urge to migrate, so only the hibernators among animals have the racial rhythm that leads to winter torpor.

One thing appears invariable: the fattest individuals begin their hibernation first and tend to stay asleep longest. The most perfect hibernators—the woodchuck in America and the hedgehog in Europe—lay up no provisions except layers of fat. In late summer, when a woodchuck is building up surplus fat, it will sometimes eat a third of its weight in plants at a single feeding. During the months of sleep the hibernator slowly assimilates this excess fat. Like oil in a lamp turned low, it is gradually burned to maintain the flame of life. A woodchuck may consume fully a third of its weight during the winter while a ground squirrel may awaken weighing only half as much as when it went to sleep. During the final days before they fall asleep, most animals eat almost nothing. The last meal eaten in fall will sometimes be still in the sleeper's stomach when it awakens in spring. During the long slumber of hibernation digestion comes to a virtual standstill.

So do other bodily processes. The kidneys cease to function. The bladder becomes tightly sealed. Some scientists have suggested that one important factor in the deep torpor of hibernating animals may be autointoxication similar to that experienced by humans in certain types of kidney disorders. Other theories have been many. Around the turn of the century, the French scientist, Raphael Dubois, announced his belief that "autonarcosis" explained the phenomenon, that the stupor of the hibernating animal was the product of carbon dioxide gas that built up in its body. However this theory has not stood the test of time. Nor has another research worker's announced discovery of a "hibernating gland." It was shown to be merely a pocket of fatty tissue.

In 1955, at the University of Wisconsin, Peter R. Morrison and A. R. Dawe observed an interesting thing about the hearts of the long sleepers. The heart of an ordinary animal, they found, would stop at the low temperatures at which the hibernators spend the winter. What, then, makes the hearts of the dormant creatures keep beating? Such organs, the Wisconsin scientists discovered, are hyper-irritable. At the slightest stimulus, at normal temperatures, they beat furiously. It is this hyper-irritability that keeps the organs slowly pulsing at temperatures at which those of nonhibernating animals would stop.

A number of research workers at various times have noticed oddities in the distribution of magnesium and calcium salts in the blood of animals that hibernate. If magnesium and insulin are chilled and injected into animals that never hibernate—cats, dogs, rabbits—they fall into a hibernation-like torpor. But it is not true hibernation; no drug known to man will produce it. And if the animal in the torpor of pseudo-hibernation does not receive an injection of counteracting drugs it dies without waking.

Some years ago the famous American surgeon, Dr. Harvey Cushing, reported the discovery that the pituitary gland of the woodchuck is reduced in size during the winter sleep. In England it has been noted that the thyroid of the hedgehog becomes shrunken in autumn and resumes its normal size in spring. Even tiny injections of warm thyroid extract will arouse a hibernating hedgehog. However if the same injections are cold the sleeping animal falls into even deeper slumber. Among the endocrine glands numerous scientists have sought the secret of hibernation. But repeated tests have proved that even when one of these glands is removed entirely it does not induce the torpor of winter sleep.

All animals were once cold-blooded. As winter approaches, some scientists believe, those with the most imperfect temperature control tend to give up the fight. They abandon their warm-blooded state and let their temperatures fall toward that of their surroundings. But they never quite cross the line, never revert entirely to the cold-bloodedness of their reptilian ancestors. They remain slightly warmer than their surroundings. Hibernation banks the fire of life but, in its mysterious way, never extinguishes it. There is, of course, a limit to the amount of cold a hibernating animal can withstand. This explains why there are no hibernators above the Arctic Circle, why the hares and lemmings and foxes all are active throughout the winter.

When the temperature, in the spring, rises to about sixty degrees F., the sleepers awake. In the autumn they enter hibernation gradually, drifting deeper and deeper into sleep over a period of days; but in the spring they leave it almost abruptly. The temperature of an awakening woodchuck may shoot up forty-eight degrees in the space of two hours and a half. There is on record an instance in which a woodchuck's temperature rose sixty degrees in a single hour. And a dormouse has been known to gain thirty-four degrees in less than three-quarters of an hour. The animals revive literally headfirst. They awake from head to tail. The blood supply to the rear is reduced until the front part—containing the brain and more vital organs—approaches normal body temperature. At Harvard, Charles P. Lyman and Paul O. Chatfield found that the electrical activity in a woodchuck's brain was nil until it reached a temperature of sixty-eight degrees. Thus the sleep of its hibernation must be a void of dreamless slumber. Before the brain temperature reaches sixty-eight degrees the movements of the woodchuck are aimless; above that point they become coordinated and brain-directed.

Violent shivering helps the aroused sleeper to equalize its temperature. At the same time it pants rapidly, expelling the carbon dioxide that has accumulated in its system. Its heart races—pounding up to 200 beats a minute for a woodchuck—to send the blood coursing through its body. Thus the winter-long sleep of hibernation comes to its swift conclusion. But the mystery of that sleep, so long eluding solution, remains with us. The marvel of migration—for the creature that travels—is balanced by the marvel of hibernation—for the creature that stays at home.

We were to see still another instance of autumn preparation for winter sleep near the end of that North Dakota day. At sunset we were driving back up the western side of the Missouri from the dusty, river-bluff site of old Fort Abraham Lincoln. There, nearly eighty years before, Custer's men had ridden away toward the Little Bighorn and their rendezvous with one of the tragic moments of American history. Between us and the river extended a narrow flood plain dense with box elder and willow and white-berried panicled dogwood. Suddenly we found ourselves in the midst of a living storm, enveloped in a wave, a cloud, a blizzard of flying insects. Each was about half an inch long, each brilliantly marked in red and black. For a quarter of a mile this winged host swept toward us, swirled around us, struck the windshield and shot up and over the car. I stopped and for a time we walked amid the thousands of insects streaming all in one direction. As in the migration of the tiger salamanders, we were witnessing something new in our lives. We were seeing for the first time an autumn flight of *Leptocoris trivittata*, the box-elder bug. Hatching from bright red eggs on the river-bottom trees, they had spent their early lives as red nymphs among the leaves of the box elders. Now, their time of growth behind them, they were gathering together, massing for the movement to the crannies of outbuildings and houses, to the dry, southward-facing crevices, where they would spend the winter in hibernation.

We waited until the insect clouds had drifted away behind us. Then we drove on—through Mandan, into the lonely dusk among the great hills north of Bismarck, toward the juncture of the Knife and the Missouri where, during the winter of 1804, Lewis and Clark had contracted for the services of the interpreter, Charbonneau, and his amazing squaw, Sacajawea. Moment by moment the purple haze deepened and the shine of the twisting Missouri dulled. A few lights at scattered ranch houses a great way off gleamed like remote and tiny stars amid the blackness of the hills. The chill of the autumn evening came swiftly. Yet even in the chill, all around us the flocking meadowlarks repeated endlessly the sweet warble of their song. And so we slipped back down the hills, back to the Missouri, back to Mandan where we spent the night.

We talked for a time that evening of all the dramatic and sudden changes that come in fall to migrant and hibernator alike. And Nellie expressed the thought of us both. We desired no migrant's year of one continued summer, no hibernator's year half lost in unconsciousness. We wanted the whole year, the twelve months complete, the year rounded with spring and summer and autumn and winter, with the variety of all its seasons.

TWELVE

WONDERFUL EIGHTY-THREE

THIS was the prairie fall. This was the "haze on the far horizon, the infinite tender sky." And it will always come back to us as we saw it then—a long, straight road stretching like a taut string toward the south, extending away across a land rolling in great tan waves beneath the high blue of the sky. It is a road we will never forget, a road we will always remember as Wonderful Eighty-Three.

Among the hills and wooded valleys of the East, the landscape closes in like a bud. Here, on the plains, it opens out, expands like a flower full-blown. Under the height of the sky and over the waves of the land, the black line of U.S. Highway 83 carried us that day southward through two and a half degrees of latitude. It led us from beautiful Apple Creek, mentioned in Audubon's journal, to Farm Island, associated with the expedition of Lewis and Clark; from near Bismarck, the capital of North Dakota, to Pierre, the capital of South Dakota. And always, just to the west, paralleling the road, the muddy Missouri, the Smoky Water of the Mandan Indians, rolled along its winding course, moving southward too.

That day started with the uncertain crows. It ended with the cautious Canada geese. Between the two it was filled with a long succession of flocks and waves and concentrations of many kinds of birds. The full tide of migration now was flowing down the valley of the Missouri to join the mightier tide of the Mississippi Flyway. For more than 150 miles that day, we overtook and moved among wave after wave of migrants. It was as though we were riding a surf-board, sweeping ahead on the crests of the great combers of the autumn flight. This was a day, as well as a road, we will always remember.

Not far from the pioneer village of Menoken we encountered the crows. In a vast assemblage they stretched like a dark scud-cloud across an expanse of open country. The cloud elongated, contracted, shifted form continually as the birds milled about in the sky. They seemed to be at the start of migration, uncertain of mind, a democracy at the polls. Some appeared set on going north, others south. The flock split apart, rejoined, divided, returned together, the babel of cawing rising to crescendos and sinking away and then swelling once more. We stopped for a long time beside the highway to watch the outcome. For minutes at a time the birds circled, apparently in screaming debate. They were like swarming bees that had lost their queen. They rose hundreds of feet into the air, descended close to the ground; they bunched and strung out. Then at last they all rose and moved away uncertainly toward the south. This almost-human hesitance and debate and final departure was our first vivid impression of this never-to-be-forgotten day.

To the Mandan Indians who lived along this part of the Missouri in the days of Lewis and Clark, all the flocking birds of autumn were going home, home to The Old Woman Who Never Dies. In their mythology this supernatural being, dwelling unseen beyond the southern horizon, was the giver of all crops and the birds were her representatives. Each fall the natives prayed and made offerings of meat and grain as the migrants departed, in order that their crops the following year might be bountiful. And in the spring when the wildfowl came back up the river the Indians greeted them as emissaries and auguries of good fortune, different birds representing success to different crops—the wild goose to the maize, the wild duck to the beans, the wild swan to the gourds.

Running south under the cloudless sky, we were at times that day in a land as lonely as the sea. We would catch glimpses of remote ranch houses across infinite stretches of country. Each surrounded by its cluster of weathered buildings, they were far-scattered, hardly more frequent than villages in the East. At times, looking ahead from the top of some rise, we would see our road, bee-lining away over the swells of land, take on a semblance to an old-fashioned spyglass seen in reverse, different sections ahead appearing beyond successive swells, suddenly narrowed by the abrupt increase in distance.

In every pond along the way muskrats were out, sleeping like kittens in the sun. A family of five slumbered in a brown cluster on top of one house no more than thirty feet from the road. They paid no attention to us. While we watched through our glasses, one lifted its head and yawned widely. Then it dozed off again. Another awoke long enough to scratch itself vigorously behind a foreleg. Two stretched, clambered down, slipped into the water and swam in a wide circle. Then they climbed out, dripping, onto the mound of yellow vegetation and curled up again, soon dry, soon part of the pile of sun-lighted, shining, sleek brown fur. These were days of warmth and well-being, the days of the early-autumn sunshine.

But down the southward-leading length of Wonderful Eighty-Three it was the birds that dominated our road and our day. Here, as nowhere else, we rode the floodtide of the autumn movement. The birds increased in number, piled up in concentrations, as we advanced. Each successive pond seemed inhabited by a denser population of coot. Swimming away as we slowed to a stop, they trailed across the water behind them a multitude of spreading V's that crisscrossed endlessly until sometimes half the surface of a pond was covered with moving, ripple-bounded diamond shapes, glinting in the sun. The sight of these many coot awakened the memory of a quaintly printed line—with f's used in place of s's in the old-fashioned way—that I once came upon in Thomas Pennant's *Arctic Zoology*. According to this famous eighteenth-century naturalist, to whom were addressed many of the letters that make up Gilbert White's classic *The Natural History of Selborne*, it was the custom of Indians around Niagara Falls to hunt coot in order to "drefs their fkins and ufe them for pouches."

One after the other, half a dozen times in the course of the day, we overtook long, straggling, southward-drifting flocks of crows. One, like a skein of windblown smoke, was strung out for more than a mile. A whole flock had landed across one hillside, and at another place the black birds of passage were crowding around a water hole to drink. Big hawks, too, were on the move. Most seemed to be roughlegs and that hawk of the prairies, Swainson's, but a number were redtails. Usually we saw them soaring southward or circling in the sky but there was one yellow slope, descending to a swale bordered by green-black rushes, where almost every one of the gray, scattered rocks held a perching buteo.

Now we were back among killdeers again. We saw them congregated together, scattered across slopes, clustered around pasture water holes, circling overhead, calling as they flew. Avocets and yellowlegs, both greater and lesser, swarmed around the edges of the sloughs; over one small lake 500 Franklin's gulls circled in great white wheels above the feeding shore birds. Then there were wondrous miles when the air all around us was filled with the sweet, flutelike song of the massed meadowlarks. Somewhere in Beaver Valley, east of Fort Yates and the grave of Sitting Bull, we came upon a bird we had never seen before. Brilliant in contrasting black and white, it shot in an almost vertical climb up the steep side of a railroad embankment—our first American magpie.

It was 12:05 P.M. when we crossed the boundary between the two Dakotas. In the southern state we were about midway between the Atlantic and the Pacific and at the same time almost equidistant from the North Pole and the Equator. Hardly twenty miles inside South Dakota, in the region of Hiddenwood Lake, we encountered the largest of all the migrants that move southward through the autumn skies along the course of the Missouri. A flock of half a dozen immense white pelicans floated near the farther shore—birds with an even greater span of wing than the rare whooping crane that sometimes crosses this land in its autumn movement from the far north to the Texas coast. As we watched, one of the pelicans flapped into the air and then, with eightfoot, black-tipped wings outspread, soared on and on over the water.

As the day advanced, small, wan clouds, few and far away, formed along the edges of the burnished sky. Little twisters ran across the open land beside the highway snatching up grass and dust. And always, seen in the hazy, dusty distance, the buttes rose along the skyline, flat-topped, roofed with a layer of harder rock that protected the softer, more easily eroded material below. The time of flowers was now past and almost every plant we saw was brown of leaf and dry of stem. In the warmth of the afternoon, grasshoppers interminably crossed the road ahead of us, some walking this way, some that, as restless as the far-scattered pioneers who roamed the area in an earlier day.

In this largely treeless land we came upon a cottonwood that must have been a landmark for a generation or more. Its lower half was clad in yellow leaves, but all its upper branches were silvered and barkless and bare. As we approached, a cloud of excited blackbirds swept toward the tree, swirled around it, descended on it. Almost in an instant the migrant host covered the bare branches and the tree seemed half clad in yellow foliage, half in black. We counted the birds perching on one limb and calculated the total number. Well over 1,000 blackbirds had settled in this single tree. Their din drowned out every other sound. This was the great adventure, for many, perhaps for most, the first migration.

At the end of five minutes the concourse of birds suddenly rose into the air. For a hundred yards or so we rode parallel to one redwing. Its speed over the ground was exactly forty miles an hour. Later in the day, near Pierre, we came within sight of a vast, flowing river of birds at least five miles long—redwings and grackles and Brewer's blackbirds—crossing the sky from east to west, toward the Missouri. Tens of thousands of flocking birds were going to roost along the river.

All that day the Missouri, unseen to the west, was a dominant feature of the land. Just below the horizon, beyond the buttes to our right, it flowed, now drawing nearer, now turning farther away in its windings. We felt its presence. We saw, in dry vegetation wrapped about fenceposts, evidences of its floodwaters in the spring. For Americans, the Missouri River has more than ordinary significance. It was the Lewis and Clark roadway into the unknown. It was the path of the early fur traders. It was the water barrier crossed by the pioneers. It carried the adventurous early naturalists deeper into a wilder West.

Just over there, on this stretch of winding river between Bismarck and Pierre, the men of the Lewis and Clark Expedition had landed their fifty-five-foot keelboat, propelled by twenty-two oars, and had examined fresh tracks of a "grizzled" bear three times as large as those of a man. There, too, they had come upon great "gangues of buffalow" swimming the river. This was in the fall of the year, in October 1804.

Only seven years later, Thomas Nuttall had wandered up the banks of this same stretch of the 2,466-mile river. It was in

June and along the stream and on the prairies beyond wild-flowers were in bloom. "Delighted with the treasures spreading themselves out before him," as Washington Irving described him on a later trip, "he went groping and stumbling along among a wilderness of sweets, forgetful of everything but his immediate pursuits." Here he found a new cinquefoil, a new figwort, a new nightshade. Where the Cheyenne River joins the Missouri—Nuttall spelled it "Shian" in his notes—he collected a prairie pentstemon new to science. This was in the fall of 1811.

Less than two decades after Nuttall, a fur-trader's canoe, following all the windings of this part of the river, carried George Catlin, pioneer painter of Indians, upstream toward his eight years with trappers and tribes of the prairie regions. This remarkable man, working under all the hardships of primitive conditions, put down on canvas a priceless collection of aboriginal portraits. But Catlin was more than a portrait painter. He was a man of vision and nobility of spirit, a friend of red men, a defender of the persecuted. And, apparently, he was the first person in America to propose the creation of a great national park in the West.

Again, a decade and a half later, John James Audubon, painting wildlife as he went, ascended the stream that flowed just beyond our western horizon. Aboard the pioneer Missouri River steamer *Omega*, he was on his way to the Yellowstone. Also on board riding with him in the wood-burning, spark-spitting paddle-wheeler were almost 10,000 pounds of gunpowder bound for frontier trading posts. At the time Audubon was in his fifty-eighth year and was described by a reporter who interviewed him in St. Louis at the start of the expedition as "an old man with silver locks and the weight of years upon him." But the entries in the journal he kept at the time show no evidence of diminishing powers. With vitality and keenness of observation they record absorbing sidelights on wildlife—how wolves came running whenever they heard the sound of a gun being fired; how antelope were so curious by nature that they would approach close to a man who lay on his back on the prairie and kicked his legs in the air; how—above Pierre, in almost the exact portion of the river that now lay due west of us—he watched a spotted sandpiper in full flight dive under the water five or six times in escaping the pursuit of a pigeon hawk.

In an introduction to a volume of his collected poems, John Masefield, the Poet Laureate of England, remarks how mention of some hillside or valley or stream in the pages of a book will invest the region with special charm and how the reader feels a quickened interest when, passing that way later on, he remembers the allusion. So it was that remembered pages from the *Original Journals of the Lewis and Clark Expedition*, from *The Missouri River Journals* of Audubon, from *Travels in the Interior of North America*, by Maximilian, Prince of Wied, had enveloped this region of the Missouri with a peculiar fascination.

We came to the river again at Pierre late in the afternoon—with Wonderful Eighty-Three, that highway of birds, behind us. Turning south we followed the eastern bank downstream to sandy roads winding among cottonwoods on Farm Island. Here, in 1804, hunters of the Lewis and Clark party killed four elk. Now connected with the mainland by a short causeway, this river island, three miles long, has been set aside as a state park. Fur traders and soldiers stationed at Fort Pierre in the early days at various times raised crops here; hence the name.

A score of chickadees were trooping along the island's edge among the cottonwoods. Savanna sparrows fed on the seeds of the pigweed. And out over the river goldfinches went past, rising and falling as though on choppy waves, while, flying farther out, a flicker loped by them in great bounds, appearing to ride longer swells of the airy sea. Under the birds and past the island, brown and swirling, rolled unceasingly the muddy water of the wide and shallow Missouri River.

Sediment of many kinds made up its burden of silt. It ranged from invisible flakes of clay, only $\frac{1}{25,000}$ of an inch across, to sandgrains of quartz, $\frac{1}{25}$ of an inch in diameter, and even small pebbles of varying size. A sluggish current, moving no more than a quarter of a mile an hour, is sufficient to support the flakes of clay. At a third of a mile an hour a stream will carry fine sand. At one mile an hour it will transport gravel the size of a pea; at three miles an hour it will move along stones as big as hens' eggs. Whatever slows the current of a stream causes it to deposit its sediment, commencing with the larger elements. The minimum gradient that will keep a river flowing is a drop of six inches to the mile. If the descent becomes shallower than that all progress ceases, the water spreads out, flow and direction are lost.

Looking across the wide brown, sediment-filled flood of the river toward the dead-appearing bluffs of its farther bank, we saw nineteen slender necks stretch up along a sandbar well out from either shore. A flock of Canada geese, settling down for the night safely beyond gunshot, had seen us emerge from among the cottonwoods. Instantly they set up a deep-toned clamor, every bird on the alert. The Missouri is one of the great river highways of the migrating geese. On "10th November Satturday 1804," among the Mandans, Captain William Clark noted in his journal that "the Gees Continue to pass in gangues." Near the very spot where we stood, John James Audubon had observed these prudent birds as they were going north in spring. They were wary then; a hundred years and more later, with the number of guns arrayed against them growing year by year, they were more wary still. From their distant sandbar this band of sagacious waterfowl watched us intently, every head erect, until we left the river bank and started back toward Pierre. Those upraised heads of the cautious geese, seen in a place so long associated with movements of their kind, provided our last bird memory of this superlative day of birds.

THIRTEEN

BADLANDS BY MOONLIGHT

SUNSET, on this day, came among the badlands of western South Dakota. We had gained an hour that morning when we crossed the wide brown Missouri and entered Rocky Mountain Time. By now we had long since, in these Dakotas, left behind the familiar, colorful eastern trees—the white oak and black oak and scarlet oak, the shagbark hickory and yellow birch, the maple and ash and beech and sassafras and tupelo. Almost the only trees we saw here were the cottonwoods that ran in straggling lines of gray and yellow, gray bark and yellow leaves, beside the infrequent streams. Just as the Indians farther west believed in Thunder-Beings among the mountains, so the plains Indians believed in spirits that dwelt within the cottonwoods. Flowing in two parallel lines, these spirit trees followed, curve for curve, the twisting serpentine of the Bad River as we ran west.

Going through the Dakotas we were cutting across a dividing zone, a region where plants of the East and plants of the West meet and intermingle. We were traveling in a land where the colors of the soil varied continually. We were traversing a country where cattle fed on a thousand hills—yellow, nibbled hills. We were journeying through an area of finer dust that hung for longer periods in the air. We were, by afternoon, wandering in the midst of a sterile world, seamed and fissured and broken, the *mauvaises terres* of the old French explorers. All around us spread that kingdom of erosion—erosion on a Paul Bunyan scale—the badlands of South Dakota.

From the vantage point of a promontory that evening, we watched this many-colored, many-formed land spreading away below us in the sunset. The water-grooved ravines, the knife-edged ridges, the fluted hillsides, the whole tortured character of the land, was accentuated by the horizontal rays streaming low out of the west. The sun sank. The salmon sky paled above the powder blue of the hazy horizon. And as we stood there in the crepuscular light, the glow of the sky was reflected momentarily from the fluttering, multi-veined wings of a slow-flying insect. It passed us, circled and landed awkwardly among the sparse grassclumps. It suggested a heavy, laboring dragonfly. But a single closer glance revealed its astonishing identity. Amid this parched and dusty land of dry ridges and gullies, it was the last insect I should have expected to see—a water scorpion.

A reddish-brown creature about an inch long, it clung to the pale yellow grass, its grasping forelegs outthrust, its long breathing tube projecting to the rear. Underwater, hanging head downward among aquatic vegetation, the tip of its air tube thrust above the surface film as it awaits the approach of its prey, a water scorpion resembles a small brownish twig caught among the plants. Scientists know it as *Ranatra fusca*. The insect we saw was one of the frontiersmen of its species. Here in South Dakota we were at the northern limit of its range west of the Mississippi.

Only rarely, and then at dusk or in the night, do the adult insects take flight. The oval eggs from which they hatch are laid in the spring and each is decorated at the top with two white, threadlike filaments longer than the egg itself. About a month after the eggs are laid, the hatching insects tilt back the tasseled caps and creep forth as baby water scorpions. True bugs, with sharp little beaks, they feed on the eggs of insects and fishes and on small aquatic creatures, often on immense numbers of mosquito larvae, attaining full size in about two and a half months.

When we were in the Kissimmee Prairie region of Florida, on our spring trip, we had been warned to look out for "alligator fleas" when wading in shallow water. But no one could describe the creature for us. It was more than a year later that I discovered its identity through a notation on an insect label in the collection of the U.S. National Museum in Washington, D.C. "Alligator flea or water dog," the notation read. "Said to bite or sting severely." The insect, collected north of Lake Okeechobee, was that close relative of our badlands water scorpion, *Ranatra australis*. Its beak, occasionally jabbed into the bare leg of a wading native, apparently is its chief claim to attention on the Florida peninsula.

We looked from the insect clinging to the grass clump out across the vast, waterless badlands. Where had this aquatic creature been born? Where had it come from to appear in the fading light of the after-sunset? Perhaps it arrived from the tortuous White River, miles to the south; perhaps from some rangeland water hole beyond the wall where the badlands end to the north. Between a thumb and forefinger I picked it from its grass stem. Its forelegs moved rapidly. They rubbed roughened patches against its body. I caught the faint, high squeak of its stridulated sound. As I continued to hold it, it suddenly ceased all movement, stiffened, feigned death in my hand. After a time it stirred. I tossed it into the air. Gauzy wings unfurled and it fluttered away. One moment it was silhouetted against the dull shine of the sky. The next it was swallowed up in the gray world of the badlands below us.

A sudden chill descends on this barren country at sundown. Almost minute by minute we could feel the air grow cooler. Standing there, alone on the promontory, we were surrounded by a silence so intense we could hear no other sound than our own slow breathing. Only twice in the transition from day to night had we seen other human beings. Once, when our eyes were wandering over the wild and lonely beauty around us, a car came speeding up the grade. It veered into the turn-out and slid to a stop amid flying gravel. Momentarily the occupants peered from the windows. Then with a roar of the exhaust they charged away. Hardly had the sound of their tires, loud in complaint on the turns, died away before another car pulled up. The driver leaned from the window and shouted: "How far to the Wall Drugstore?" Then he was gone and we were left alone in the silence and the deepening dusk.

As the sky grew velvet and the last of the daylight ebbed away, in the darkness the stars seemed hanging low all across the heavens. The illusion of nearness at times became so intense in this dry, clear atmosphere that we appeared to need but a slightly higher promontory to lift us into the midst of that shining multitude of heavenly bodies overhead. They spread away in all directions. They clustered together. They glittered in constellations. They ran across the firmament in the heaven-wide galaxy of the Milky Way—that great silver river of the sky, believed by the old Egyptians to be the source of the Nile and by the ancient Hindus to be the fountainhead of their sacred Ganges. Here were the stars—the autumn stars—as we had hoped to see them at Delphos.

In lush, far-off Tertiary times, the stars no doubt shone less brilliantly here. For vapors filled the warm and humid air above the great marshes that extended across the region. Then the Thunderbeast, the giant brontotherium, wallowed amid the steaming vegetation, lived and died and left its fossil bones to be unearthed more than 100,000,000 years afterwards. In the badlands of South Dakota scientists have found a rich graveyard of prehistoric life. Beginning with the pioneer Thaddeus A. Culbertson, who roamed the region in a lumber wagon in 1850 looking for "petrifactions" for the Smithsonian Institution, through the later paleontologists, Professor O. C.

CINDER FIELDS in southern Idaho appear scattered with
doilies where bunched eriogonum has gained a foothold.

ARID highlands at the Dinosaur National Park, in Utah.
From these rocks have come fossils of many prehistoric animals.

Marsh of Yale, and Henry Fairfield Osborn of the American Museum of Natural History, men of science have discovered the remains not only of dinosaurs but of giant tortoises, three-toed horses and the prehistoric ancestor of the camel.

In the badlands, fossil birds' eggs have been found so perfectly petrified that the thickness of the shell can be measured and the yolk and white distinguished within. Here too are unearthed fragments of trees that millions of years ago turned to stone. Fossil eggs and fossil trees bring to mind the tall story of Jim Bridger, pioneer western trapper and scout, who reported seeing "peetrefied birds on peetrefied limbs singing peetrefied songs." Oddly enough, technological advances since Bridger's day have, in truth, made petrified bird songs of modern species available to all—preserved in the hard, grooved disks of phonograph records.

Under the expanse of the stars we drove deeper into the badlands. Jack rabbits bounded deerlike across our path—silvery, shining creatures with eyes glowing red as coals. Straightening out on the curves, our headlights would often bring to life a sudden glare of round, baleful eyes where beer cans had been tossed aside in the ditches. Moths, and more than once a bat, flitted in and out of the beams. And as we drove, the moon, now more than half full, ascended slowly toward the zenith of the cloudless sky.

On every rise we pulled aside, cut the lights and sat for a long time gazing in silence over the scene around us. All across this scarred and tormented land the moon was spreading its tranquil light. Velvet darkness filled the ravines, but the strangely eroded hills, like sheeted shapes, lifted above them. They rose with the moonlight full upon them. Yet they seemed to glow and glimmer, to be illusory and insubstantial. The whole surrounding scene extended away in the silvered light vague and dreamlike and spectral.

Back to Dillon Pass, almost back to Big Foot Pass, we rode through a still world magic with moonlight. At times we had the eerie sensation of looking from a moon toward the moon. The silence, the dead hills, the lonely, forsaken air of the unpeopled miles around us, created the illusion we were moving across a moonscape on earth.

As strange and unfamiliar as these badlands by moonlight seemed to us, for many a creature of the night they represented merely the commonplace surroundings of home. We caught glimpses of some of these winged or furred local inhabitants from time to time as we drove slowly along. Once we were drifting down a long slope when I pulled up sharply. There beside the road, bobbing in the light, was a small brown owl. Instantly a picture of the wide Kissimmee Prairie in Florida came to mind. It was there that we first encountered the ground-dwelling burrowing owl. Like the dry prairie lands of the Kissimmee and the plains of Texas, the badlands of South Dakota form one of its far-separated habitats.

As we watched, the bobbing stopped. The owl leaped into the air, twisted above the road, pounced into the grass at the opposite side. For a moment it stood there. When it lifted, a small victim—a mouse or insect—was clutched in its talons. Turning, wings widespread, it was brilliant in the headlights. Then it swept into the dark and was gone.

For nearly half an hour on the way back to the promontory we paused on one high elevation, our eyes roaming over the vast stretches of the patchy, light-and-dark, broken land lying spread out in the moonlight below us. When I switched on the lights again their sudden glare picked out a pale-colored mouse, white beneath, scurrying onto the road. Spotlighted by the beams it whirled and, tail up, scuttled back to the shelter of the roadside grasses. It was, perhaps, one of the white-footed mice that range, with many a variation, across the continent. We might, we thought, have marked our progress from coast to coast with the milestones of the white-footed mice. For there is a Monomoy Island white-footed mouse on Cape Cod; a badlands white-footed mouse in this portion of South Dakota; a sagebrush white-footed mouse in western Wyoming; a Puget Sound white-footed mouse in northwestern Washington; and a redwood white-footed mouse in northern California.

In the economy of some of the plains Indians these abundant little rodents played an important part. Captain Clark, in his journal entry for October 11, 1804, records, concerning a visit to the Mandans: "Those people gave us to eate bread made of Corn & Beens, also Corn & Beens boild. a large Been which they rob the mice of the Prarie which is rich and verry nurrishing." These beans served Lewis and Clark by the Indians were the underground seeds of the "hog peanut," one of the wild legumes, *Amphicarpa monoica*. Every fall the squaws of the Mandans collected considerable quantities by pillaging the nests of the white-footed mice.

We were back on the same promontory where we had watched the sunset die and the stars come out and the early moon begin its ascent of the sky. In misty light the badlands reached away to the south where they merged, at last, along an indefinite horizon line, with the splendor of the heavens. The harshness was gone from the raw land. A luminous sheen clothed its desolate hills. We looked for a long time, lost in the enchantment of the scene, impressing it indelibly on our minds. Then we turned away, thinking we had seen the utmost beauty of the night.

But, swinging to the north, our eyes met new nocturnal beauty, more delicate, more ethereal, more unearthly than any we had yet encountered. For there, lifting into the sky in long streamers and shafts, ascending high into the heavens, tilting toward the center of the firmament, rose the glory of the aurora. We had seen no sign of it before. An arc of silver-white, glowing and insubstantial, curved across the northern sky. Sometimes extending above it, sometimes dropping below it, the vertical streamers wavered and shimmered.

Their light at times was tinged with yellow, at times with green. They varied in number. At first there were only four; later they increased to twelve. Beginning more than fifty miles above the earth, the electrified particles of these auroral streamers extended perhaps for hundrds of miles into the rarefied outer atmosphere.

Such disembodied light, shifting and rippling in upper spaces, has stirred the superstitious awe and the mystical imagination of primitive people wherever the aurora is seen. To the Eskimos the northern lights were made by spirits playing ball with a walrus skull. And to the old Norsemen they were formed of the flickering beams shed by the armor of the Valkyries as they rode through the sky carrying dead heroes to Valhalla.

Once, as we watched, a falling star drew its fine, bright line deep into the aurora. The Great Dipper towered above the shafts of light. And, bisecting the cope of the heavens, the Milky Way descended into the north and passed through almost the exact center of the glowing arch. In the whole expanse of the star-studded sky there was not a cloud—only these clouds of celestial light, diaphanous and ever-changing, moving in the northern sky.

Under the stars, under the moon, under the aurora, we turned at last toward the little town of Wall and our cabin for the remainder of the night. Sunset and moonlight, stars and the aurora, burrowing owl and badlands mouse—vivid memories of them all went with us. As we rode through the silence I remembered how, years before on a page of *The Lost Woods*, I had set down the things I would most want to see and hear and experience in the natural world during a last day on earth. And I fell to considering again the beauty of the world, so hard to think of leaving, and all the things I would want most to have during a last night in the out-of-doors.

They came crowding in: The song of a whippoorwill, the

calling of a katydid, Orion glittering aloft, the smell of new-mown hay at dusk, the mellow music of snowy tree crickets, the aurora shimmering in the northern sky, lowland mist shot through with the weaving lights of summer fireflies, the perfume of violets, the sound of a train whistle far away in the night—these, all of these, but more than any of them the moon and the light of the moon—shining on breaking waves along the shore, extending a path across a forest lake, glittering on crystalline fields of winter snow—the moon bringing to the world and the nighttime the never-ending wonder and magic of its light.

FOURTEEN

TUMBLEWEED WINDS

SOMEWHERE along the Cheyenne River, the next morning, we rode through a valley of magpies. The spectacular black-and-white birds were suddenly all around us. They were climbing and turning in the sun. They were spreading their great tails into dark diamonds as they slanted down to land. They were bouncing like bluejays along the ground. Once we came upon nine magpies clustered about what seemed to be a special delicacy, the most malodorous carcass of a skunk we met in all our travels. At other times we saw the birds feeding on porcupines, on deer, on innumerable jack rabbits killed along the road. These were the days of the autumn harvest. The whole wildlife population is at its yearly peak in early fall and fresh meat lay on the highways, awaiting the magpies, at every dawn.

That afternoon we glimpsed through shining, dusty haze, a dark line running low along the horizon. It was the line of the Black Hills, the first of the Western mountains. Recalling the events of the next day on roads that climbed and twisted, zigzagging higher and deeper into a tumbled landscape, we can visualize again, in sharp little vignettes of memory, special moments along the way.

There was the golden eagle riding the towering updraft beside Mt. Rushmore. In its breathtaking ascent—each swift circle carrying it hundreds of feet aloft—it passed the titanic carved heads of Washington, Jefferson, Lincoln and Theodore

Roosevelt, lifted above the mountaintop, ascended up and up into the blue until, still turning, it was only robin-sized in the sky. There was the great blowdown of a cyclone swath, miles on miles of dead, fallen trees extending the length of a mountainside. There was a twisting climb by switchbacks to nearly a mile above sea level where thin, airy music rose and fell around us, the aeolian strains of wind in the needles of the ponderosa pines. There was the sound of autumn we had never heard before, the bugling of a bull elk. Fall is the mating time of the wapiti and over and over again, in the zoo enclosure of the Custer State Park, a bull lifted its head in the mighty bugling bellow that we could hear far down the road after we had driven on. At 2:10 P.M. that afternoon, we crossed the line into Wyoming.

At this far western edge of South Dakota, along the line of the Wyoming boundary, we were in the land of a fabulous white wolf. Like "The Traveler" of western Arkansas and "Lobo" of the Currumpaw country of New Mexico, the Custer Wolf was one of the most famous of the animal outlaws of the West. Accompanied by two coyotes that trailed along like bodyguards, feeding on the leavings of his kills and, no doubt, helping warn of danger, the white wolf ranged over more than 2,500 square miles. In the last half dozen years of his life, the Custer Wolf was credited with killing $25,000 worth of livestock. Whole communities hunted him. A bounty of $500 was offered for his scalp. Yet year after year—even down to 1920— this last of the celebrated renegade wolves continued to prey on ranchers, escaping dogs and guns and traps and poison bait.

Then, in the spring of 1920, the U.S. Biological Survey sent into the region a professional hunter, H. P. Williams. His instructions were to take up the trail and follow it, no matter how far, no matter how long, until the white wolf was dead.

It was March when Williams arrived in the Black Hills. It was April when he first caught sight of his quarry with the two coyotes trailing a hundred yards or so behind. In the weeks that followed he killed first one, then the other coyote. Now he and the wolf were pitted against each other. Day after day, month after month, he followed the trail continuously over an area of rolling rangeland sixty-five miles long and forty miles wide. Rarely he saw the white wolf. Always it eluded him. Spring passed, summer passed, autumn came while the relentless pursuit continued. It was in October, after nearly seven months of unbroken trailing, that Williams at long last killed the Custer Wolf. On that day, one record of the time reports, the telephone lines of the region were busier than they were on the day the armistice was signed at the end of the First World War.

A few miles beyond the Wyoming line, near Red Bird Creek, we came upon the first extensive stand of a plant that was to accompany us during most of the thousands of miles of wandering that still lay ahead. This was that bushy, many-branched member of the sunflower family, the sagebrush. Whole hillsides were soon covered with the massed gray-green leaves washed with their bloom of silver down. This is the great indicator plant of the West. Where it grows the land is neither too salt nor too alkali; the soil is suitable for grazing and irrigation farming. Across the tops of many plants, like a sprinkling of darkened sulphur, ran clumps and sprays of tiny flowers. Far into the fall the sagebrush blooms.

Coming out of the walled-in valleys of the mountains into the open rangeland of Wyoming was like sailing from a fiord into the ocean. In great swells the rolling land stretched away for immense distances, broken only by infrequent, toy-sized clusters of ranch buildings. It was a long time before our eyes and minds adjusted to the new dimensions. Only when we noticed how tiny were the cattle that seemed feeding in the foreground of the scene, did we comprehend the vastness of the sweep of land that led our eyes across each trough to the succeeding wave beyond.

Rising and falling with the road, we drove west to Newcastle, where once a stagecoach loaded with cats had stopped on its way to rat-ridden Deadwood. Then we turned south past the Morrissey Road—a track leading away among sagebrush—along which mysterious lights, their origin still unexplained, were reported for years. And so through this highland autumn of tan ranges and gray-green sagebrush, we rode down the eastern edge of central Wyoming, past Bob Cat Creek and Mule Creek Junction, south to Lusk, once the northern terminus of the Texas Trail. As many as 800,000 bawling long-horned cattle a year, in the 1880's, plodded through this area at the end of their epic trek to spread out across the newly opened rangeland of Wyoming.

We wandered, later on, over the Nebraska line into that strange, picturesque region that forms the state's northwestern corner. Not far below us flowed the North Fork of the Platte River. Along its banks, in the springtime of 1834, Thomas Nuttall had found himself in an untouched Eden of wild-flowers. A vivid picture of this scene is given by John K. Townsend, Nuttall's young ornithologist companion, in his *Narrative of a Journey Across the Rockies to the Columbia River*, published in 1839. The party had come to an area of innumerable mounds of hard yellow clay. Extending for three miles, these mounds rose to a height of from six to eight feet high and were set so close together that the men could barely ride between them. "Along the bases and in the narrow passages," Townsend writes, "flowers of every hue were growing. It was a most enchanting sight; even the men noticed it, and more than one of our matter-of-fact people exclaimed, *beautiful, beautiful*. Mr. N. was here in his glory. He rode on ahead of the company, and cleared the passages with a trembling and eager hand, looking anxiously back at the approaching party, as though he feared it would come ere he had finished, and tread his lovely prizes underfoot."

The Nebraska hills were shrouded in twilight, then pale in moonlight, on the evening we rode back toward Wyoming.

Here, far from the stretch that had carried us into Joliet, we were once more on the Lincoln Highway. In 1913, when it was completed, its course for 405 miles, all across Wyoming, was marked by a chain of bonfires. For a time, east of the Nebraska line, we found ourselves among great whitish rocks, oddly shaped. They loomed up, pale and ghostly, around us. There was something brooding, druidical about them. We seemed visiting the ruins of some Stonehenge of the New World. Here was a land that formed a fitting habitation for extinct forms of life, for the prehistoric camels and the pigmy two-horned rhinoceroses whose fossil remains, mined in this region, enrich the collections of eastern universities and museums.

The hills were no longer shrouded, no longer dim in moonlight, when we headed west into Wyoming in the morning. The sun was brilliant on the mile-high land. And all across it the wind swept up and down the slopes and rode over the crests of the swells. All day it blew. And as it blew it rolled before it the first of the autumn tumbleweed.

Beginning in the Dakotas, we had seen old tumbleweeds, dry and brittle and silvered by weathering. They had filled culverts under railroad tracks, congregated into porous dams in ditches, caught in ash-gray billows against fences. Dusty cars came into cattle towns with tumbleweeds dragging beneath or riding on bumpers. And once a tongue of wind had scooped a dozen from a roadside depression and sent them rolling single file across the road like a line of bounding deer.

These were old tumbleweeds, the product of other seasons. Only a few of the new crop had broken free. We saw them anchored in place, like unreleased balloons—millions of them —all across Wyoming. Their seeds were ripening, their tiny leaves drying, and in some storm of the latter days of autumn or in winter their stems would break in a ragged fracture just above the ground and their travels would commence. For these plants "a time to keep" would end and "a time to cast away" would begin. The rolling tumbleweed, almost in the manner of a pepper shaker, scatters its seeds across the land. A botanist once counted 180,220 minute, glossy black, lens-shaped seeds on a single plant of the common tumbleweed, *Amaranthus albus*.

For man, autumn is a time of harvest, of gathering together. For nature, it is a time of sowing, of scattering abroad. Seeds are shot away as though from tiny cannons. They are transported by running water. They ride long distances in mud adhering to the feet of birds. Travelers on the prairie in early days were mystified by great circles of plants like giant pixie rings. It developed that buffalo cows bedded down for the night in a circle, enclosing the calves, and in this position shook free from their shaggy manes seeds that had collected there during the day. William T. Davis, the Staten Island naturalist, one autumn examined two small turkey feathers that were being blown along the ground by the wind. Attached to both, ten to one and fourteen to the other, were the seeds of bidens or beggar-ticks.

Among the many devices employed in the seed-scattering of autumn—the bur that adheres, the nut that rolls downhill, the fluff that takes wing—one of the simplest and most effective of all is the wandering of the tumbleweed. It seems to saturate the ground with seeds. Every fallow field, every roadside excavation, every scar on the earth was thickly dotted with a stand of the globular plants. We had seen them leaning out over the precipitous bluff above the Missouri at Fort Abraham Lincoln. We had seen them clustered about the base of the statue of Sacajawea, the Indian woman of the Lewis and Clark Expedition, on the capitol grounds at Bismarck. Plowed fields had a reddish edging of tumbleweeds. Earth-formed erosion dams on hillsides were solidly covered with tumbleweeds. Where firebreaks had been plowed along the roads in rangeland, the bare earth, mile after mile, was hidden by one long band of tumbleweeds.

Following blacksnake roads—hardtopped, shining, twisting

—we passed cattle sheds that penetrated far under great hay-stacks that formed, to north and west, ramparts against the winter storms. We went by small water holes with drinking birds—sparrows, larks, pipits and bluebirds—massed around them. Once we stopped to spend a quarter of an hour watching seventeen pronghorn antelope feeding on the long slope of a hillside. Always mountains rose on the far rim of the horizon. And always tumbleweeds grew along the way, drawing their wiry blanket over every scar on the earth. Like the rag-weed of the East, the tumbleweed of the West is the first plant to invade soil laid bare.

No doubt their rooted stems and shielding mass of branches help check erosion in summer. And on the heels of these first invaders, other annuals and perennials take root. Some plants, in fact, associate so closely with tumbleweeds that botanists have found their stems growing upward amid the massed branches of the larger species. As a consequence they, too, are carried off, riding with the tumbleweeds, pinwheeling over the ground and scattering their own seeds along the way.

Not only does the tumbleweed run in a bumper crop across every field left fallow. It also gets a toehold in even the slightest crevice where earth is found. Outside Casper, when we swung north toward Sheridan, we passed a half-deserted wartime air-port. Down the length of all its black runways extended lines of reddish-green where, side by side, tumbleweeds were anchored in cracks between the strips of asphalt.

Somewhere north of Casper we came to a sign: "Caution. Wildlife Crossing Next 50 Miles." All along our journey we saw animals that had been killed by speeding cars. Our list, growing daily, already included squirrels, skunks, muskrats, opossums, mink, raccoons, ground squirrels, chipmunks, por-cupines, foxes, white-tailed deer and pronghorn antelope. But most of all were the jack rabbits. Our autumn, apparently, came in a "rabbit year." In every dusk we saw them by the roadside now, red eyes shining in our headlights. Near one water hole in sagebrush country, where the animals crossed the road to drink, we counted almost a hundred killed in less than a mile. Another time, for the space of twenty miles, we were never out of sight of a killed jack rabbit. Often their flattened bodies looked like newspapers scattered down the highway. We estimated—in a figure we are sure is far too low—that we saw 10,000 jack rabbits killed on the road in our travels through the fall. The world never cares much what happens to a rabbit. As Nellie put it, some place should be—but no place is—labeled "Rabbit Crossing."

There was a time that day when, overwhelmed by the heavy smell of crude oil, we rode for miles among the straining derricks and the bobbing pumps—like nodding hobbyhorses—of the great Teapot Dome field. Beyond, north of Kaycee, in a land of rimrock and gulches—in the country of the notorious bandit stronghold, Hole-in-the-Wall—we crossed a creek with the ominous name of Corpse Draw. We were, on this and succeeding days, riding on a high road through autumn. With the wall of the Bighorn Mountains reared along the west, we passed a hillside late in the afternoon where crows and Brewer's blackbirds fed with a flock of tame turkeys in a cut-over grainfield. From end to end this stubble field was washed with the reddish tinge of autumn tumbleweeds.

The West, in song and story, has given a prominent place to the tumbleweed. Yet it is not *the* tumbleweed. It is several tumbleweeds. The plant most often referred to is *Amaranthus albus*, the white pigweed or tumbling pigweed. This ball of whitish, many-branched stems bears minute, green-tinted flowers in crowded clusters. From them the black seeds develop. In autumn, when the seeds are ripened and the stems have become rigid and leafless, the plant is ready for its wanderings. Weeds are weeds—in other words particularly successful plants—partly because of their enormous number of seeds. One plant of *Amaranthus albus*, a scientist once calculated, starts its travels with sufficient supply to sow eleven seeds on every square foot of an acre of soil. Moreover these seeds, like those of the ragweed, are remarkably long-lived. Tests have shown, in the case of one species of *Amaranthus*, that the seeds could germinate after being buried for twenty, or even forty, years.

A second member of the tumbleweed clan is the winged pigweed, *Cycloloma atriplicifolium*. Its interlacing branches are rarely white, occasionally green, most often purple in the fall. Confined to country west of the Mississippi, it stands out in gaily colored balls amid the tans and yellows of the autumn landscape. Other plants sometimes referred to as tumbleweeds are the buffalo-bur, *Solanum rostratum*, a member of the night-shade family; the Russian pigweed, *Axyris amaranthoides*; and the tumbling mustard, *Sisymbrium altissimum*. The first of these is native, the second was naturalized from Siberia and Russia and the third, introduced from Europe, has spread widely and rapidly during the past half century.

But it is another tumbleweed from abroad that has made the swiftest advance of all. This is the Russian thistle, *Salsola kali*. It is also known as Russian cactus, prickly glasswort, Russian tumbleweed, tumbling thistle and wind witch. Introduced accidentally with imported flax seed into Bon Homme County, South Dakota, near the Nebraska line about 1873, its conquest in eighty years represents one of the outstanding weed success stories of the world. From Canada to Mexico and to the Pacific it has penetrated throughout the West. More sparsely it has moved across northern states as far as the Atlantic Coast. In numerous places in the West we found it the dominant tumbleweed of the area.

The loose globes of these plants not infrequently have a diameter of three and occasionally four feet. One that Nellie and I measured on Farm Island, in the Missouri south of Pierre, was slightly more than four feet tall. The small leaves of the Russian thistle are stiff and prickle-tipped. Sharp-pointed bracts jut out at their bases. The flowers, minute and hugging the stems, are often greenish, sometimes red, pink or white.

The wind-borne pollen is highly toxic for hay-fever sufferers. Allergy experts rank the Russian thistle close to the ragweed as a cause of discomfort during the time of its pollen-shedding.

Unlike other tumbleweeds its seeds are enclosed in a paper-like calyx with converging lobes. These lobes, together with numerous twisted hairs, hold the spirally coiled, yellow-brown, snaillike seeds loosely in place. After the hard, woody plant has rolled over the ground all winter it still may retain some of its seeds. If shaken over a cloth at different stages of the winter, a Russian thistle will rattle down a succession of showers of falling seeds. The last to develop are the first to be shaken free. The first to ripen, near the base of the plant, may never leave the stem. Occasionally the rolling balls are partially buried in dust or sand. Under such conditions the seeds still attached to the stems sprout and produce plants in the spring. This provision of the plant for scattering its seeds in installments, rather than in a quick dispersal, may well have speeded up the advance of the species across the continent. No doubt the swiftest advance of all occurred along railroad right-of-ways. There we saw tumbleweeds, caught on jolting freightcars, scattering their seeds for many miles along the tracks.

Not all of the 50,000 or so seeds of the Russian thistle are planted in its wind-blown travels. A good many go to nourish varied forms of wildlife. The gamebirds, songbirds and mammals that feed on them include the ring-necked pheasant, the valley quail and the Gambel quail, the horned lark, the lazuli bunting, the redpoll, the white-crowned sparrow, the grasshopper mouse, the brown pocket gopher, the prairie dog, the antelope ground squirrel and the kangaroo rat. In addition elk, antelope and mule deer browse on the plants in early stages.

We noticed in several places that the tumbleweeds appeared larger where they grew out of the reach of cattle. But they seemed such stiff, prickly, unappetizing plants that we could not make up our minds whether livestock would eat them. I asked an old rancher we met at a filling station. They do, he said, but only in the spring when the shoots are young and soft. Oftentimes, in the wake of the melting snow, a well-seeded area will become covered with a dense carpet of green sprouts suggesting a luscious stand of new grass. In fact, the scientific name of the Russian thistle, *Salsola,* is derived from a Persian word meaning carpet. Because of their high protein content, these sprouts are often preferred to grass by the browsing cattle. It is, however, in years of drought and depression that tumbleweeds are pressed into service on a large scale. Farmers and ranchers then cut and stack them while they are still green, to provide emergency winter rations for their livestock.

A painstaking census of all the parts of a good-sized Russian thistle was once made by a laboratory scientist. He reported that the plant had some 12,000 minute leaves. It had forty-five feet of branching stems. The length of its underground root system was sixty-three feet. One important factor in the plant's ability to withstand drought is its particularly long roots. During years of little rain in the western Dakotas it is the most conspicuous plant, the last survivor among the parched annuals. In semidesert conditions, it often is still green in midsummer when all the neighboring plants are dry and brown. To produce one pound of dry matter, experiments have shown, a Russian thistle uses about 340 pounds of water. Flax or alfalfa uses two or three times as much.

The amount of green in a Russian thistle varies considerably. Its spiny stems are tinged or lined with pink or purpled-red, the depth of the color increasing toward the top. Several times tumbleweeds rolled across the highway where men with scythes had been at work along the roadside, and the two colors, green and red, alternated as they rolled. The red, apparently increasing in the autumn, makes these rooted globes one of the most brilliant features of the high-country fall.

Dry, a large tumbleweed weighs only six or seven pounds. But not infrequently the rolling spheres pile up in immense windrows against the wire fences of the open range. Then comes some gale of winter or a chinook—that wind of dramatic change, rising in the night and lifting the mercury as much as thirty degrees in a single hour. Hurled across the rolling land, its great gusts meet the wall of tumbleweeds, push wide gaps in the fences and release the bounding, leaping balls that go racing away until, many miles downwind perhaps, some other obstruction halts them.

The immense number of these airy globes that roll before a winter gale is reflected in an event reported in *Natural History Magazine* by H. E. Prentice of Johnson, Kansas. The worst dust storm ever recorded in the area swept over the southwestern portion of that state in February 1954. Along Bear Creek and the Cimarron River, where the velocity of the wind rose to seventy-five miles an hour, range animals were driven into the protection of the dry gulches. There many of them were buried under immense piles of tumbleweeds weighted down with dust. "The fate of hundreds of beef cattle," Prentice wrote, "will remain a mystery until the tumbleweeds have been burned or removed from the dry gulches by future winds."

Our wind, a mountain wind, blew steadily all that day across endless miles of tan range grass, red-tinged tumbleweeds and gray-green sagebrush. Late in the day, in the region of the Tongue River, we found ourselves suddenly in honeybee country. In clusters of white dots, the hives appeared on the hillsides. All down the slopes the sagebrush grew as thick as a cultivated crop. These were the bee pastures of fall. Still in bloom, the sage was providing the final nectar of the autumn harvest. The next day, with the red rock ballast of the Burlington Railroad's single track paralleling the highway, with black road and red right-of-way running side by side, we drove north and crossed the line into a new state, one we had not seen before—the nineteenth state of the trip, Montana.

FIFTEEN

ANTS OF THE BATTLEFIELD

NEVER say never.

We learned that rule of natural history, learned it over again, early on our first morning in Montana.

All through the high cattle country of Wyoming, all along the Cheyenne Valley of South Dakota, we had seen magpies. We had seen them pumping their long bronze-green tails, balancing themselves in the wind on the top wires of fences. We had seen their cannily constructed nests, usually with more than one entrance and often made with a dome of thorns to repel invaders. We had watched them feeding on killed jack rabbits along the way. We had noticed how the slow-flying birds took wing while we were still a good way off. Nowhere did we see a single magpie killed on the highway. So, in the rashness of insufficient experience, I had set down in my journal the observation that magpies are probably too smart to get hit, that never are they killed by automobiles on the highway. That particular "never" came to an abrupt end at 9:34 A.M. on this morning. For at that moment on a long stretch of open road through a rolling land of grass and sagebrush, we came upon the crushed body of a magpie beside the crushed body of a rabbit upon which it had been feeding.

A little later we passed two young men pulling a miniature covered wagon that resembled a doghouse on wheels. Along the side they had painted in irregular letters: "Walking in all 48 States." We have often wondered what lay before them and how many of the forty-eight states they actually saw in their pedestrian adventure. Driving northward through rangeland we came, from time to time, upon old tumbleweeds congregated into gray islands in water holes. The product of these same small ponds, dark dragonflies hawked about over the sagebrush. Once we passed a cattail marsh where not a bird was visible but where the air pulsated with the uproar of Brewer's blackbirds hidden among the stems. Thus on this bright fall morning small memories of our journey were being laid down in our minds, layer on layer, like the successive strata of fossil-bearing rock.

About mid-morning we crossed a meandering river where ripples glinted in the sun among the gravelly shallows and long quiet pools reflected the yellow of the overhanging cotton-woods. Each sandbar was edged along its upstream end with a kind of golden fringe where drifting leaves had stranded. Beyond the cottonwoods a long sweep of sunlit sagebrush ascended gradually to a ridgetop. The stream was the Little Bighorn. For three miles along this Montana river, in June 1876, Sioux and Cheyenne warriors had camped 4,000 strong. For the slope beyond, now stretching away in peaceful sunshine, was the most famous of all the battlefields of the frontier, the scene of Custer's last stand.

"My every thought," General George A. Custer once wrote, "was . . . not to be wealthy, not to be learned, but to be great . . . to future generations." In one of the paradoxes of history, this seeker of glory is known to these future generations of which he thought not for what he achieved in life but for the spectacular disaster that marked his death. Rash, arrogant, quarrelsome, callous to the suffering of others, he led a stormy life that lasted for thirty-six and a half years. Time and again luck saved him from his impetuous folly. And, in a way, luck was with him on that Sunday in June when the waves of screaming, painted Indians, almost invisible in clouds of dust, swirled around him, firing and vanishing and, in the end, wiping out every living member of his command. The tragic finality, the mystery of events in those last hours, with no single man to say, "I only have escaped alone to tell thee"—these circumstances have surrounded Custer's name with a kind of somber splendor, symbolic and ironic. And beside the river, among the cottonwoods on that Sunday of slaughter, Lonesome Charley Reynolds—the scout whose disregarded advice might have saved all—had died alone with sixty-eight empty cartridges beside him.

Since that day floods have shifted the course of the Little Bighorn slightly. But the dry slope beyond is dominated by sagebrush and grass, yucca and tumbleweed, just as it must have appeared to Custer when he swept the landscape with his glasses on the morning of that twenty-fifth day of June. Meadowlarks flew down the slope over the white markers that indicate where Custer's men were slain, and red mounds of tumbleweed billowed up beside the iron fence that encloses the spot where the general and his officers fought on until, one by one to the very last, they were cut down.

Wandering along the edge of this old battlefield in the tranquil sunshine we heard around us the crackle of grasshopper wings. Once when we bent down to obtain a bit of perfumed resin from a gum plant, a dark, nondescript dragonfly rattled up out of the dry vegetation and shot high into the air above us. And wherever we went along the hillside, we came upon the circular patches of cleared ground and the low mounds of the harvester ants. Ages before a moving cloud of dust along the ridgetop advertised the coming of Custer and his men, grasshopper and dragonfly, gum plant and harvester ant had formed part of the life of the valley of the Little Bighorn.

Of these it was the harvester ant that interested us most that morning. Throughout the higher, dryer western autumn, we were to see their mounds—thousands and hundreds of thousands, millions, no doubt—on both sides of the Continental

Divide. But it was here, at this historic site, that we were able to examine them closely for the first time.

Each mound, when we bent to inspect it, seemed formed of minute pebbles. We were, in fact, looking down on the gravel roof of the nest. This protective layer is from a half inch to an inch thick. Along western railroad tracks the insects frequently roof their mounds with bits of coal, cinders and fragments of ballast. Beside the Platte River pioneers sometimes found small Indian beads intermixed with the pebbles. And at a site where several old houses had been demolished, the outer layer of near-by harvester-ant nests contained bits of glass, pieces of mortar and fragments of rust. Below this protective roof there is a layer of solid earth. Then the innumerable galleries of the underground city begin.

About one third of the way up from the base, the side of each mound we examined was pierced by a funnel-shaped opening. This was the doorway into the subterranean labyrinth. While all of the mounds we saw had but one entrance, the 10,000 and more insects in the largest colonies may come and go through as many as eight. In some species of harvester ants the doors are carefully closed with pebbles soon after sunset on summer evenings. They are opened again the next morning, usually between eight and nine o'clock. The portals are also blocked up before heavy rainstorms. It has been noticed that while only a few ants engage in the leisurely process of locking up for the night, many ants scurry about to complete the work in the shortest possible time when these weather-wise insects sense the approach of a violent storm.

The ants we saw were, I should judge, about three sixteenths of an inch long. They were reddish in color and large of head. Housed within those heads were the muscles that operated the powerful, seed-crushing jaws. Each of these two curved mandibles possesses seven serrations or teeth. Thus the jaws of the gleaning ants can be employed for cutting, sawing or crushing. A cluster of hairs beneath their heads is characteristic of the bearded harvester, *Pogonomyrmex occidentalis*. Here in Montana the species was almost at the northern limit of its range. All the harvester ants of the world—those found in Africa, Australia, the Near East and the Orient, as well as those native to America—are dwellers in desert lands or regions of comparatively little rainfall. This particular genus, *Pogonomyrmex*, is not infrequently a mountaineer ant as well as a harvester ant. It thrives at elevations of 6,000 and sometimes even 8,000 feet.

We made no effort to pick up any of the foraging seed hunters. I had been forewarned. Each worker has not only powerful jaws but a sting as potent as that of a bumblebee or yellowjacket. In ancient Mexico prisoners were sometimes tortured by binding them to the mounds of the harvester ants. The pain produced by the injected fluid is fiery and numbing and sometimes lasts for hours. It seems to run along the limbs and settle in the lymphatics of the groin. The poison of these ants is still something of a mystery. Formic acid is commonly supposed to be the pain-producing fluid. But when A. L. Melander and C. T. Brues, the American entomologists, made a careful chemical analysis of the poison of a *Pogonomyrmex* worker they found not the slightest trace of formic acid. The fluid is known to be a protein, but exactly how it produces its painful effects is but incompletely understood.

Fortunately these armed ants are comparatively mild-tempered. They attack only to protect themselves or their stores. In fact, so tolerant are they that they sometimes permit smaller ants to live in the cleared spaces around their nests and even sidestep the attacks of these midgets when, aroused by the close passage of some harvester, they rush forth to defend their diminutive anthills.

It is these cleared areas about the mounds that make harvester ants so conspicuous in the West. Across some long slope of range country we would often see thousands of such round bare spots standing out amid the darker vegetation. In maintaining their clearings in alfalfa fields, the ants sometimes destroy as much as 2 per cent of the crop. Half a century ago, in their classic study of the harvester ants of western Kansas, T. J. Headlee and George A. Dean found that most clearings were almost perfectly round while a few were elliptical. Their size varied considerably. In buffalo grass, the circle of bare ground had an average diameter of nine feet. Among Russian thistles it was eleven feet. And in alfalfa it was twenty feet. The largest cleared area that Headlee and Dean encountered was in a corral. It had a diameter of forty-five feet.

Every blade of grass, every twig and slightest obstruction, is removed from these clean-swept dooryards of the mound builders. Apparently the cleared areas provide a number of benefits for the colonies. In the first place they are like the clearings of the pioneers; enemies are in the open when they approach the nest. Again, and far more important, the bare area retains less moisture than would ground covered with vegetation. Moreover, the roots of plants growing close to the nests would penetrate the galleries and, on decaying, would provide channels for water to enter the caverns.

This is always of great importance in the economy of the seed gatherers. Living in dry soil they can store their grain underground with little danger of its becoming damp or mildewed. It is only when heavy rains soak into the earth that their stores are imperiled. Under such conditions harvester ants have been observed bringing out their collected seeds and spreading them in the sunshine to dry. On rare occasions seeds will sprout underground. But the ants themselves usually forestall this. In an amazing example of instinctive sagacity and foresight, the insects bite the radicle from each stored seed and thus prevent its germination.

Watching these ants of the battlefield on their slope above the river and the yellow cottonwoods, we were seeing some of the last gleaning of the year. The days were shortening and the foraging workers were utilizing what might well be, in this high country, one of the last of the days of sunny warmth. Some species of harvester ants march out along regular well-trodden paths, sometimes a hundred feet or more in length, when they go afield in search of seeds. But the bearded *Pogonomyrmex* workers scatter as soon as they leave the nest. They radiate out in all directions from their clearing into the wild grain-fields beyond.

There they garner any seed they come upon. William Morton Wheeler, the famous ant authority of Harvard, found eighteen different families of plants represented in the seeds stored up in a single nest. Headlee and Dean found the harvesters of western Kansas bringing in seeds from such varied sources as pigweed, sunflowers, lance-leaved sage, lamb's-quarters, knotweed, green foxtail, dog fennel, wild flax and from millet and other cultivated grains. In at least one instance, the amount of grain carried across a boundary line and stored underground by the ants was sufficient to become the subject of litigation.

Each of the red workers we watched returning across the clearing and climbing the steep pebbly slope to the entrance carried a seed of some kind clamped in its curved jaws. The mound into which it disappeared is only the cupola, or at most the top story, of the underground nest. Chains of linking galleries descend deep into the earth beneath it. The granaries of the colony extend all the way from the mound to the lowest chambers of the labyrinth. Most of the seeds, however, are stored in cavities below the frost line.

Almost always—but not invariably—the jaws of the returning worker hold a seed. There are rare exceptions; apparent mistakes. Wheeler observed one ant coming home with a rose petal. Another brought in a small flower. A third returned with part of a ripe raspberry. In cattle country harvester ants sometimes come back from foraging trips carrying later-discarded bits of dried cow manure or bird droppings. Hardly any of these seed gatherers is exclusively vegetarian in diet. It will take a piece of meat, usually that of some other insect, if the opportunity occurs. This fact was capitalized on during pioneer times by overland stagecoach drivers along the south fork of the Platte River. During stopovers it was their custom, in hot midsummer weather when vermin multiplied rapidly, to spread out clothing on a harvester-ant mound in the morning and get it again in the evening. The interval was sufficient for members of the colony to strip every garment clean of unwanted insect life.

The jaws of some of the ants we saw issuing from the mounds held tiny papery husks. They had been removed from seeds within the nest. These are carried to a kind of kitchen midden along the outer edge of the cleared circle. With all their instinctive wisdom, the harvester ants occasionally make a mistake coming out of the nest as well as going into it. They will bring, at rare intervals, a seed along with the husks and deposit it on the accumulated refuse. As a result around some of the ant nests a kind of fairy ring of vegetation springs up. Sometimes plants grow on such rubbish heaps that are not found anywhere else close by. They have sprouted from seeds brought from a considerable distance by the foraging workers. It has even been suggested that in this way, little by little, the ants may advance the range of different species of plants when they are active along the edges of their zones. Two species of grass in Texas, from their long association with the seed gatherers, have become known as "ant rice" or "ant grass." But in this case, as with all similar instances, scientists have concluded the planting is accidental rather than deliberate.

Driving northward again, beyond the Custer battlefield and the mounds of its seed-gleaning ants, we crossed the Yellowstone River a little below Billings. Soon afterwards a gray tiger beetle flew in the open car window. It rode with us, like some local guide, through the city and left us as soon as we reached the open country beyond. On the way to Red Lodge we passed through a Joliet, so far from the Illinois Joliet of my boyhood. We rode by fences snowy with the white, plumed seeds of the virgin's bower. We passed a succession of cattle-country railroad sidings, each with its corral and chutes. All the western streams we crossed now were little streams in big beds. They were like small children sleeping in four-posters. They had room to grow in the sudden freshets of spring. Somewhere before Red Lodge we passed over an invisible boundary and entered the Middle Rocky Mountain Province of the geologists. With grasslands replaced by stretches of golden aspens we began to climb. Rearing just ahead loomed the towering range of the Beartooth Mountains with its sixteen miles of switchbacks that would carry us zigzagging upward to the top of a pass 10,942 feet above the level of the sea.

Climb any mountain in the Northern Hemisphere and you make a telescoped journey toward the Arctic. Every thousand feet you ascend is, in its effect on the vegetation around you, equivalent to traveling 600 miles to the north. From lodgepole pine to Engelmann spruce to fir that became blasted and twisted and dwarfed as we ascended, we passed from zone to zone up Primal Switchback, up Deadwood Switchback, up Frozen Man's Curve, slowly climbing up and up toward timberline and the tundra plateau at the top. The needle of the altimeter our banker-entomologist friend, Rowland R. Mc-Elvare, had given us for the trip edged into new territory around the face of the instrument. Below us a vast granite panorama expanded. The lower mountains, and the snowfields along their tops, sank away. Deep in the tremendous V of a valley, we could follow for forty or fifty miles the shining, twisting thread of a stream. In a slow drift, clouds moved the islands of their shadows across the lined, seamed face of the landscape spreading away below us. Built with Federal funds in the 1930's at a cost of $2,500,000, the climbing road that lifted us upward among these wild and craggy mountains follows the ancient path of the Nez Percé Indians over Beartooth Pass.

At 8,000 feet a western robin appeared and disappeared

among the evergreens. At 9,000 feet a gray-bodied Clark's nut-cracker, with white flashing on its wings and tail, labored up the slope and crossed above us. Before 10,000 feet the alpine firs had shrunk until they lay prostrate on the ground and we were among small tarns of melted snow water. Then fir and tarn were left behind and we were creeping across the treeless, rock-strewn, russet tundra land at the top of the pass. We were more than two miles high.

I swung into a turnout and stopped. There—as we walked about momentarily light-headed in the rarefied air—we saw, almost in as many minutes, two surprising things. The first was a horse. It appeared, going over the pass in the opposite direction, riding in a stall-on-wheels behind a light Ford truck. The second was a hawk. It flashed up over the brow of the tundra top, curved away, rocketed down out of sight again. It was a swift, slender-winged falcon, probably a prairie falcon, for, surprisingly enough, it is this species rather than the peregrine that hunts the highest among the Rockies.

It was nearing sunset when we started down the steep descent beyond, twisting and turning while the altimeter needle slowly retreated around its circular course. The evergreen forest rose around us. Every westward-leading stretch of the tortuous road brought a vista of golden, shining motes where gnats danced in the backlighting of the sunset. The smell of the coniferous trees, the sight of their legion spires descending the slope before us, the sound of waterfalls tumbling down the mountainside—such perfumes and vistas and wild music accompanied us as we slipped lower to reach, in the gathering dusk, the village of Cooke nestled with its hundred or so inhabitants at the bottom of a narrow valley surrounded by towering peaks. We were still 7,500 feet above sea level.

In mountain moonlight, after we had found a log cabin for the night, we walked down the single long street of the village. The rumble of a gold mine, like the sound of a train crossing a trestle, echoed from a shadowed mountainside. Coming back in the chill of the night we overtook the dark form of a man, bent far forward, plodding beneath the weight of an enormous back-pack. We passed without speaking and it was only later that we learned that this shadowy figure was one of the most interesting men to cross our path during all our westward trip. A graduate of a leading Eastern university, he had chosen the life of a mountain recluse. For a dozen years, winter and summer, he had lived out-of-doors, coming only rarely to Cooke for needed supplies. Of the many adventures of his solitary life only a few were known. Once, skiing down a snowy slope under the stars on a winter night, he had plunged without warning into the trampled path of a mooseyard. All around him in the darkness he could hear the snorting of the alarmed animals. Fortunately none was close by, and pulling himself cautiously up out of the runway he was able to make good his escape.

With thoughts of his lonely winter life, now close at hand, and with the sound of the gold mine continuing its unbroken and raucous lullaby, we went to sleep that night. The next morning at 9:10 A.M. we crossed the line into Yellowstone, that far-famed, fabulous first in the national park system of America.

SIXTEEN

ROCK RABBITS

THIRTY-FIVE miles from the Continental Divide. Seventy-five hundred feet above the level of the sea. In the high autumn of the Rockies. There we first encountered the charm of the pika.

It was at sunset. We were sitting amid the vast jumble of an ancient rock slide. White and marked by bubbles and seemingly formed of hardened dough, the blocks of stone ranged from a few feet in diameter to the bulk of a cabin. This rock cascade, now long stilled, had tumbled down the steep descent below a cliff of travertine. The drop plunged away below us while other rock slides ran in spreading inverted V's down the brown sides of a peak beyond. We were near the Silver Gate on Terrace Mountain, not far from Mammoth Hot Springs, in the northwestern corner of Yellowstone.

We were also now in the wonderful month of October, that perfect month of fall. In October calm and sunny days prevail. High winds are almost unknown; thunderheads are rarely seen; the season of tempests and cyclones is virtually over. In October the same temperature is found over a greater portion of the United States than at any other time of year. Medical records show that babies conceived in October are heavier than the average. Ellsworth Huntington of Yale, after a lifetime of research, reported that in the autumn, in October, our creative mental ability is at a peak. In this Leaf-Falling Moon of the Indians our general health is best, we feel most fit.

Sitting there on the rock slide in the calm of that October evening, in the quiet of the mountain heights, the sunset glowing above the white line of the cliff behind us, valleys and mountains—with grass embrowned and aspens golden, all in autumn dress—spread out below us, we became conscious of a sound like an elfin horn blown far away. It came down the slope across the labyrinth of rocks. We listened. It came again. This time it was answered more loudly to our right, below us to our left. Then all at once half a dozen of the elfin horns were blowing back and forth across the avalanche debris. We swept our glasses slowly from rock to rock. Almost at the same instant we discovered the diminutive horn blower. It was in the very act of sending forth the short blast of its little bleat.

Sleek, plump, brownish, about half a foot long, with short, rounded ears, with no visible tail at all, the animal sat on the flat shelf of a projecting rock. Just as it came into focus it lifted its head, opened its little mouth, stretched out its neck and then, like an old-fashioned auto horn with the rubber bulb squeezed, it jerked and propelled forth the small trumpet-note of its call.

We were looking for the first time in our lives at the animal Thomas Nuttall once described in a letter to John James Audubon—that famous haymaker of the rock slides, the pika, the cony, the calling hare, the slide rat, the little chief hare, the rock rabbit. No other animal we had ever seen, no puppy or kitten or chipmunk or flying squirrel, had ever had so much charm-at-first-glance as this little caller of the mountain tops. We saw it later in other avalanche areas, among the talus of more than one mountain cliff near timberline, and each subsequent meeting strengthened this initial impression of the endearing charm of the pika.

Each of the mountaineer animals we watched had its own particular porch or backward-slanting slab of rock where it sat surveying its surroundings and calling from time to time. Because its forelegs and hind legs are almost of equal length the pika is often mistaken for a species of mountain rat. It is, however, a true member of the rabbit clan. Its range extends from the mountains of western North America across Siberia to the Ural Mountains of Russia. In New Mexico it has been found inhabiting bleak, windswept heights 13,500 feet above sea level and in the Himalayas colonies have been encountered as high as 21,000 feet. At the other extreme, near the Columbia River, in Washington, pikas live at an elevation of less than 500 feet above sea level.

King Solomon, almost 3,000 years ago, wrote in *Proverbs*: "There be four things which are little upon the earth but they are exceeding wise." These Four Little Things were the harvester ants—"a people not strong, yet they prepare their meat in summer"; the conies—"but a feeble folk, yet they make their houses in the rocks"; the locusts—that "have no king, yet go they forth all of them in bands"; and the spider—that "taketh hold with her hands, and is in kings' palaces." Locust and spider had long been familiar to us. The harvester ant—the First Little Thing—we had just seen foraging over the Custer battlefield. And here, as we looked about our rock slide in the sunset—although the pika, the so-called cony of the New World, and the true cony, the daman or hyrax, of Palestine, are not the same animals—we might well be seeing Solomon's Second Wise Little Thing. For the pikas—"a feeble folk"— like the conies of the Old World, find their safe refuge among the rocks.

There, too, in the stone barns of the crevices, these provident rabbits store the hay they harvest during summer days. Grasses, sedges, flowering plants, even small twigs clipped from the lowest branches of shrubs and trees, go into the piles. Sometimes haycocks containing a bushel or more of this material can be seen curing in the sun in sheltered places among the rocks of a slide. The harvested plants are added little by little to the pile, in layers, so they have time to cure without molding. One of the superstitions of the early trappers and mountaineers was that the severity of the winter could be foretold by the size of the haycocks. Although the exterior of such piles may become brown, the interior remains vividly green and fragrant. Agricultural scientists from a western university at one time studied the hay-making methods of the pikas in search of improved ways of harvesting and curing fodder on farms.

The plants the mountain rabbits gather for their winter food vary greatly with the locality. In the Grand Tetons, near Jackson Hole in Wyoming, Alexander Wetmore found the piles consisted almost entirely of elder leaves. At Yellowstone, Vernon Bailey noted that one haycock made by pikas consisted of about one-half grasses and about one-fourth huckleberry stems and leaves. Sagebrush is the principal source of supply for pikas in the broken lava beds of Idaho and eastern Oregon. On a mountainside in New Mexico, Bailey identified thirty-four different species of plants in one pile of pika hay—including nettles, roses, lupines, syringa, snowberry and phacelia. On the long list of plants garnered by the pikas you find fireweed, stonecrop, cinquefoil, goldenrod, saxifrage, yarrow, thistle, knotweed, aster, gentian, Indian tobacco, sweetgrass, ferns and clover. They sometimes even gather the needles of fir and pine. Some colonies of pikas seem to concentrate on two or three plants; others to harvest almost everything that grows near the rock slides where they live.

Although we searched in the sunset and returned and searched next day we saw none of the pika-made haystacks among the rocks. Here at the northern edge of Yellowstone the growing season between killing frosts sometimes is as short as thirty days. The harvest of the pikas had been cured weeks before. By now it was housed deep in protected crevices among the rocks. We saw where stems had been clipped off—the stubble remaining from the harvest—but regretted missing the harvest itself. At such times the pikas often return with bunches of bright mountain flowers carried crosswise in their mouths. Sometimes a haymaker will come home bringing so

LOST DOG found. Gerald W. Wear, at Alder Creek, Oregon, with Poncho, the object of his long search among the mountains.

SALMON leap up the falls at Celilo on their return from the sea. Here every autumn Indians fish with dip nets.

large a bouquet, with head held high and mouth open to the limit, that it can hardly see ahead. At other times a worker will bring back a single lengthy stem, gripping the butt between its teeth as it drags it along the ground. One sedge stem forty-five inches long was found in a pile of pika hay. It had been folded several times before it was added to the mound. On several occasions observers have seen the little harvesters tightroping along low horizontal branches of trees to clip off twigs and leaves.

Several weeks later and several thousand miles farther on in our wandering with the fall, Nellie and I spent the better part of an afternoon in northern California talking with a man who probably knows more about the pikas from first-hand observation than anyone else in the world. For two years, while he was doing graduate work at the University of California, J. Harold Severaid devoted part of every month, except the three coldest in winter, to studying the thousands of pikas that lived in a half mile of talus below an abandoned mine in Mono County on the eastern side of the Sierra Nevadas. Roughing it in a deserted shack 8,000 feet above sea level, he lived in the very midst of the rock rabbits. For so many days he sat motionless and silent among the rocks that he was accepted as part of the scenery. At the end of his field studies Severaid brought back twenty of the animals and succeeded for the first time in history in raising pikas in captivity. On the day we visited him, we saw the last member of this original colony, a patriarch pika still living in a small artificial talus behind the laboratory.

The longer Severaid watched the pikas the more he was impressed by their engaging personalities. Gentle, friendly, filled with curiosity, rarely quarreling among themselves, industrious and provident, they fill a special niche in that world of lonely heights above timberline. The rock jumbles in which they dwell provide a ready-made labyrinth of interconnecting tunnels. And the unstable character of the slide protects them from any creature, including man, that would dig them out.

Remove only a few rocks and a new avalanche begins. Consequently the life of the pikas, as it is lived deep in the rock slides, has never been seen by any man.

Ordinarily, Severaid noticed, the hay-gatherers rarely ventured more than a hundred feet away from their stronghold of rocks. Before they crossed any open space they looked around carefully. In several instances he saw them vary their route to and from their hayfields instead of following the same beaten path each time. Like the man who carries the payroll from the bank along different streets to reduce the chances of a hold-up, they avoided making a well-worn path that would attract the attention of enemies.

The chief enemies of the pika are three: the least weasel, the mountain weasel and the pine marten. There are no snakes near timberline where most of the pikas live and their lookouts, providing a wide view and a quick retreat, are usually overhung by other rocks that shield them from the air attacks of hawks and eagles. Sitting there hunched up, with backs higher than heads, about the size of a half-grown cottontail, they survey their surroundings with bright little eyes set on either side of a Roman nose. Let a weasel approach and they come to instant attention, heads up, noses twitching, feet shuffling. From lookout to lookout the alarm spreads. Then pika after pika whisks downward into the catacombs below.

To see these plump, silky-furred creatures at ease—as we saw them among the white rocks of Yellowstone—to see them stretching out their necks and giving their little calls, to see them washing their faces like kittens, to see them sitting motionless as lumps of moss on rock, it is difficult to conceive of their astonishing speed and agility. Once when we were eating sandwiches, leaning back against one of the rocks, a cony on a lookout slab commenced a sudden run of a hundred feet or more down the slope, disappearing under rocks, popping up again at the mouth of some natural tunnel, streaking across a weathered shelving of travertine, speeding up at every open space, and shooting at last, in a catapulting leap, into the maze of corridors threading a lower jumble. A pika runs like a rat and bounds like a rabbit. When pursued it can hurl the six to eight ounces of its body from rock to rock in leaps as great as ten feet. At the base of each toe it has a naked pad and on the sole of its foot the hair is swirled into a gripping tread that provides such good traction that it is sure-footed even among icy rocks. In emergencies a pika can swim rapidly for a distance of fifty feet or more.

One July day in 1930, at Milner Pass on the Continental Divide, in the Rocky Mountain National Park in Colorado, the western mammalogist, Joseph Dixon, had an unusual opportunity to observe the activity of pikas when a weasel invaded their rock slide. Almost at his feet, Dixon saw a young pika race by between two rocks with a streak of brown behind it.

"I had always believed," he writes in *The Journal of Mammalogy* for February 1931, "that nothing could thread the maze of winding passages between the boulders of a rock slide quite as fast as a pika can and does. However I found myself mistaken for the weasel could, and did, outrun the pika. I watched the weasel closely from a distance of ten feet and found that it apparently followed the pika entirely by scent, dodging in and out among the rocks with unbelievable speed and following the winding course of the cony with ease and accuracy. Then when it seemed that the weasel was just about to capture the young pika, one of the old adult pikas cut into the race ahead of the weasel and just behind the young pika, which was becoming exhausted and which dodged out of the race at the first opportunity.

"My first thought was that the second pika, while in a panic of fear, had fled blindly and had accidentally gotten into the race. But while I watched, a third pika, distinguishable by a scar on its side, deliberately entered the race but was not successful in diverting the weasel from the second pika, which was getting weary. A few minutes later a fourth pika joined in the relay race. By this time the weasel showed marked signs of fatigue and gave up the unequal contest."

The way of a pika with a weasel in a rock slide, it appears, is something akin to the way of a flock of birds with a hawk in the sky. By swirling continually and preventing the hawk from concentrating on one bird the whole flock is saved. By criss-crossing in the corridors of the rock slide—by design or by accident—the pikas similarly distract the bloodthirsty weasel. They upset its intense concentration on one victim and often save the lives of all.

Such desperate emergencies are only occasional. Most of the time the pikas' home among the rocks is a house of peace. The maze of interconnecting corridors may carry them down into the talus as much as sixty feet. Occasionally a few of the mountain rabbits, instead of living in avalanche debris, burrow under rocks in alpine meadows. There are also a number of oddity records such as one small colony that lived among stored lumber and another colony, on Goose Prairie, below Mount Rainier in Washington, that was found inhabiting a log jam that had been piled up by a spring flood some years before.

But wherever they live, winter and summer, the little rock rabbits continue to be active. They do not hibernate. During winter months they spend most of the time snug in their rock tunnels under the snow. But occasionally a pika will come to the surface amid the white mountain world, leaving the tracery of its tracks across the drifts like the trail of a small snowshoe rabbit.

Safe from blizzard, safe from snowslide, safe from icy wind, the cony enjoys the bounty of its summer harvest in winter. The fragrant piles of hay, stacked in dry and airy caves, provide them with an apartment as well as a food supply. The pika burrows into its haymow and eats from the inside out. Some of these stacks house a number of animals, probably a family.

Six pikas have been found, snug and warm and well fed, within a single mound of stored-up hay. The young—in litters of two to five; an extremely low birthrate for a member of the rabbit tribe—are born in spring. They are darker than the adults and have disproportionately large heads and feet. Like the mountain flowers, they have a short growing period and increase in size rapidly. Pikas may sometimes breed twice a year. Usually the young remain hidden in the rock slide until they are about half grown. Looking across the talus below the abandoned Sierra mine, Severaid once saw hundreds of young conies emerge into the May sunshine almost at the same time.

Courtship season, which continues for weeks, usually begins in March. Then the voice of the pika gains strength. Its call carries through the rarefied mountain air for half a mile or more. All through the moonlit nights, at this season of the year, the animals sit on their lookout slabs and send forth their little serenades.

In describing the sounds produced by pikas authors have varied widely. One refers to the call as a squeak, another as a mewing note, a third as a bleat, a fourth as a bark, a fifth as a high-pitched stony sound, a sixth as a nasal squeak resembling the bleat of a very young lamb while a seventh compares it to the cry of a rabbit when hurt. All agree that it has a ventriloquial quality that makes it difficult to trace to its source. "The voice of the pika," one authority sums it up, "is impossible to describe, but once heard it is never forgotten."

Part of the confusion over the sound the animals produce is due to the fact that the same sound evokes different images in different minds; part is due to the fact that the same pika may produce several sounds; but more than either of these reasons is the fact that the thirty-two races of the two species of pikas found in North America all apparently have characteristic "dialects," noticeable differences in the sounds they produce. Some years ago a scientist studying pikas among the western mountains heard a call unlike any he had previously encountered. He felt sure he had come upon a new race of the animals. Without mentioning this belief, he forwarded a specimen to government mammalogists in Washington. Word came back that the animal fitted into none of the previously named categories and represented a race of pikas new to science.

Different kinds of pikas may vary also somewhat in their haying methods. Those on the eastern slope of the Sierra Nevadas studied by Severaid usually took the harvested plants directly into the dry interior of the rock slide. Only a few piled it in the sun to cure. Yet other observers at other colonies in different areas have watched the animals not only spreading the gathered plants out in the sunshine to dry but, when the shadow of a rock fell on them, moving them into the sun again.

Early in September one year, C. Hart Merriam and Vernon Bailey camped on a rock slide above timberline in the Salmon River Mountains of Idaho. Little cocks of pika-hay crowned many of the boulders. That night rain commenced, changed to hail, turned to snow. By morning the slide was sheeted in drifts and all the haycocks were gone. During most of that stormy night the two naturalists heard the almost continual calling of the pikas as they scurried to get their harvest into the safety of the sheltered caves within the slide.

In contrast to this feverish activity, Severaid several times saw his Sierra rock rabbits go inside themselves when a shower began, leaving their hay—and Severaid—out in the rain. Nor did he ever see, as many people have reported observing, the pikas spreading their hay out to dry after a storm had passed. Like most living things, the pikas—although they look so much alike it is impossible to tell one from another except after long and close observation—have many differences. They vary greatly as groups and as individuals.

Our last glimpse of this engaging rabbit mountaineer—whose tribe in Yellowstone is enrolled in the registers of science as *Ochotona princeps ventorum*—came under another sunset sky. We had descended to the road after clambering upward among the blocks of travertine, some splashed with blotches of orange algae; over low junipers decorated with the blue berries of fall; among the tarnished gold of late-blooming mountain goldenrod; past beds of haircap moss with delicate umbrellas shaking where breeze eddies swirled in spaces between the rocks. One little grotto, near a rotten stump that had been clawed apart by a bear, was roofed over by a slab that jutted out like a white awning. A wild gooseberry bush arched over it. As we looked back up the slope, a rock rabbit suddenly appeared on this slab. It was its porch, its lookout post. It surveyed the slide for a minute or more, called twice, stopped suddenly, scratched its right ear and then, like a chipmunk, stood on its hind legs and thrust its nose upward to pick some morsel from the gooseberry bush. It nibbled away for a moment, then turned and leisurely disappeared.

Driving, with infinite regret, away from the cony heights that night we seemed very close to one of the pioneer naturalists who had followed the westward trail more than a century before. No one but a naturalist, he had observed, can know the joy of a new discovery in the wild. And no one but a naturalist can know the sadness of having to leave so soon the thing so much enjoyed.

SEVENTEEN

HIGH AUTUMN

I N mountain sunshine, at midday, we leveled off at the top of Craig Pass, 8,262 feet above sea level. The hood of our car dipped and for the first time in thousands of miles of wandering our wheels rolled on the western side of the Great Divide.

All around the Great Lakes, all across the Great Plains, among the badlands and the Black Hills, over the windy highlands of central Wyoming and southern Montana, even when we were nearly 11,000 feet above sea level in the Beartooth Range, we had always been in the eastern two-thirds of the nation where all moving water flows toward the Atlantic or the Gulf of Mexico. Now beyond the serpentine crest of the Divide, mountain brooks and lowland streams alike moved toward another objective, the Pacific.

In sunshine by day and sudden chill by night we wandered, now on one side, now on the other, along this backbone of the continent. Set aside as the first national park in the history of the United States, the Yellowstone country in the northwestern corner of Wyoming has special fascination for anyone with even the mildest interest in natural history. For hundreds of miles we wound among its hot springs and mud pots, its fumeroles and geysers. Here geology sheds its ancient, static mask. It advances to the present tense; becomes a thing active and alive. Here we were amid wildlife that, in a thousand ways, had adapted itself to this bizarre environment. Here we were on the highroad of the hummingbirds that, weeks before, in an early movement of fall, had started down the long chain of alpine meadows, feeding as they flew among the late-blooming flowers of the upper Rockies. Here we were in dry lightning country where bolts sometimes flash from an almost cloudless sky. Here the roads carried us among moose and bear and elk and bison roaming wild. And here we were in the homeland of that largest of all North American waterfowl, the magnificent, almost-vanished trumpeter swan.

"Its total extinction," Edward Howe Forbush wrote in 1912, "is now only a matter of years." With a wing expanse of as much as ten feet, with a snow-white body as long as five and a half feet, weighing as much as thirty-six pounds, this great bird had once bred as far south as Missouri and had been familiar throughout most of the United States. But decades of unremitting persecution, of gunning, even of chasing flightless young swans through the tule of western lakes and lassoing them from boats, had reduced its numbers and had pushed back the species until, when conservation laws in 1924 gave it belated protection, it was making a last stand in remote mountain lakes and in the Canadian wilds. It has been estimated that hardly half a hundred individuals remained then in the whole United States. After eleven years of protection the number had reached seventy-three. By 1952 a census revealed there were 571 trumpeter swans in the country, an increase of thirty-six over the year before. And in 1954 the number was 642, a twelve-month gain of sixty-five.

We first saw this bird that came so close to being numbered among the beautiful lost species of the continent near Soda Butte Creek. We had pulled to the side of the road to watch a coyote hunting mice beside the stream—in the brilliant sunshine stalking, pouncing, stalking again, tail up, ears forward, yellow fur merging with the yellow of the autumn grasses. Starting up we rounded a turn and came upon a little lake encircled by the handiwork of the early frosts, by slopes clothed in infinitely varied, infinitely intermingling shadings of tan and russet and gold. Close to the farther shore floated a pair of the hugest white birds we had ever seen. They tacked about restlessly, turning this way and that in stately maneuvers. Their necks, unlike the curved neck of the familiar mute swan, rose straight up to heads that remained turned our way in alert attention. The long persecution was over but the inbred uncertainty and caution remained.

This shyness of the swans appealed to us far more than the importunate boldness of the bears that beg along the roads of Yellowstone. We encountered these mendicants wherever we went, lolling by the roadside, padding toward every car that came to a halt, considering each machine a kind of rolling cafeteria. What oddities of diet the summer season must bring to the Yellowstone bears! Yet of all animals they are probably best equipped to survive on a fearful and wonderful menu. For, in the wild, the food of the omnivorous bear ranges from berries to fish, from honey to carrion, from acorns to insects. Among the Mission Mountains of Montana, some 200 miles northwest of Yellowstone, one spring, a naturalist came upon twelve grizzly bears turning over stones and scooping up and devouring the bushels of hibernating ladybird beetles underneath. Black bears have been known to dine on grasshoppers stranded on mountain snowfields. And beside far northern lakes, bears sometimes gorge themselves on those most ephemeral of flying creatures—seemingly the most airy and least substantial form of food on earth—the mayflies that at certain seasons pile up in windrows six inches deep along the shore.

There is a tale by Herman Melville that deals with the meeting of two men who were born in houses looking across a valley from opposite mountainsides. All their lives they had wondered about the inhabitants of the opposite faraway dwellings. Then, meeting at last, they find the imagined, the mysterious, the often-wondered-about suddenly become the visible and the known. So it was in our travels through the high autumn of the mountain country. Often, across some lonely valley, we would catch a glimpse of a remote scene of special beauty or interest. Usually we saw these distant scenes but once. They remained in our minds as luminous memories. But on a number of occasions some farther winding of the road carried us back to the opposite side of the valley and we found ourselves face to face with the very scene that had been glimpsed so far away.

One such experience returns with special vividness. Slanting across the upslope beyond a valley, a grove of aspens cut through dark evergreens, extending for half a mile or more like a vein of shining gold. And later, still in brilliant sunshine, we stood in the very midst of this expanse of autumn gold, new minted. We walked as through a grove of fabled trees, such trees as grew "with yellow leaves and yellow branches" in the garden of Venus's temple and supplied Atalanta with her golden fruit.

All the hours of these autumn days were spent amid shining and sometimes eerie beauty. Once, in the moonlight, we watched Old Faithful rise higher and higher until it towered in a glowing plume of white lifting 150 feet into the air. Another time, in midafternoon, we came upon the Giant Geyser in full eruption, supporting twenty tons of water in the air at one time, sending its billowing clouds of steam and scalding spray 250 feet above the ground, while in the midst of this superheated fury shone the delicate, ephemeral beauty of a rainbow.

The sudden chill of the October nights carried the mercury down as much as thirty degrees below the high point of the day. And all around the hot springs and fumeroles the clouds of steam increased. As we walked amid the bubbling kettles of the hot spring basins by moonlight we saw wherever we looked wraiths of vapor that rose and wavered and shone in the silvery light. The whole land seemed restless and alive. Chilled and shivering we would hurry from the warmth of one drifting steam cloud to the next. Only two sounds broke the stillness of the mountain night. One was the steady, uneven bumbling and bubbling of the hot springs. The other—to our amazement—was the loud and confident chirping of crickets beside the path. Their burrows in the ground were steam-heated apartments and, so far, they had defied and outlived the frosts.

These nocturnal musicians are only one of many kinds of creatures that benefit in one way or another from the heated earth and heated vapor and heated water of Yellowstone. Bird nests warmed by steam and bear dens heated by near-by springs have been observed more than once in the park. Trout are active all winter long in the warmed water of Firehole and Gibbon rivers. And every year a few kingfishers remain at Yellowstone in spite of the snow and ice and low temperatures. Their rattling call has been heard in the midst of snowstorms close to the top of the Great Divide and they have been seen diving through rising vapor of the warmed rivers when the mercury stood as low as thirty degrees below zero.

At dawn one day when all the fields of deer-colored grass were pearly with the night's heavy rime of frost, we came upon two mallards taking advantage of the Yellowstone warmth. They floated on a small, rush-bordered pool formed by the runoff of a neighboring spring. They were not feeding as they rode about with wisps of vapor curling up around them. They seemed merely enjoying the warmth. I rummaged around in the glove compartment until I found the thermometer. It showed that the temperature of the water was eighty-eight degrees F.—sixty degrees above that of the surrounding air.

In the autumn ducks come more and more to the warmed pools as the nights grow colder. Some mallards overwinter on the open rivers that carry away the flow of hot springs, on the Gardiner and Yellowstone as well as on the Firehole and the Gibbon. During some years green-winged teal and Wilson snipe, as well as mallards, winter around the warm overflow at the foot of Jupiter Terrace. Here is food and warmth even in the coldest weather. And wild ducks have been observed circling above the Giant Geyser when it was in full eruption in winter, apparently enjoying the warm air rising above it.

At Orange Mound Spring, where the deposits of years of flowing, mineral-laden water have engulfed and killed trees as a moving dune buries them among sandhills, we watched a red-breasted nuthatch obtaining a drink in an unconventional way. It darted down to the tip of a dead twig on a tree whose whole lower trunk was encased within the slanting wall of rock. Then it leaned far out and, dipping its upcurved bill into the thin sheet of descending water, drank repeatedly. I touched the flow with a forefinger. The water was warm but not hot. The largest of the birds we saw drinking at a hot spring was a magpie. It rode past us in a long toboggan, lifting or depressing its extended tail as it checked or accentuated the angle of its glide, until it dropped down beside one of the shallow pools on the terrace of Mammoth Hot Springs. There, with steam curling thinly up around it, the bird lowered its head and began to drink.

In some small pools near Mammoth Hot Springs where birds come to drink, carbon dioxide gas bubbles up continually. Unless the breeze blows it away it hangs in a poisonous cloud just above the water. On still days, this invisible, colorless gas is often fatal to birds. As many as a score or more may lose their lives around the edges of one small pool. Even species as large as screech owls and Clark's nutcrackers are sometimes numbered among them.

Some of the birds we watched in the vicinity of geysers and hot springs had come not to drink but to feed on the insect life that multiplies in the warm waters. Milton P. Skinner, a former park naturalist and author of *The Birds of Yellowstone National Park*, tells of snowshoeing on a day of zero weather and finding flies running about on the surface film of water flowing away from a geyser. When he held a thermometer a quarter of an inch—the height of an insect—above the water he found the temperature, instead of being zero, was that of a summer day. The small creatures were living in a summer-in-winter close to the surface of the heated geyser water.

Thirty years ago, Charles T. Brues of Harvard University collected six different species of beetles from Yellowstone pools where the water temperature was between 90 and 100 degrees F. He found pond snails living in 96-degree water and the larvae of one of the horseflies thriving in pools with a temperature of 100 degrees. Tadpoles of one of the *Rana* frogs swam about in even hotter water—ranging from 104 to 106 degrees. And *Chironomid* larvae, immature gnats, were swarming in pools that had a temperature of 120 degrees. Writing in *The Canadian Naturalist* in 1891, H. G. Hubbard told of seeing tiger beetles racing along the fluting of the terraces of Mammoth Hot Springs, sprinting through almost scalding water an eighth of an inch deep, in order to feed on these gnats emerging from pupa cases that had collected in rafts along the edges of the pools.

For a long time, during one sunny October afternoon, Nellie and I watched a minute black beetle creeping upsidedown along the bottom of the surface film—as on the ceiling of a room—where small pools had collected on the brilliant-colored terrace of an unnamed little hot spring. Here, too, a myriad tiny, thick-shouldered flies engaged in some mysterious rite of their own. On the sheets of water, seemingly tissue-paper thin, that descended the terrace, they continually leapfrogged over one another or flew in short hops from place to place. They suggested Lilliputian checker pieces being moved rapidly about on a rainbow-hued board. For each descending step of the terrace was gaudy with greens and reds and browns intermingling —each bright hue the product of a living pigment.

There is no stranger phase of life in and around the hot springs of Yellowstone than the growth of these organic pigments. They are the creation of those primitive and remarkable plants, the algae. North of the Arctic Circle some species of algae live all their lives on ice and snow. Here at Yellowstone other species thrive at the opposite extreme, in the water of the hot springs. On the upper terrace of Mammoth Hot Springs they grow where the thermometer rises to 168 degrees F. Elsewhere the plants have been found enduring even higher temperatures. The record was set at Pluton Creek in California. There a scientist obtained a reading of 200 degrees from water in which whitish algae grew.

There appears to be a direct connection between the reading of the thermometer and the color of the algae. This was first noted by one of the earliest scientists to investigate the vegetation of the Yellowstone hot springs, Walter Harvey Weed. Reporting his findings in *The American Naturalist* in 1889, Weed noted that at 185 degrees the alga was invariably white; at about 180 degrees, it tended to be flesh pink; at about 165 degrees, pale yellow; at 155 degrees, yellow green; between 135 and 140 degrees, emerald green; at 130 degrees, dark green; at 125, orange; at 110, red; at 90, cedar brown. These colors merged into one another but the sequence, he reported, held true. Along one of the channels that carried away the flood of hot water from Old Faithful, he found that as the water progressively cooled the color of the algae altered, beginning with yellow, merging into orange, then turning red and finally assuming a brownish hue.

The brilliant coloring of the hot spring walls is not entirely a coating deposited on the rock. The algae grow not only on the surface but within the outer layers of the deposited stone. They are, moreover, often an important factor in the production of that stone, particularly in the case of travertine, the porous lime rock of the cony heights that forms the terraces of the largest springs. From the heavily charged water, lime is deposited in the gelatinous material surrounding the cells of the algae. Thus, tests have shown, a layer of travertine as much as a millimeter and a half thick may be added in the course of only three days—the algae adding their own particular tint to the white stone. It lasts as long as the minute plants live. When they die, the color fades.

In an entirely different manner algae contributed to the colors at Yellowstone some years ago. Green snow fell on parts of the park during the spring of 1936. When the drifts melted that June the algae that formed the coloring matter collected along the edges in a brilliant rim of brighter green. Red snow, also caused by algae, is a more common occurrence. The first recorded instance of green snow was reported from Spitzbergen in 1838 by two French explorers. Until 1936 brought the green-tinted drifts to Yellowstone the phenomenon had never been observed on the North American continent. The cause, in this case, was determined to be immense quantities of a minute alga with a lengthy scientific name: *Chalomydomonas yellowstonensis.*

During this period when we were following the high roads of the Wyoming Rockies, everyone was talking about the wonderful fall. The days were abnormally warm and sunny. The snow that usually arrives well before the park closes officially on October 15, was still to come. We had hurried to reach and cross the high passes before the drifts closed in. But now in a kind of high country Indian summer we wandered about in days of lingering warmth.

Indian summer, that halcyon time of fall, comes in different years and in diverse parts of the country at varying times of October and November. It has no fixed date, no definite duration, this time of golden haze and glinting gossamer with its sense of drifting and reprieve. The very nearness of winter accentuates its charm. It also underscores its swift and transient nature. Thomas De Quincey described the season as "that last brief resurrection of summer in its most brilliant memorials, a resurrection that has no root in the past, nor steady hold upon the future, like the lambent and fitful gleams from an expiring lamp." It has many names in many parts of the world: Second Summer, Counterfeit Summer, St. Martin's Summer, The Fifth Season, Fall Summer, All Hallow's Summer, Summer Close, The After Heat and The Summer of Old Women.

Greek mythology accounted for a somewhat similar period
of calm before winter as a special gift of the gods to the king-
fisher, or halcyon, a bird that was believed to build a floating
nest at sea and to raise its brood during these "halcyon days" of
sunshine and warmth. Early settlers in America assumed that
the autumn fires of the Indians, burning off the prairies, caused
both the hazy atmosphere and the abnormal warmth. Hence
their name for the season: Indian summer. Meteorologists
credit warmer air masses moving northward from the Gulf
with producing this succession of tranquil days.

Our weather held. Nights brought heavy frost but the days
warmed quickly. Once we came upon a silver tree spread out
on the floor of an opening where the sun had etched away all
the frost except where the tree's shadow lay on the grass. And
one morning we ran for a mile or so down a road that was
barred with the shadows of slim evergreens just as, in Illinois,
we had ridden past cornfields in the sunrise—cornfields that
by now held long rows of tentlike shocks or lay empty with the
autumn harvest hauled away.

We left behind Two Ocean Pass where twin creeks, only a
quarter of a mile apart, begin their flow toward opposite desti-
nations. The pressure to cross the Rockies was now behind us
and we drifted with the drifting days down into beautiful
Jackson Hole—along U.S. 6 once more—below the range of
the Grand Tetons. Winding with all its twistings, we followed
the gorge of the upper Snake River over the line into the
twentieth state of the trip, Idaho.

Sheep were coming down from summer pasture in the
higher mountains. Children were playing in new strawstacks,
and brown burlap bags of sacked potatoes ran in ragged rows
across miles of open fields where killdeers circled and called.
Some of the filled sacks seemed bags of cats, so large were the
famed Idaho russets. We passed schools closed for a week and
school busses carrying children to help in the fields. This was
the height of the autumn harvest and trucks laden with bagged

potatoes and empty trucks returning to the fields passed us all day long.

Then we were on roads running south down the eastern edge of Idaho, in tumbleweed country, in the land of the Blackfeet, sometimes surrounded for miles by strange ebony volcanic formations. We came to Cache Valley where long ago Jim Bridger had hidden his store of furs and where now two golden eagles hung in an updraft as though pinned to the sky. We found ourselves amid the green of irrigated fields and rows of white beehives. Thus we descended from the Continental Divide into the Great Basin, advancing toward Utah's desert flats, the Great Salt Lake and a day with a million ducks.

EIGHTEEN

OUR MILLION-DUCK DAY

ONE autumn day in the year 1824, a bullboat formed of buffalo hides stretched over a willow framework floated on the slow current out through the marshes of the Bear River delta. The lone occupant noticed his craft suddenly riding higher, gaining buoyancy. He trailed a forefinger over the side, tasted brine, and was convinced that he was drifting on the Pacific Ocean. Thus more than a century and a quarter ago Jim Bridger, pioneer trapper and scout, discovered the Great Salt Lake.

Twenty-five miles of marshes extended across the delta of the Bear River in Bridger's day. Eighteen years later, in the fall of 1842, John C. Frémont followed the tortuous channels across the marshes with Kit Carson and reported: "The whole morass was animated with multitudes of waterfowl rising for the space of a mile round about at the sound of a gun, with a noise like distant thunder." In an orgy of killing by sportsmen who complained that they got "only 325" ducks in a day's shooting and by meat-hunters who sold mallard for a dollar-and-a-half and teal for a dollar a dozen, vast numbers of the waterfowl were slaughtered in the 1890's. Today the marshes are replaced with shallow lakes rimmed by nearly forty miles of dikes. Fanning out across the delta they provide one of the greatest migratory bird refuges in the world.

We first saw this impounded water through the shining, dusty haze of afternoon. For fifteen miles west of Brigham we drove across flatlands where black-and-white cattle fed amid patches of crimson salicornia, past dark tule marshes, the home of yellow-headed blackbirds and white-faced glossy ibis, beside the Bear River, at an altitude of more than 4,000 feet meandering and brown and lazy like some lowland stream approaching the sea.

Along the dike tops twelve miles of open roads led us into a wonderland of waterfowl. Never in our lives had we seen such concentrations of birds. And we were to see still greater numbers the next day when John Bauman, refuge biologist, took us into areas closed to the casual visitor. For the Bear River delta is a kind of watershed for migrating waterfowl. In days when the ducks and geese stream southward in their autumn flight some continue south down the Great Basin, but others turn east at this point toward the Central Flyway while still others turn west toward the Pacific Coast.

Vanez T. Wilson, refuge manager, showed us that day maps and charts and some of the amazing records of birds that had been banded at Bear River. Since the refuge was established in 1928 more than 36,000 individuals have received numbered metal leg-bands. They have been recovered in twenty-nine of the forty-eight states as well as in Canada, Alaska, Mexico, Honduras, and even the Territory of Hawaii. One pintail, banded on August 15, 1942, was found eighty-three days later on the tiny island of Palmyra, part of the Hawaiian group far out in the Pacific. The distance between this island and Bear River is 3,600 miles.

Because this sanctuary is the most famous nesting ground of the redhead duck, individuals of this species have provided some of the most interesting records. Returns have come in from twenty-two states. They show that when autumn comes some of the redheads fly 500 miles or so west across Nevada to California and move south, beyond the Sierra, along the Pacific Coast Flyway. But others that have hatched in nests almost beside them migrate in the opposite direction, over the Continental Divide of the Rockies, to descend along the Central Flyway to the Gulf or to join flocks from Canada and move across the land to the flyway of the Atlantic Coast, three-quarters of a continent away.

It was still dark the next morning when, at 5:30, we climbed into Bauman's jeep. But by the time we had finished our ham and eggs and emerged from an all-night restaurant in Brigham the whole top of the Wasatch range was glowing in the dawn light. And a little later when we swung into the side roads of the refuge, the upper levels of the Promontory Mountains, west of Bear River Bay, were already bright with the first sunshine of the morning. Then the valley, too, became illuminated. And all across the 50,000 and more acres of the sanctuary the wings of great clouds of waterfowl shimmered and glinted in the sunrise.

Pintails predominated. Thousands at a time they leaped into the air, climbed steeply, turned in the sky or trailed in scudding clouds low above the water, or skittered along the surface as they landed amid a myriad flashing drops of thrown-up spray. This was autumn. This was the beginning of migration. The birds were immaculate in new plumage, at the peak of their powers. Everywhere we looked ducks were taking off and landing. An electric atmosphere of energy and vitality filled the air around us. Wherever we went that day—along the ridge called Molly's Stocking, past the high abandoned lookout tower where ravens have built their nest, on the dike tops, along the skirts of the mountains, tan or tawny with dry Junegrass —always we were within sight of waterfowl. Through the sunshine and drifting milkweed fluff and gossamer showers of this autumn day we saw a million ducks.

Once we climbed to the top of a hundred-foot observation tower for an eagle's-eye view of the delta. All the wide, dike-bordered ponds were stippled with the massed dots of rafts and banks and shoals of floating waterfowl. Our field glasses showed us other rafts beyond the vision of our unaided eyes and our Balscope, with its twenty-power lens, brought still more remote concentrations into view—like nebulae and galaxies and island universes thickly strewn over the reaches of outer space. A still higher eyrie is that employed by one of the refuge men who makes a weekly census of waterfowl from a lightplane that is housed in a hangar near the observation tower. Estimating with a practiced eye the number of ducks and geese below him, this flying census taker probably has more waterfowl within his sight in the course of a year than any other man in America.

Most of the redheads had already gone south on that October day. They are early migrants. So are the gadwall and the cinnamon teal. Here and there we saw a few gadwall as we saw shoveller, mallard, canvasback, baldpate and ruddy ducks. But this was the time of the pintail. And next to the pintail the green-winged teal. These beautiful, swift, vibrant forms of life, turning and flashing in the sun, darting upward, whirling in sudden circles, slanting downward in arrowy descent, moving together in perfect time and unison, these tens of thousands of small waterfowl were active all across the sanctuary. Almost all of the green-winged teal of Bear River overwinter in the Sacramento Valley of California. We saw, no doubt, some of these same birds when, weeks later, we visited that valley of the west.

For us who, among the depleted, overgunned ponds of the populous east, were accustomed to counting our flocks of migrant ducks in dozens and scores, the wonder never diminished in these thousands and tens of thousands and hundreds of thousands of waterfowl. It was, for a glorious day, a return to older times, to times when the country was new. And if the sound of the rising waterfowl was not quite like distant thunder the glint and shine of their myriad moving wings provided one of the inerasable memories of our trip.

Another link with earlier days was the dessert we had when we dined with the Baumans that noon. Wild currant pie. Then we were out on the dikes again with wildfowl all around us.

Distant objects now shimmered in the heat waves—rafts of lesser snow geese and Canada geese, long flotillas of white pelicans, the dark islands of the varied ducks. And as we looked down the dike ahead of us the dry vegetation—sunflowers, thistles, milkweed and tumbleweed-shaped *bassia*—growing on either side of the road seemed on fire. Dense black smoke appeared pouring above it, rising in twin clouds, ascending thirty feet in the air, mysteriously hanging there without changing form or size, without drifting away. What we were seeing was not smoke but billions of dark little midges hanging in the air all along the miles of vegetation, forming, when viewed down the dike's length, clouds so dense they stood out black against the sky.

Just as never before had I seen so many ducks of a kind, so never before had I seen so many insects of a kind at one time. Heads of cattails, needles of tamarisk trees, the fluff of burst milkweed pods, all were burdened with resting midges. They darkened the white-painted railings of the spillway bridges. They coated the thousands of roadside plants like a covering of dust. Along the length of every thread of stranded gossamer, midges clung like swallows sitting side by side on a telephone wire. At times the plants seemed half animal and when we disturbed one it appeared partially to dissolve into a dark cloud that puffed upward into the air. And all down the dike the living clouds merged with one another into a continuous swarm. My brain grew weary trying to calculate the astronomical number of the more than thirty-five miles of midges we saw that day.

Mile after mile the fine, high humming of the *Chironomids* accompanied us, a sound so small, so fairylike, it would have to be, I think, multiplied a thousandfold to be barely audible. But here the thousandfold was multiplied a thousandfold. This thin, steely sound encircled every pond, ran along all the dikes, spoke of the prodigality of Nature which here, among these small creatures, had reached one of its autumn peaks.

At times the whole scene around us, the distant mountains and the nearer lakes, wavered behind a diaphanous curtain of hovering midges. We walked in the midst of the clouds, saw the insect hosts above us, below us, around us. Later in the afternoon, whenever we swung toward the lowering sun, these dark insect swarms became suddenly, in the backlighting, dancing clouds of golden motes. All the millions of midges hung in the gentle breeze like tiny minnows stemming the current of a sluggish stream. They moved forward and backward, up and down. This was their great aerial dance, their mating time, the climax of their lives. And it would continue day after day, on after sunset each day, far into the dusk.

Theirs was not the only mating flight that afternoon. For all across the delta red harvester ants drifted on wings soon to be discarded, navigating the air for the only time in their earthbound lives. And here and there in the sun we came upon dark clusters of flesh flies, insects that have increased since the mysterious "western duck sickness" first swept through Bear River forty years ago. A form of botulism, a bacterial poisoning produced by germs incubating in the mud, it has brought death to hundreds of thousands of waterfowl. We saw one great trench excavated by a bulldozer into which the bodies of dead ducks were heaped for burning. In some instances gulls have been stricken after eating contaminated flesh flies and there is one case of a red-shafted flicker falling prey to the disease as a result of feeding on flesh-fly larvae. Oftentimes if the stricken waterfowl can be transferred to fresh water in the early stages of the sickness it will recover. But many die on the outer mudbanks beyond the farthest dike. Looking out toward the shimmer of the Great Salt Lake we could see their bodies scattered across the bars and shallows waiting to be collected.

The lake beyond, a lake of brine, a dead sea so salt no fish swims in it, stretches north and south about eighty miles and east and west about forty. It is the shrunken remnant of the great Lake Bonneville of prehistoric times. Howard Stansbury, the army engineer who made the first thorough survey of the area a century ago, has left a vivid account of a night spent floating in the eerie quiet of this inland sea:

"The silence of the grave was around us, unrelieved by the slightest sound. Not the leaping of a fish nor the solitary cry of a bird was to be heard, as in profound darkness the boat moved on. Even the chirp of a cricket would have formed some link with the world of life; but all was stillness and solitary desolation."

The entire flora and fauna of this lake of salt consists of one minute kind of plant life and two minute kinds of animal life. Just as in the hot springs of Yellowstone we had found brilliant-colored algae growing, so here, where the saline content of the water is almost at the saturation point, the blue-green alga, *Apanothece packardii*, makes its home. Underwater pastures of this alga provide the only food of the animal life of the lake—the quarter-inch-long brine shrimp, *Artemia gracilis*, and the larvae of two species of brine flies, *Ephydra gracilis* and *Ephydra hians*. Both shrimp and flies, in the aquatic desert to which they have adapted themselves, are free from parasites. Each summer they develop in enormous numbers. So transparent are the minute shrimp however that, although they are everywhere in the midsummer water, they are rarely noticed by bathers. It is the pupa cases of the flies that attract amazed attention.

Frémont waded ashore on the island that was later given his name through a band of these cases twenty feet wide and as much as a foot thick. Yet each brine-fly pupa is no larger than a grain of oats. Forming on the bottom of the lake and becoming buoyant with gas, they rise to the surface where hornlike projections link them together into solid floating masses, sometimes acres in extent. Although we saw none of these spectacular concentrations in October, there are years when, in July and August, the currents shape these masses into disks and ribbons and occasionally into serpentine forms as much as a mile in length. Waves toss them on the shore in great red-brown windrows. And all around these windrows are the countless hordes of the emerging adults.

J. M. Aldrich, writing in *The Journal of the New York Entomological Society* for June, 1912, reported that mile after mile along the shore in mid-July he found the big-eyed, big-headed, stubby-abdomened little brine flies resting on the surface of the water in a band almost twenty feet wide, a dark, winding ribbon of insects that he could see from a distance of several miles. So densely were they massed together that he counted twenty-five, and sometimes as many as fifty, to the square inch. The minimum figure for the flies along a mile of beach, he calculated, was 370,000,000. We saw, in October, only small and scattered concentrations of the little flies.

At the height of their midsummer season these insects have alighted on the rails of the Southern Pacific cutoff across the Great Salt Lake in such numbers they have stalled gasoline handcars. Trainmen hastily slam down windows in coaches approaching the cutoff to prevent the clouds of flies from being sucked inside. Known locally as "buffalo gnats" or "salt flies," the tiny creatures never bite and have little interest in human beings. But for centuries before the first white man reached the Great Salt Lake the brine flies were the object of an autumn pilgrimage that brought Indian tribes from distant points to camp along the shore. This was "the time of koo-tsabe," the time when the larvae of the flies were collected, dried in the sun, and stored away like yellow kernels of grain as a staple winter food.

Old hunters used to say that "everything fattens in the time of koo-tsabe." The teeming larvae of the salt waters were a favored food of ducks as well as of Indians. Near the mouth of the Bear River a scientist once observed a band of shoveller ducks two miles long and a quarter of a mile wide busily gobbling down such larvae in an especially rich feeding area. The celebrated California gulls that saved the Utah pioneers by devouring a plague of Mormon crickets—and that are reproduced at the top of the famous Seagull Monument in Salt Lake City—also dine on the larvae and pupae of the brine flies. When we had come down from Yellowstone into the Great Basin, we had met these gulls moving north, as they do early each fall, up Cache Valley. One flock of a hundred or more was fluttering down into a field of sprouting winter grain. The gulls might well have been in search of the Mormon crickets that they still eat in Mormon fields.

Above the ponds and dikes of Bear River on this day of a million ducks ring-billed gulls had replaced the California gulls. This was one of the innumerable facets of change that marked the season. Already a few mountain bluebirds had come down from the higher levels. Every fall and spring this species engages in a vertical migration such as we found the Carolina juncos making amid the Great Smoky Mountains of the east. By this October day the ducklings and goslings of the eleven species of ducks and the Canada geese that breed at Bear River were as large as their parents and ready for migration. All the nestlings of the delta, the avocets, the Forster's terns, the black-necked stilts, the yellow-headed blackbirds and great blue herons all now were grown birds. So were the eared grebes and western grebes that, only a few months before, had ridden on their mothers' backs while their parents fished in the troubled waters of the spillways. We saw them now scattered over the open spaces of the ponds. Arresting in black and white plumage, its head rising high on its slender neck, its bill brilliant yellow, its eyes fiery red, the western grebe was a new bird for us. It is the largest of its kind, twice the size of the familiar pied-billed. When first we heard its curious creaking call, like the sound of a rusty pulley, we confused it with the shorter creak of the green-winged teal. It was a sound that was all around us in the sunset that evening.

The coming of night amid the waterfowl of Bear River is a

wild and impressive time. The water lies flat, tinted, reflecting the purple of the mountains, strewn with the constellations of the floating ducks. The clamor of the wildfowl rises and falls away. Restless flocks—pintail and green-winged teal, snow geese and white pelicans—turn in the air with the whistle of wings, their plumage stained with the red of the western sky. And all around us, under the purple-tinted mountains, on the pink-tinted water, beneath the flame-colored sky, there was the almost continuous creaking of the western grebes.

Here and there as we drifted along the dikes at sundown that evening, we came on a glowing mudflat where killdeers ran and teetered and trilled and where dowitchers fed with sewing-machine movements of their long bills. Once when I slammed the car door every dowitcher in a flock of more than fifty flipped its wings in unison but continued feeding. How amazing is the uniformity of response in such birds. Not one individual leaped into the air; not one failed to flip its wings in exactly the same manner. All the birds, and each and every one of them, was alarmed so much and no more. We wondered later about this feeding flock that reacted like a single organism composed of many cells. Were the birds so nervously alike that the same stimulus instantaneously produced an identical response? Or had we seen a contagious reaction, an imitative movement that was started by one individual and ran from bird to bird with a time lapse so slight our eyes could not record it?

Curving into the west over our heads, their snow-white plumage suffused with glowing pink, twenty-two pelicans followed each other in single file. When these huge birds are nesting on the islands of the Great Salt Lake they fly from 30 to 100 miles to fresh water for the fish they feed their young. Although this catch consists almost entirely of carp and other so-called "trash" fish—which by its removal actually helps the gamefish the sportsmen favor—the pelicans of Utah have been the objects of a long persecution. As late as 1918, masquerading under the often-abused term of sportsmen and with the active cooperation of the state fish and game department, gangs invaded the island nesting grounds and shot and clubbed to death several thousand white pelicans including the helpless nestlings.

One of the last birds we saw that night against the darkening sky was a pelican moving overhead in silent silhouette like some creature out of the prehistoric past. When we switched on our headlights and started back along the dike-top roads, out of the space ahead a black blizzard of midges continually swept toward us.

That night, as in all the months that have followed, when we closed our eyes and reviewed the scenes of that wonderful day we could see these myriad tiny forms dancing through the air just as we could see once more the rivers and constellations of the million ducks of Bear River and the shine and shimmer of waterfowl wings over the wide expanse of the delta.

NINETEEN

WHITE DESERT

UTAH lies midway between Canada and Mexico just as Wyoming lies midway between the Mississippi and the Pacific. Four times in its history it has been submerged beneath inland seas. All of its major cities occupy the level benches cut by the waves of prehistoric Lake Bonneville and its wide salt flats, where man has attained the fastest speed on wheels, are formed of sediments laid down on the bottom of this ancient body of water.

After days of lingering in the vicinity of the delta of the Bear, we began swinging this way and that over the once-submerged land—north to Logan Canyon, east to Vernal and Dinosaur and over the Colorado border, west across the white glitter of the salt barrens to the Nevada line. Here we were in a new kind of fall, autumn in the dry country, the third season as it comes within the rain shadow of the Great Basin.

Around Salt Lake City the annual precipitation is only about five inches compared to the forty-two inches of rainfall for New England and the 140 inches for the western slopes of the Olympic Mountains in Washington. Here water is always at a premium. Its presence or absence is dramatically revealed. At first, retracing our steps up the Cache Valley, we were amid woods and irrigated fields. The waters of the Bear and its tributaries gave life to the land. Farther up this same river, a hundred miles from its mouth, Thomas Nuttall and his young scientific companion, John K. Townsend, had camped on July 8, 1843. They noted that at this point in their travels numerous white pelicans and "hooping cranes" flew overhead.

Probing eastward into the deep gulch of Echo Canyon we rode where the ill-starred Donner Party in 1846 struggled for twenty-three days over rocks and fallen trees before they escaped into the open Cache Valley beyond. Then with two congenial companions, George F. Knowland, the Utah entomologist, and his wife, we traversed the length of beautiful Logan Canyon and climbed to high Bear Lake, overlooked by the mountains of three states. All of these side canyons of the larger Cache Valley run roughly east and west. And in consequence they have a peculiar seasonal history. Spring, for example, comes first to the northern side of Logan Canyon. The rays of the sun, as it mounts the sky toward the peak of its summer solstice, reach this side of the deep valley first. Only later do they shine on the southern side. Thus wildflowers unfold their blooms first in the hastened spring of the northern side. By the time the sun reached the southern wall, plants that bloomed on the opposite side of the narrow canyon may already be brown and dry. In this manner the different sides of the canyon—so close together in space—may, at the same time, reveal characteristics of different seasons of the year. Similarly, wherever we went among these western mountains, we found local conditions retarding or advancing the seasons, producing climatic effects in miniature.

The tide of spring and the tide of fall have, in many ways, reverse characteristics. Spring moves north; autumn south. Spring races ahead down the valleys, creeps slowly up the mountainsides; autumn comes first to the highlands, runs fastest into the south along the high ridges and the mountain chains and then sweeps southward more gradually down the valleys and over the lowlands. In spring, to ascend a mountain is to go backward in time, back to the latter days of winter. To ascend a mountain in fall is to go forward in the seasons, to advance into later autumn or early winter. On the map, up is north and down is south. Similarly, among the mountains going up is the equivalent of going north so far as seasonal conditions are concerned while going down is the equivalent of going south.

Among the painted forests of the east we had seen a multitude of colors in the autumn foliage, crimson and scarlet and gold and orange and lemon yellow and burgundy red. In the high autumn of the Continental Divide yellow had predominated. Now in Logan Canyon we saw the red of the bigtoothed or western sugar maple and, when we traveled south —past turkey farms where birds were fattening for Thanksgiving, past roadside stands laden with apples and pears and plums and grapes, the fruits of fall, on through Salt Lake City and east toward Strawberry Daniel's Pass—we came to rolling mountains that were covered with a low chaparral growth that ran on and on in a vast tapestry of colors as though all the hills were covered with Indian blankets, richly hued.

As it ran east our road paralleled the 125-mile chain of the Uinta Mountains, the only range in the United States that runs east and west. It carried us through canyons, pink-soiled and red-rocked or gray of soil and rock, sometimes with a silver stream of thistledown riding through on the wind. It crossed dry creek beds and rivers of stones. Magpies alighted in treetops beside the road, balancing themselves with long tails bobbing up and down like pumphandles. More than once we passed weathered log cabins with sod roofs, some with tumbleweeds rooted in the roof soil. One that combined the old and the new was wired for electricity. Most stood in the shade of cottonwoods, the trees whose scraped inner pulp once provided the hard-pressed pioneers with a confection called "cottonwood ice cream." Red foliage once more lay behind us. But aspen gold, pure, brilliant, shining, was scattered all around us. It covered the steeps, flowed down the declivities, massed along the creek banks. Then the gold, too, dropped behind us and we were among silvery sagebrush and juniper forests so

SNOW-COVERED Mt. Rainier. Below, forest ferns remain green the year around in the mild climate of coastal Washington.

MISTY FOREST scenery is familiar along the paths of the Olympic Peninsula where fog is common and rainfall heavy.

darkly green the trees looked black along the mountainsides.

It was late in the afternoon when we reached Vernal. Ringed by gaunt, sterile mountains, the green cup of the Vernal Valley of northeastern Utah is an oasis of plenty. The nectar of its alfalfa fields is the source of its famed Vernal honey. Utah, with a bee-skep on the seal of the state and with the honeybee, Deseret, prominent in Mormon teachings, has always been an important producer of honey. Now many of the Utah swarms are active almost the year around. Each January, thousands of colonies ride on trucks that roll virtually nonstop all the way to California. There they are rented to orchardists to fertilize the blooms of fruit trees. By late spring the hives are heading back home on board other trucks to begin harvesting the nectar of another summer in Utah.

That night a wild west, Indians-and-Pioneers movie played at the Vernal theater. The town was crowded with Ute Indians from a neighboring reservation. Oftentimes in the past when I have heard people mention "The Indian Problem" I have waited hopefully for them to speak a word in defense of the red men we have robbed and penned up in reservations of our own choosing. But always they have spoken of the faraway Indians of India, of somebody else's Indians, not ours. The Utes, however, had received not long before, at the end of long-drawn-out litigation, a large award from the government for what had been taken from them. Many drove into town that night in new and shiny cars. While waiting for the show to begin the children looked at comic books and the men and women ate popcorn. Here, as in the log cabin with the sod roof and electric lights, the old and the new were joined.

Only a few months before, another instance of the old and the new in juxtaposition had led to an odd tragedy on the desert road west of Vernal. Four Indians were driving home in a Buick late at night. Just over the brow of a hill the engine stopped. The fuel tank was empty. Instead of pushing the machine off the road, the Indians did what their ancestors had done when a horse went lame or night overtook them at a distance from home. They simply rolled up in their blankets and went to sleep. Before dawn a milk truck roaring through the dark at sixty miles an hour burst over the hilltop, crashed into the stalled car and instantly killed all of its occupants.

A dozen miles or so east of Vernal, the next morning, a dusty side road led us north to one of America's oldest graveyards, a burial place of prehistoric monsters. A million pounds of fossil bones, the skeletons of extinct creatures ranging from the size of a house cat to thirty-ton dinosaurs eighty feet long, were quarried from this area before it was set aside by the federal government as a national monument. This land of desert hills and desert plateaus will be remembered also as one of the great battlefields of the conservation movement in America. The invasion of national parks—"owned by the people of the United States"—by private interests, by cattlemen, by lumbermen, by powermen, is the goal of a continual and unrelenting pressure. It reached a peak in the Echo Park Dam project of the Dinosaur National Monument, a project that, in the early 1950's, promised to set a precedent for raiding public lands and destroying the purpose and promise of the whole national park system. Its defeat came only after half a decade of stubborn fighting that aroused conservationists from coast to coast.

About 140,000,000 years before it became a conservation battleground, this desert highland was a marshy, tropical lowland. Here the "Terrible Lizards," the dinosaurs of the Mesozoic Era, wallowed and browsed and fought. Ponderous and slow moving, some were trapped in quicksand, others drowned in sudden floods. Their bodies congregated, were covered by earth and eventually their skeletons became part of the forming rock. At the time the Uinta Mountains were formed, this rock was lifted, tilted and folded. Subsequent erosion brought to light the rich fossil beds it contained. Thus, some 50,000,000 years after the last dinosaur had disappeared from the earth, man found here twelve different species of these prehistoric creatures that, at one time, inhabited all the continents of the globe and yet were never seen alive by any human eye.

In the yellow rock we examined some of these fossil bones a million centuries old. Then we looked away—from the skeleton of the dinosaur to the skeleton of the earth. All the land of this dry country of the west appears gaunt. There is little meat on its bones. And often its skeleton is showing. Around us the reared and folded hills of the arid upland were almost entirely bare. Their rocks were yellow and brown and red. Some of the slopes were sliced by erosion. Others ascended formed of different-colored strata like the layers of a cake. Dabs of black-green, far-spaced and tiny, showed where tenacious junipers, stunted and twisted, were anchored with roots plunged deeply into small fissures in the rock.

As I write these words, two thousand and more miles from Dinosaur, a smooth greenish stone lies on the desk beside me. It is a gastrolith obtained at the Vernal Museum. Because the dinosaurs had no grinding teeth they swallowed stones, somewhat as a chicken swallows pebbles, to aid in the digestion of their food. The piece of greenish rock that I have just laid down, about as long as my thumb, was once such a "stomach stone." It rode about within the body of a giant, lumbering creature that saw the world as it appeared 50,000,000 or 100,000,000 years before my remotest ancestor arrived on earth.

Looking at it now I can see vividly again the desert surroundings of that graveyard of ancient giants. I can see the bare, colored hills and the green water of the Green River winding away below us toward Desolation Canyon. I can see the dusty-colored grasshoppers exploding into the air, a Say's ground squirrel racing over the hard, baked earth to its burrow, red harvester ants endlessly coming and going, and a magpie cutting scallops in the air as it repeatedly checked its speed in a long tobogganing descent. But most of all I can see a modern descendant of the dinosaurs, a desert whiptail lizard, clinging to the rock, gray and diminutive, close beside one of the great fossil bones of its prehistoric ancestor. It cocked its head to look at me as I stood looking at it. I moved a step nearer; it disappeared in a flick of movement into a crevice.

Continuing through aeons of time, the smaller lizards have outlived the dinosaurs. Perhaps the end of their mighty ancestors came because the land rose, draining the swamps they inhabited, perhaps because they grew too large for their food supply, perhaps because the climate grew colder and they, being cold-blooded, became too sluggish to obtain sufficient food—at any rate because they could not adapt themselves to new conditions. This inability is called by biologists "racial old age." But the gray whiptail lizard that popped from its crevice again when I remained motionless was far from racial old age. It, and its kind, had adapted itself to its environment in many ways.

I observed one such adjustment as it turned broadside to the sun on this autumn morning. Desert lizards, as well as desert grasshoppers, regulate their body temperatures to some degree by taking different positions in relation to the sun. They point directly at it, so they are parallel with its rays, when they are reducing the amount of heat they absorb; they turn at right angles to it, so more of their body is exposed to the rays, when the air is chill. A scientist who recorded the temperature of a grasshopper when it was parallel to the sun's rays and when it was at right angles to them, found that in the latter position the reading was higher by more than six degrees F.

In his *The Natural History of Selborne*, Gilbert White tells how his old Sussex turtle adjusted itself to take full advantage of the waning sunshine in autumn. "In the decline of the year," White notes, "he improves the faint autumnal beams by getting within the reflection of a fruit wall: and, though he never has read that planes inclined to the horizon receive a greater share of warmth, he inclines his shell, by tilting it against the wall, to collect and admit every feeble ray." To get enough heat but not too much heat from the sun is the dual problem of every cold-blooded creature.

In the southwestern desert, some years ago, two American herpetologists, Charles M. Bogert and Raymond B. Cowles, found that no lizard they tested could survive a temperature of more than 117 degrees. To avoid fatal overheating the cold-blooded creatures of desert areas use many stratagems. Some insects, for example, walk almost on tiptoe to keep their bodies as far as possible from the sun-heated earth and to permit air to circulate beneath them. During the more sultry hours of the day grasshoppers of the Great Basin are often found massed together on the shady side of fenceposts. And, in northern Arizona, a collared lizard is able to change its clothes, so to speak, according to the temperature. In the hottest weather it is very light colored, almost white, thus reflecting the sun's rays; but in chill weather it turns slaty black, its body in consequence absorbing a greater amount of warmth from the sun.

The year before we visited the area winter had come to Vernal in late September. Ours—by great good fortune—was an abnormally warm, wonderfully prolonged, autumn. Snow first fell on the fields weeks after its normal time of arrival. Because the seasons vary so greatly, one time being shortened, another time lengthened, exact dates on such a trip as ours might well be misleading. The same date in a different year may present altogether different conditions. Hence in this account the definite dates are few. They have been replaced mainly by general dates which, in truth, in the end may be more exact than exact dates would be.

Every autumn, from time uncounted, the calendar of the Ute Indians contained as one of the great, gala events of the year the annual expedition to the mountains for the nuts of the pinyon pine. It occurred just after the first frosts of the season. As we drove back from Vernal, west along the skirts of the Uintas, we saw the low, round-headed pines extending away across the dry foothills. Half a dozen times we stopped

and picked the pitchy cones, pried open the scales, and ex-
tracted the thin-shelled nuts. But almost every time another
nut-eater had been there before us. A small round hole in the
shell told of the insect that had consumed the contents within.
Our hands grew progressively more gummed up with pitch.
When we tried to wipe it off, bark and leaves became glued in
place. We felt as though we were tarred and feathered before
we had gathered a handful of sound nuts.

But the delicate, unforgettable flavor of those seeds of *Pinus
edulis* was reward enough. Vernal honey and pinyon nuts—
that was the food we dined on beside the road that day. These
seeds of the pine, we decided, were our favorites among all the
infinite variety of nuts that in those autumn days were being
harvested in woods and fields and groves and among the mountains all across the land.

Just as the wild rice of the upper Mississippi, the buffalo
of the Great Plains and the salmon of the northwest provided
special foods and influenced the way of life of the aboriginal
inhabitants of those regions, so the pine nuts or Indian nuts of
the dry areas of the west played an important part in shaping
the lives of the Indians there. Abundant, nourishing, keeping
well, they formed the staple food of winter. In times of early
shortage, pioneers kept horses alive till spring by feeding them
pine nuts as grain. And all over the west even today the nourishing seeds are sold in country stores and city groceries. We
bought pounds of them along the way, never tiring of their
wild and indescribably delicate flavor. During years of special
abundance as many as a million dollars' worth of pine nuts
go to market in western states.

Although only a few days had gone by since we drove to
Vernal, a great leaf fall had taken place among the aspens of
Strawberry Daniel's Pass, 8,000 feet above sea level. In place
of the shining gold, a silvery shade of gray that seemed to have
been laid on with light, vertical brush strokes, extended across
the mountainsides. It was the gray of the crowding mul-

titude of the slender trunks of newly leafless aspen trees.

Running west past the Indian blanket mountains, past valley cattails where the lower stems seemed dipped in whitewash with their coating of alkali, past the Seagull Monument in Salt Lake City, past the Pavilion at Saltair and the southern end of the Great Salt Lake, we came at evening to the one street town of Grantsville—five miles long and one street wide—on the eastern edge of the Great Salt Lake Desert. In the dusk we pulled up before a silent, darkened structure of yellow brick. Its windows were broken. Dust lay thick on the wide concrete steps that mounted to massive front doors. Above the entrance, cut in stone, were the words: "GRAND OPERA—1900." We have often thought since of that dark and lonely building, its lights and its life gone out. And we have tried to imagine what happened there when its lights were lighted and what life was like on this desert frontier for those who, half a century ago, climbed those steps and entered those doors when they were new.

The crowing of a rooster, that wild, stirring sound that seems more nearly allied with nature than any other domestic sound, awoke us in the morning. By seven-thirty Grantsville —known to the pioneers as Twenty Wells from the score of water holes in the vicinity—was receding behind us. Ahead lay the white desert, the dry floor of the ancient sea, a shimmering plain of salt and alkali. No stream enters it. No plant grows on it. No animal burrows in it. Here at its heart, it is the desert lifeless, the desert deserted.

In the beginning, while we were still on the border of this vast white waste, pipits in small bands took off, bounding through the air like corks riding turbulent water. Here the salicornia—the pickleweed or burro weed—ran the scarlet of its autumn brilliance along the roadside just as, over the salt meadows of Cape May and below the hills of Shinnecock, now so far away, it was aflame amid the tan-gray waves of the cordgrass. Four ravens, following the road partway into the desert, passed over us, one with the heavy broadax of its bill turned to one side as it peered down at us.

The sparse greasewood shrank, became stunted, disappeared. All the trailer trucks coming off the desert now carried water bags slung on the front bumpers. Long drifts of white, like snowbanks, stretched away, grew more numerous, merged at last and we were in the midst of the wasteland, stopping often beside the straight black ribbon of the single road that stretched on and on before us.

Until almost ten o'clock the desert air was surprisingly cool. Then the swiftly mounting heat of the day began. Mirages formed all around us. Distant mountains took the form of islands rising from a shimmering lake. Cars came down the road toward us seemingly riding on air high above the pavement. One illusion of a body of water to the north was so vivid that Nellie got out the map and searched for an arm of the Great Salt Lake in that direction.

Almost without a curve for fifty miles the road ran on. The whole land seemed glazed with a white frosting. The apparent snowbanks and ice fields were formed of unmelting crystals, of hot ice without moisture. The glare increased. Without sun glasses, even on this October day, it would have been unbearable. We thought of the slow ox teams plodding through the dust and heat and dazzling brilliance of midsummer, following the deadly Hastings Cutoff across this parched, ominous land. We thought of Jedediah Smith, the twenty-eight-year-old Bible-carrying trapper, adventurer, crackshot and former divinity student from New Hampshire who, in 1827, with two companions first made the perilous crossing. We thought of young William D. Rishel and C. A. Emise and their daring ride across this naked desert in 1906 on bicycles. We remembered the pioneers who failed to make the other side and we talked of how vivid is the suffering of the few when the people are few and how the suffering of nameless millions in two world wars is blurred over by numbers.

Walking out on the desert we found that in some places the surface was like a pie crust. When we broke through, the layer beneath resembled heavy grease or wet and slippery clay. The crust seals in the moisture. And when rains fall in winter the mirage of lakes on the desert is no longer an illusion. The water, without penetrating the crust, stands in shallow pools, some of them remaining until summer dries them up. But so dry is the area in midsummer that rain, falling from the clouds, is likely to disappear before it reaches the ground, evaporating into the air.

Not far from the Bonneville Salt Flats, where racing drivers, in straightaway runs over the floor of the desert—here level and hard-packed—have reached speeds as high as 394 miles an hour, we came upon a riddle of erosion. The stump of an ancient telegraph pole, about three feet high, had been worn thin and smooth to within six inches of the ground. This lower section was a mass of ravelings or fibers fluffed out like the shavings at the end of a stick. Why had the winds that had eroded away the hard upper wood failed to carry away this mass of flimsy fragments? The answer, we decided, lay in the fact that the fluffy mass was solidly packed with gritty material, that it had thus, like an abrasive tool, become more resistant to wind and flying sand than the wood itself.

Before us now the brown mountains of the Pilot Range rose higher at the western edge of the desert. But we were still well out on this dead, flat, shimmering land when we encountered one of the most amazing sights of our travels.

Three monarch butterflies drifted by, then two more appeared in sight—five monarchs winging their way across the desert on their long migration south. More than fifty barren miles of salt and alkali lay between them and the southern boundary of this desolate, plantless waste. How, amid heat wave and mirage and blinding glare, could these insect voyagers find their way? They were not using landmarks for there were no landmarks to use. All was one white, level, featureless plain. They were not following the terrain—the lay of the land, as in a river valley—for the desert stretched before them to the horizon as level as the sea. How were they orienting themselves? We pondered that question during succeeding days. By the time I reached the famed butterfly trees of the Monterey Peninsula in California I thought I had an answer.

East of Wendover we met the first stunted clumps of greasewood, this time crowning a host of small knolls like haycocks in the desert. We looked back on that land of desolation —the end of the world surrounded by mountains—and thought how long a time it would take to feel at home in all this dry country of the west, so lonely and overwhelming. And in that moment I was aware of a curious mental reaction that, no doubt, a psychologist would find revealing. There swept over me a fierce hunger for books, for libraries, for all the worn favorites on my shelves at home, for the commingled smell of old paper and glue and ink that surrounds the stacks of every public library. I longed for Keats and Shakespeare and Conrad and Thoreau and Hudson. I had, for that day, enough of wilderness, enough of remote and inhospitable land.

This mood went with me all the way to Wells, the old wagon-train oasis in Nevada, all the way north among the gray and yellow mountains of the eastern edge of that state, through sagebrush and jackrabbit country where we counted as many as eighty-nine of the animals killed on a measured mile of road, through nearly a hundred miles of dust devils where ten or fifteen at a time mounted and spun around us, into the curious yellow light of a gathering dust storm, and over the line into Idaho. It is easier, we decided that night, to accept the message of the stars than the message of the salt desert. The stars speak of man's insignificance in the long eternity of time; the desert speaks of his insignificance right now.

TWENTY

CRATERS OF THE MOON

I STARTED out that morning with a dull mind fit only for entering figures in our expense account. But we had not gone far before a change in the country around us kindled to life vivid memories of an experience 2,000 miles away, on the border of North Carolina and Tennessee, in the spring of the year. Then we had come from lush Appalachian forests into the blighted, manmade desert of the Copper Basin. Now, once again, we rode through a stricken land. As far as we could see around us extended only hills and plains of cinders and barren lava. We seemed to have slipped swiftly backward through immense reaches of time. We were in the third day of creation. We wandered in a land new made.

For 200,000 square miles across south central Idaho, in the region of the Craters of the Moon, the earth presents a face hard, almost untouched by time. It is America's newest landscape. Only a few thousand years ago, in some cases only 500 years ago—a mere second as geological ages run—the molten, smoking lava had welled from fissures in the earth. The blue glaze of its exterior was still unmarked by storms. The centuries of gradual transformation and breaking down, of erosion and decay, were only just beginning. In the Copper Basin of the east the topsoil had been carried away. Here the soil had never been. Here was a hard, lifeless land. Or so we thought. Here was a countryside untouched by the seasons. Or so it seemed. The great adventure of this day was the discovery of life where life appeared impossible, the revelation that, in hundreds of ways, even in this dead land the turning wheel of the seasons had left its track.

By midmorning we reached the roads and trails of the Craters of the Moon National Monument, an eighty-square-mile area near Arco set aside by the federal government in 1924. It was autumn. The tourist season was over. We wandered almost alone through its black, eerie world of broken lava, tree molds, cinder cones and natural bridges. We had gone but a short distance before we were reminded afresh of how almost pathetically small are the basic requirements of life. Put a teaspoonful of dust in any crack and some seed will find it. All across this land of seeming emptiness and desolation seeds had discovered little accumulations of airborne dust. Even clumps of that bushy western relative of the goldenrod, rabbitbrush, here and there amazingly rose from the lava, rooted in invisible soil.

Our first surprise came when we entered a stretch of open cinders, our feet crunching along as though we were walking on dry toast. These cinder fields are formed of the froth or molten spray thrown off by fire fountains during volcanic activity. Sometimes they have a brownish cast, occasionally a reddish hue as though they were still uncooled, but most of the time they are ebony black. From a distance they look like rich loam plowed and harrowed and ready for planting. As we emerged on this sloping plain of cinders we saw scattered across its surface hundreds of what appeared to be small, white, lace doilies. Each was from three inches to a foot across. Each, on closer examination, proved to be composed of low-lying, silver-hued, woolly-textured leaves. Variously known as the umbrella plant, the silver plant and woolly knees, these cinder dwellers were one of the wild buckwheats. Long since the yellow flowers had withered. The upright stems were now dry and shriveled. Only a few more weeks and this year's installment of the life of the plant would be rounded out. But the perennial roots below, as well as the seeds, already formed and hardened, insured that its blooms would appear again the following summer in this arid and improbable garden.

Looking down at these silver clusters of the wild buckwheat we were, once more, making contact with the eccentric pioneer naturalist whose trail we first encountered at Cape May. For it was Thomas Nuttall who, a century ago, bestowed on this western plant its scientific name, *Eriogonum ovalifolium*.

There were other plants—small, sere, sparse, widely spaced —growing on the cinder fields. Only the *Eriogonum* now showed signs of life. But in June and July the white of bitter-root blooms and the red of monkey flowers are scattered over the black background of the cinders. Growth, blooming and seedtime come swiftly here as they do on a mountain meadow. Down some of the slopes of the cinder cones that favorite food of bears, the wild parsnip, grows almost abundantly. And in shaded cracks and recesses in the lava the dainty *Woodsia* fern sometimes obtains a foothold. Lichens, liverworts, mosses and algae—primitive plants all—are widely scattered in the Craters of the Moon. All through the so-called Devil's Orchard we found the ragged, jumbled masses—the slag of primal furnaces—splotched with brilliant patches of algae, orange and scarlet and sulphur yellow.

It was while we were wandering through this colorful, eerie landscape that we came upon the juncos. They were no ordinary juncos. They were juncos our eyes had never encountered before. A little flock of a dozen or more flitted about, calling, alighting on the ground, feeding. Each bird was brownish of back, grayish of head, with a flush of rusty pink running back along its sides and across its breast. Amid these bizarre surroundings we were meeting our first pink-sided juncos.

As the afternoon advanced the wind rose. It pummeled us on the rises and raced overhead in long screeching blasts when we descended into the hollows. It drove cinder dust into our mouths and ears and noses. Once we struggled for an eighth

of a mile—like flies on the rim of a bowl—around the edge of
a deep cinder crater. In this exposed position the fifty-mile-an-
hour gale caught us full force. We struggled down into a depression beyond, pounded and panting as though we had
battled our way through heavy surf. There, protected from the
great gusts and warmed by the sun a dancing, yellow-winged
grasshopper crackled in the air. And above the sound of the
wind we caught low cricket music somewhere amid the sparse
vegetation.

It was in this depression that I picked a fernlike leaf from
a low shrub. Absently, I crushed it between my fingers. Fragrance filled the air around us. For hours afterward my hand
was scented with the perfume of this redolent leaf. The low
shrub was that medicinal plant of the pioneers, mountain mis-
ery, bear clover, bearmat, tarweed, kittikit or kit-kit-dizze. Its
aromatic leaves are evergreen. Where the white-petaled blos-
soms of summer had been, autumn had brought the dry, one-
seeded hips of this curious relative of the wild rose.

When the early pioneers first came to the Craters of the
Moon region they were mystified by low mounds found here
and there among the lava fields. Each mound consisted of
alternating layers of cinders and sagebrush. The riddle was
solved when an aged Indian at the Fort Hall Reservation recalled that it was thus his ancestors had marked their paths,
the sagebrush being laid lengthwise to indicate the direction
of the trail. For three miles, past Great Owl Cavern and on to
the tree molds west of Big Cinder Butte, we followed one
of these ancient Indian trails. The path led along the line where
lava fields and cinder slopes met. Here and there, dwarfed and
wind-wracked limber pines huddled together, their branches
contorted and grotesque. One of these trees, in 1926, was
struck by lightning near Big Crater. When park service men
felled it they found it measured thirty-four and a half inches
in diameter. Its annual growth rings numbered 461. It was
rooted there, already a good-sized tree, before the *Santa*

Maria sailed from Spain on its epic voyage of discovery.

The sun was well down in the west by the time we passed Great Owl Cavern. Not far beyond we came upon deer tracks in the cinders and near by, where a dry, fallen tree lay shaggy in a brilliant sheathing of green lichen, a chipmunk had dug its burrow. Twice we glimpsed these striped rodents scurrying away across the rolling waves of lava. On occasions they explore the lava plains as much as half a mile from their cinderfield homes. We, like the chipmunks, emerged on the open lava as we neared the tree molds. There a remarkable sight met our eyes, as beautiful as it was unexpected.

All across the black, wind-buffeted expanse to the west— shot through with the iridescent, metallic glintings of the lava beneath—was a streaming sea of silken threads. A vast multitude of ballooning spiderlings had come to earth in this forbidding place. Across thousands upon thousands of acres the silver of the autumn gossamer was streaming in the wind, catching the low rays of the sun, shimmering and flickering in constant motion—the ephemeral silk of a few days' duration bringing its delicate beauty to the hard, enduring, centuries-old face of the lava.

It was amid this gossamer that we came at last to those almost miraculous features of the lava beds, the tree molds. At this spot, once upon a time, a group of trees had stood in the path of the molten flood. The round holes, where the trunks had been, extended deep into the hardened lava. When that lava had issued incandescent from fissures in The Great Rift, its temperature had been about 2,000 degrees F. How then did the trees avoid being consumed like celluloid? What enabled them to survive long enough to leave their forms in the hardening rock? Scientists believe the lava was slowing down and cooling rapidly when it reached the spot. Moisture and sap in the trunks formed a layer of steam that accelerated the cooling process and formed a protective shell of rock around the wood. Later the tree trunks rotted away leaving the molds behind In a few rare instances, the top of a burning tree would fall on the surface of the cooling lava and leave there, by the same sequence of events, a perfect mold of its upper branches.

Retracing our steps in the sunset, we stopped on the flank of a cinder cone to watch a slim bird flitting flycatcherwise along the slope from pine to sagebrush and back to pine again. Each time it landed its support reared and bucked in the wind while the bird gripped its twig and rode out the great gusts. White feathers ran down either side of its tail. Brown patches stood out on its dark gray wings. And a white line encircled each eye. Here, in this solitary place, we were seeing for the first time a Townsend's solitaire. And once more we were touching the life of Old Curious.

For it was during the 1834 Wyeth Expedition across the South Pass of Wyoming to the Columbia River that Nuttall's young companion, John Kirk Townsend, had collected the first specimen of this bird known to science, a bird named for its discoverer by John James Audubon. It is the only North American representative of a group of thrushes, mostly tropical, famed for their glorious voices. Here, in the Craters of the Moon, the two pioneer naturalists who had journeyed west so long before were, after a fashion, united again, one remembered for the silver plant he had named, the other for a dark, slender bird christened in his honor.

At one point I tried a short cut across an arm of the open lava. I learned in a dozen steps how slow and laborious and hazardous is the walking. In places the lava is jagged and broken. No horse can be ridden across it. Snakes are entirely absent from the region. The local belief is that they cannot stand the abrasion of the hard furrows. Pioneers who penetrated the area on foot often returned with their shoes nearly eaten away by the rasp of the lava.

Out of the fastness of this dangerous land they brought tales of ice-cold pools surrounded by sun-heated rocks too hot to touch. And, unlike those legends of hidden treasure with which the region abounds, these reports were true. Here and there are small water holes where the temperature rarely exceeds thirty-four degrees. They are not springs. They are not connected with subterranean streams. Their origin, for a long time a baffling mystery, is now known to be associated with caches of winter ice and snow. Packing into deep pits and fissures during the seven months of cold weather, the frozen water in time forms a solid base of impermeable ice. Lava is a poor conductor of heat. Only the upper layers of the snow and ice melt in summer and the resulting water never gets much more than two degrees above the freezing point. Yet in this frigid water green algae sometimes grow.

At first the riddle of these water holes was believed to be connected with another mystery, a mystery of lost rivers. For all this area of the Craters of the Moon is a land of disappearing streams. Beneath the lava run the subterranean conduits of rivers flowing underground. Not a single stream flows across the surface of the whole Snake River Plateau. Fifty miles to the north of us, as we followed the trail back, rose Borah Peak, the highest mountain in Idaho, its summit 12,655 feet above sea level. And all along the horizon in that direction we saw the lofty rampart of the snowclad Sawtooth Mountains. Down their slopes the Big Lost River, the Little Lost River, and numerous other streams descend until they reach the lava plain. Then they sink out of sight. Draining into innumerable cracks and crevices they flow beneath the lava layer across a gently tilting plain to the gorge of the Snake River. There, in some cases after running unseen for upward of 200 miles, they emerge near Hagerman in the spectacular display of a host of fountains gushing from the sheer face of the river wall. These are the famous Thousand Springs marveled at by the early pioneers as their covered wagons crept along the opposite bank of the river on the road to Oregon.

Looking across the greenish water of the Snake from this same vantage point the next day, Nellie and I spent an hour watching the emerging rivers plunging down the rocks in sheets of spray. Some descended in long plumes and veils, others dropped to the river in walls of white water. The year around the temperature of the emerging flood is between sixty and sixty-two degrees. All the way from the Salmon River to the town of Bliss, a distance of eighteen miles, fountains flow from the northern wall of the canyon. But it is in a stretch of hardly more than half a mile near Hagerman that the dramatic display of the Thousand Springs is concentrated. Here the precipice towers as much as 185 feet above the river and some of the springs pour out their long-pent-up flood close to the top.

At the turn of the century it was estimated that water flowed down the face of the canyon wall at this point at the rate of 20,000 cubic feet a second. At the lowest point of the Snake, during the latter days of summer, the fountains of the Thousand Springs were said to add a volume of water that equaled the entire previous flow of the river. What we witnessed, half a century later, while still beautiful was only a maimed and diminished show. Where some of the falls had been there were now the slanting metal flumes of a power company. We remembered Thoreau's observation when owners began cutting down the beautiful Walden Woods: "It concerns us all whether these proprietors choose to cut down all the woods this winter or not." The wild beauty of America is a national possession. The preservation of this heritage is everybody's affair. No land on earth has been more superlatively blessed with varied and priceless forms of natural beauty. Whatever mars or destroys it robs the future as well as the present. What "These Proprietors" choose to do—even in a far-off corner of the land—is of more than personal, more than local concern. It is the concern of all.

By this fifty-fourth day of our trip we had already traveled more than 8,000 miles, more than the equivalent of the diameter of the earth. And the Oregon Trail, the great northwest, the Olympic Peninsula, upper California, all still lay before us.

TWENTY-ONE

LOST IN THE MOUNTAINS

MILE-A-MINUTE Diesel trucks, those modern covered wagons of the Oregon Trail, thundered around us when we slowed to read a sign on a hillside strewn with oval rocks: "Petrified Watermelons. Take One Home to Your Mother-in-Law." Not long afterward we crossed the Snake into Oregon near the Malheur River—where Indians once sought the wild syringa for their arrow shafts. Later we climbed above a steep valley—where a golden eagle went rocketing past us in a scalp-tingling plunge. Then, following all the windings of the twisting Snake we came, with the morning behind us, to Farewell Bend.

Here the covered wagons of the pioneers bade good-by to the river and turned west toward the dreaded Blue Mountains of eastern Oregon. And here the river swung away to the north, carrying its green-tinted waters toward the Seven Devils Mountains, the Wallowas, and, between the two, Hell's Canyon, the deepest and narrowest gash on the face of the continent.

The next day, driving from Baker, Oregon, we followed the Powder River to its juncture with the Snake. Then for another thirty miles we rode the bank of the larger stream—traveling north beyond the ghost town of Homestead, to the only steel bridge over the Snake in a hundred miles, close to the narrowing mouth of the canyon. Our dusty road, clinging to the side of a steep descent, was marked on our map: "Dangerous Road. Use Caution." It was built on the one-track right-of-way of an abandoned railroad. On either side tawny mountains rose above us so ribbed with horizontal cattle trails they seemed made of corduroy. Little side canyons flamed with the red of autumn sumac and where deserted shacks marked the site of Homestead, once bustling with copper and gold, now the gold of a single straggling peach tree shone in the sun. Robins, a migrant flock of fifty or more, the first we had seen in many days, darted and called and fed among the branches of riverside hackberry trees. And always beside us flowed the Snake, that stream of many moods, sliding silently around pure white sand bars crisscrossed with cattle tracks, tumbling down the Wild Horse Rapids, turning in lazy slicks above the deeper reaches.

We stopped, before turning back, by the bridge that crosses to the Kleinschmidt Grade, a towering zigzag road of switchbacks that in ten miles ascends 6,000 feet up the Idaho mountainsides. Below the bridge the surface of the Snake had a smooth, oily appearance, swirling and turning as it slid with steady speed toward the entrance, only a few miles farther on, of one of the greatest chasms cut by any river in the crust of the earth. For forty miles the Grand Canyon of the Snake has an average depth of 5,500 feet. From the top of He Devil Peak to the floor of the chasm the measurement is 7,900 feet. Pinched together by walls of granite until it is often less than a hundred feet wide and dropping an average of ten and a half feet to the mile, the torrent tumbles down the long passage of the gorge.

To the right, as the river flows, seven serrated peaks rise in a semi-circle—the Seven Devils Mountains of the northwestern Rockies. To the left, lifting ten peaks above 9,000 feet and almost as many more above 8,000, the wild jumble of the Wallowa Mountains extends in a highland wilderness across the northeastern corner of Oregon. The Wallowas, as William O. Douglas points out in *Of Men and Mountains*, are roughly in the form of a wagon wheel with Eagle Cap the hub and the various ridges running from it the spokes. So knife edged are some of these ridges that it is impossible to ride a horse along their tops. Few roads penetrate the area, only the tracks of remote ranchers and of hunters threading the interior. Months later, when I tried to buy a topographical map of the region in New York, I found that even today it has never been completely surveyed, that still it is marked "unmapped."

All of our glimpses of this forbidding land are now linked in our minds with images of a dark shepherd dog, of a man with a shy smile and an enduring affection; with memories of a long and lonely search. For, on the night of October 24, 1950, in these wild Wallowa Mountains, America's greatest dog hunt began.

On that October day Gerald R. Wear, an elk hunter from the village of Alder Creek, south of Mount Hood, had followed a primitive road far into the interior of this isolated region. Riding beside him in his light delivery truck was Poncho, a German shepherd dog that, for nearly ten years, had been his daily companion. It was after nine o'clock when Wear made camp. Poncho, cramped from the confinement of the long day's ride, ranged over the surrounding country. Exactly what happened in the next hour nobody knows. Perhaps Poncho raced after some jack rabbit or other quarry, followed it too far in the darkness and became confused in unfamiliar territory. At any rate when supper was ready Poncho was gone; when Wear went to bed he was still missing; when morning came, somewhere in the immensity of jumbled peaks and broken gullies Wear's dog was alone and lost.

The man who set out to find him faced odds that seemed insuperable. He could not hear his dog's bark. He was entirely deaf. He could not call his dog's name. He was mute. The area around him formed one of the wildest spots in all the United States. It is a land of long winters with killing frosts coming, on the average, before the second week in September and with the thermometer, in the late October nights, dropping close to zero. The menace of early blizzards is always present. Time was short. But it was not these considerations so much as another that drove Wear to frenzied search. It was the knowledge that, at first glance, Poncho would be mistaken for a coyote. Every rancher's and hunter's gun would be against him.

Snow had fallen during the night and the ground was white when Wear started out at dawn. For fourteen hours that day he hurried this way and that seeking the trail of his lost dog. He clambered up ridges and climbed the skirts of the surrounding mountains and scanned the country below. Nowhere did he see a moving thing that resembled Poncho. It was long after dark when he returned to camp. He was too tired and worried to eat. All that night he kept a campfire roaring in the hope that Poncho would see it or would catch the smell of its smoke. At daybreak he was on the trail again. All that day and the next and the next he searched. And each night he kept the beacon light of his campfire burning. He had combed the whole of the wild Billings Meadow area before he admitted defeat. Poncho, he knew, had gone beyond the vicinity. He was wandering somewhere, but no one knew where, in the Wallowa wilderness.

What happened in the days and weeks that followed I learned from Wear, himself, when I visited Alder Creek.

"If you blink when you go through," a waitress in near-by Sandy told us, "you'll miss Alder Creek entirely."

Set amid forests and mountains, it consists mainly of the weathered roadside restaurant owned by Rose Moody. Here, where he works, I found Wear, a square-jawed, pleasant-faced man in his early forties. From a pocket he fished a small peach-colored pad and a stub of yellow pencil. Through the intermediary of scribbled questions and answers on this pad I learned the story of the succeeding days of search.

Hurrying out to the nearest town—Enterprise, Oregon— Wear got in touch with highway officials. He notified the state police. He visited the government men in charge of the Wallowa National Forest. He pleaded with everyone to tell all hunters going into the area that his dog was lost and not to shoot it. He enlisted the help of the local newspaper, the *Wallowa County Chieftain*. Issue after issue carried stories on the progress of his lone-handed hunt for his lost dog.

Then he drove the 250 miles back to Alder Creek, stocked his truck with provisions, put a cot in the back where he could sleep during the cold nights, purchased a new compass, and with general maps of the area and virtually all the money he had in the world, he returned to the hunt. Poncho, he knew, was shy of strangers. No matter how lonely or hungry he got he was not likely to go to a ranch or hunters' camp for help. He was a one-man dog. And, as events amply proved, Wear was a one-dog man.

November came. Wherever a track led to an isolated ranch Wear followed it to ask about his dog. By the middle of the month almost everyone in the Wallowa area was looking for Poncho.

"What was the weather like?" I wrote.

"All the time snow. Two to six inches of snow. Temperature twenty degrees above zero to two degrees below zero."

He pointed out the light delivery truck he had used, a red machine, enclosed in the back, the kind of delivery truck used by butchers and grocers. Sleeping in the rear of this machine, Wear was protected from wind and snow but not from the cold. Day after day he drove himself, losing weight, sleeping fitfully, often going supperless to bed. Twice he came close to a nervous breakdown from exhaustion.

"Too much worry. Too little rest," he scribbled on the pad.

But reports began to trickle in. A rancher here, a hunter there, had sighted the dog. But none could get near him. The first report came from Cold Spring, less than ten miles from the Washington line and hardly six from Hell's Canyon and the boundary of Idaho. Wear roamed over the area for days seeking some sign, some trail of Poncho. But he was too late. The dog had moved on. Next hunters reported they had seen him in the vicinity of Buckhorn Spring, some twenty miles to the south. Wear spent days, with the temperature close to zero all the time, searching from dawn to night. And in the dark at the end of each day he returned to the cold truck discouraged and alone.

"But I wouldn't give up," he wrote.

As each report came in he marked the spot with a penciled cross on his general map of the area. He brought out this map, creased and worn and marked with half a dozen widely scattered crosses. The third report came from a rancher near Zumwalt, twenty miles south of Buckhorn Spring. Hunters next glimpsed the dog near an abandoned campfire in wild country to the west of Zumwalt. Then he was seen near Tope Creek, thirty miles away and still farther west; then near Mud Creek, to the north. His erratic wanderings were carrying him in a great hundred-mile, clockwise circle back toward the spot where he had first become lost.

Out of his movements a pattern began to emerge. Although Poncho was avoiding hunters he was going to the remains of their campfires in search of his master. By now Wear had tramped hundreds of miles among the mountains. Each lead he received came out of the remote interior days after the dog had been sighted. Always by the time he rushed to the area the trail had grown cold. Although he cannot speak a word, Wear is able to utter a thin, shrill cry that Poncho knew. From the top of each elevation he repeated this cry over and over again. But never once in all the weeks of his lonely quest did he catch a glimpse of the dog he sought.

Thanksgiving Day came. Then a month had gone by since Poncho disappeared in the darkness. Time had almost run out. It was only a matter of days now before the northern high country winter closed in. Then search would be impossible. The lost dog would be overwhelmed by drifts and cold.

In desperation Wear went aloft in an airplane piloted by an

Enterprise aviator. Circling, following the valleys, climbing over the ridges, skimming close to each wide stretch of open country, the plane carried him in a wandering course across the wilderness. For 375 miles this aerial search continued. Every second he was in the sky Wear peered intently down, scanning the ground for the small, dark shape he sought. But nowhere did his eyes catch a glimpse of Poncho. He landed again at Enterprise at the lowest point of his despair.

It was in the final week of November when word came from a rancher that only the day before he had seen the dog in broken country some twenty-five miles east of Mud Creek. Wear raced north. This, he was well aware, was almost his last chance. His money was virtually gone. His strength was nearly exhausted. In his lone-handed hunt he had walked more than 450 miles, had flown 375, had traveled a total of 1,752 miles, more than the equivalent of a journey halfway across the continent. And every step and every day had been marked by failure.

This was the situation at the dawn of Sunday, November 26. All morning Wear hunted and called. It was nearing mid-afternoon when he climbed to the top of the highest elevation where he could survey all the surrounding country. Nothing moved below him. His voice was nearly gone but he kept giving his shrill cry in the desperate hope that Poncho might catch it somewhere in the country spread out below him. He had called for nearly two hours when, a mile or so away, his eyes caught the movement of a small black speck on the snow.

Wear redoubled his calling. The speck moved slowly toward him. Three times it disappeared entirely, twice descending into gullies and once being swallowed up in a stretch of woodland. But little by little, stopping and inching ahead, so weak from cold and hunger and fatigue it took nearly two hours to cover the mile, Poncho kept coming on. When he appeared in the last opening Wear ran down the slope to meet him. It was 4:20 P.M. when he threw his arms around him and America's greatest dog hunt was over.

For a time Poncho lay on the ground, his ears down, completely exhausted. Then he revived and together the one-man dog and the one-dog man descended to the red truck that carried them home.

"Where is Poncho now?" I wrote on the pad and slid it along the counter to Wear.

He led me outside. As soon as we opened the door a dark German shepherd dog, sleek and strong, came bounding across the road and over the frosty ground. More than twelve, a little gray around the muzzle, Poncho is solid and healthy, all signs of his ordeal gone. He sniffed me briefly and let me scratch his ear. But his interest in me was scant. As soon as I was done he nuzzled close to Wear. He was his friend—the finest friend a dog ever had.

TWENTY-TWO

HORSE HEAVEN HILLS

F OR thousands of miles now far horizons had crept closer
and then had slipped to the rear. Always they had been
replaced by other far horizons—the low skyline of the prairies,
the soaring jagged rim of the Continental Divide, the shimmering edge of the salt desert, the furry line of forest tops. Rising and falling, curving with the rivers and valleys, we had
ridden over the uneven surface of the earth, moving in zigzags
head-on into the roll of the spinning globe.

The far horizon on this October morning lifted in a hazy
rampart against the western sky. The wilderness of the Blue
Mountains of eastern Oregon rose before us, as it had risen
ahead of the lumbering ox-drawn wagons of the pioneers—the
final barrier before the valley of the Columbia River. Each
morning, during these wonderful days in a country we had
never seen before, we pulled out on "the long trail, the trail
that is ever new." And on this morning we had set our watches
back another hour. First in Eastern Standard Time, then in
Central Standard Time, then in Rocky Mountain Standard
Time and now in Pacific Standard Time—the last time zone
of the continent—we had moved, as the sun moves, toward the
west, toward the far edge of the American autumn.

There is a valley on the eastern flank of the Blue Mountains,
some hundred miles west of the Snake where, in the fall of the
year, the Oregon Trail climbs upward in long loops and curves
through a fairyland of golden Christmas trees. Hundreds of

larches on either side of a river gorge lift glowing yellow spires against the somber green of spruce and pine. Their deciduous needles, clumped in spreading clusters of a score or so, change color before they drop away. Adorned with the bright yellow of these clusters, the trees appear crystalline, seem covered from top to bottom with a golden frost. That strain of giantism that runs through all the forests of the northwest is apparent in these larches. They lift their spires to a height of 150 feet or more. And the long slow cycle of their lives may span seven centuries.

We had climbed out of the valley of the larches and were ascending the gradual tilt of a little plateau among great ponderosa pines when we encountered an Indian demigod in black and blue. It was the first Steller's jay we had ever seen—a bird that ranked high in the mythology of northwestern tribes. A trio of these jays moved about among the pines. Their crests were high and black. Black, too, were their heads and forebodies while wings and tails and underparts were a deep purple-tinted blue. One of the birds thrust its bill beneath a piece of cinnamon-colored bark and pried. The fragment, shaped like some piece from a jigsaw puzzle, fell spinning to the ground. I picked it up. It roughly resembled a fish or whale. For a time after that we amused ourselves, as we had done under other ponderosa pines, by examining the pieces of fallen bark littering the ground beside the trunk. Even the most stolid imagination can see in these oddly formed fragments the shapes of birds and fish and animals.

As we drove on, leaving the Steller's jays at work, we talked of the varied men who have been commemorated in the names of birds and trees: Georg Wilhelm Steller, himself, naturalist on Bering's pioneer voyage to the Arctic; David Douglas, "The Man of Grass" who roamed the northwest for London's botanical garden and for whom the noble Douglas fir is named; William Clark, second in command in the immortal Lewis and Clark Expedition, the Clark of the Clark's nutcracker; George

Engelmann, St. Louis physician and botanist, remembered in the beautiful Engelmann spruce of the Rockies. These and those others—painters, explorers, army officers, scientists, patrons of scientists, fortunate men all—have these living monuments to keep their memories fresh.

Through Meacham. Past Emigrant Spring. On to Dead-man's Pass. Here in the Blue Mountains we were amid Oregon's oldest land, the ancient "Shoshone Island" of the geologists. Once, as we climbed on the curve of a steep ascent, we skirted a fence, long weathered by storms and falling into decay, but turned into a thing of superlative beauty by the brilliant green of a solid masking of lichen. We were in damper country now. The chill of the mornings affected us more than in the drier desert air and the static electricity which all across the Great Basin had sparked when I put the key in the ignition lock now was gone.

Climbing thus in new country, we recalled an idea that had occurred to us more than once in our travels. All day long the motorist reads Burma Shave and Coca-Cola, beer and gasoline signs. Why not an occasional tree and wildflower and geology sign? Why not a nature highway for motorists as there are nature trails in sanctuaries for walkers? Prominent trees and arresting outcroppings of rock could be identified in a word or two so that even he who runs could read and learn. The northwest, with its outstanding trees and easily indicated features, would be an ideal location for a sample stretch of such a nature highway.

It was past midday when we topped Deadman's Pass and came to Emigrant Hill and the switchbacks and hairpin turns that drop away down the steep slide of the western edge of the mountains. At the rim of this titanic wall we stood for a long time gazing in silence over the vast patchwork of grain-fields and pastures that stretched away into the haze-dimmed distance so far below us. This land of ranches and farms was the vision the pioneers saw as they peered into the wilderness ahead. How many of them had stood at this very spot shading their eyes in the autumn sunshine, seeking a glimpse of the Columbia, that river gateway to a Promised Land!

Standing there we thought of something else. Our minds went back to other eyes that also must have looked away from this eyrie into the vastness beyond. They were large, weary, patient eyes, the eyes of those unsung heroes of the westward trek, the long-enduring oxen.

There were many reasons why these great beasts—weighing often three-quarters of a ton—dragged so many of the covered wagons over the 2,000 miles of the Oregon Trail from Independence, on the lower Missouri, to The Dalles, on the lower Columbia. In the first place oxen cost less than horses. But even more important they could thrive on forage that horses would not touch. Often they kept going on cottonwood twigs and leaves when no grass was available. They moved slowly, traveling only twelve or fifteen miles in a day. But they had the strength to drag the great prairie schooners, with their wheels often six feet in diameter, across rivers and through deep mud. Three yokes of medium-sized oxen could haul a load of more than a ton through roadless country. To the Indians horses meant wealth, oxen only food—like buffalos. Moreover, the red men could not run off the oxen as they could horses on their night raids. To the pioneers, pushing into unknown land, the oxen also represented food on the hoof; they could eat the animals if faced with starvation. And finally, when the end of the trail was reached, oxen were better adapted to pulling the heavy plows that first broke the rough, untamed land of the wilderness homesteads.

How many oxen thus played their part in winning the west no one knows. But in the year 1850, by July—only three months after the start of the season—30,616 oxen had passed through Fort Laramie, Wyoming, plodding west in the great emigration of the Oregon Trail. The hardships endured by these patient giants is legendary. Through heat and thirst and dust so thick the wagons were lost to sight they trudged on. Into choked ravines and up mountainsides and across rivers and through endless miles of mud they struggled ahead. One appeared, ready to be yoked one morning, with an Indian arrow buried ten inches in its shoulder. Even when their strength began to fail and their owners were forced to whittle down the massive wooden yokes to lighten their load by even a few pounds, the oxen labored on, keeping pace with that slow, epic procession moving always toward the Columbia.

The pioneers who journeyed with them came to have a profound respect for these long-suffering companions of the trail. Their future and not infrequently their lives depended upon them. During the mountain nights they sometimes kept warm by sleeping snuggled against the great backs of their oxen. They came to know every peculiarity and trait of the animals —how they showed fatigue by sticking out their tongues, how they plunged into streams until only their muzzles were above water in order to soak up the coolness, how they tended to give up and resign themselves and go down without a struggle in quicksand unless goaded into action. Ordinarily placid and obedient, in times of extreme thirst they became headstrong and intractable when they scented water in the distance. John Wood, in *Along the Emigrant Trail*, tells of oxen that would begin moving noticeably faster when they were still ten miles away from water. Often the huge animals would run the last mile in spite of every effort to stop them, plunging, wagon and all, down the river bank and into the water. Among the hot springs of the western mountains many a burned muzzle resulted from the impetuous rush of thirsty oxen.

Individual animals often had individual traits. John Muir, as a boy on a Wisconsin homestead, was fascinated by the way one of his father's whitefaced oxen, Buck, broke open the pumpkins the animals were fed in the fall. All the other oxen stood about waiting for someone to split open the hard shells with an ax. But Buck would select a large pumpkin, kneel before it, place his flat forehead against the top and press downward until the shell shattered. He alone among the oxen of the farm did this. And he did it every time.

Because they have no upper teeth, oxen cannot nibble short grass as horses do. Consequently the ox teams had to make a later start from Independence in the spring. There are places along the Platte where the Oregon Trail is more than thirty miles wide. Here the trains of prairie schooners spread out and advanced on a wider front, thus insuring sufficient forage for all the animals. It was along the Platte that pioneers were especially alert for stampedes. Severe electrical storms sometimes set them off. At other times buffalo herds, thundering past a camp, infected the oxen with panic and sent them charging across the prairie, often to be lost for days.

But here at the western edge of the Blue Mountains the Platte and its stampedes lay far behind. Behind, too, was the dreaded climb through wilderness to Deadman's Pass. Forty men hacked for five days at underbrush and trees to clear a trail just wide enough for oxen to drag the first wagon to the top. But when that point had been reached only the zigzag descent to the floor of the valley remained. We tobogganed down the twisting modern highway and out onto the gently rolling ground where a century ago—as Irene D. Paden describes it in that invaluable mixture of research and personal experience, *The Wake of the Prairie Schooner*—the battered, pitching wagons advanced in line, a source of unceasing wonderment to the Indians who called them "Horse-Canoes."

Men were burning tumbleweeds beside the road. The smoke from the mounds of red and pink and yellow and brown globes rose hundreds of feet into the air. Then, as though it had encountered a ceiling in the sky, the smoke spread out in a level blue-gray layer miles in extent. We had observed similar occurrences in a number of places in recent days. In Idaho, on the Snake River Plateau, the smoke behind a laboring freight engine had stretched in a line more than ten miles long and as

RAIN FOREST sunshine brings a glowing, misty light to the path Nellie follows not far from the bank of the Hoh River.

STREAMLINED bushes at the top of Oregon's windswept Cape Blanco. Below, a dense stand of Darlingtonia pitcher plants.

level and as straight as though the smudge had been drawn above the skyline with a ruler. This phenomenon is often encountered in the fall. It is caused when two layers of air of different temperatures and densities meet in a definite boundary line. This meeting place forms the transparent ceiling beneath which the smoke collects and spreads out.

Somewhere in this valley, beside the Umatilla River, Nuttall and Townsend had camped after traversing Deadman's Pass. There, in anticipation of approaching civilization, they had shaved for the first time in many weeks and discovered they had bicolored faces, swarthy with tan above the whisker line and pale, almost white, below it. There, too, on a day of short rations, Townsend returned to camp after making a meal of wild rose hips to find his botanist friend dining on an owl the ornithologist had collected the night before.

Beyond Pendleton, on our way to the Columbia, the road rose and fell on the stilled billows of a pale yellow sea—mile after mile of cut-over grain fields. There were no trees, no fences. The wheat grew in dooryards, pressed close to the unpainted sides of the infrequent houses, ran between houses and barns, between barns and outbuildings. The whole land seemed buried beneath a flood of grain with here and there a white elevator thrusting up, lighthouse-like, out of the stubble sea.

Then in bewildering succession grain fields gave way to pastures and pastures to a land of sage and cactus. The nearer we drew to the Columbia the more desert-like became the land. The rain shadow of the Cascades extends across much of eastern Washington and Oregon. The great trees and lush, well-watered lower reaches of the Columbia—the ultimate goal of most of the pioneers—lie on the western, the seaward, side of these mountains.

Standing at last beside the Columbia, watching its green-tinted water—now at its autumnal low—slide and twist among the sand bars, we were at an elevation of less than 300 feet. Not since Pennsylvania had we been so near the level of the sea.

Beyond the precipitous wall of the opposite bank, hills trooped away, rank on rank. The toasted, golden brown of their flanks turned a delicate shade of pink in the sinking light of late afternoon. Enclosed within a great curve of the river, beyond these eminences, lay the Horse Heaven Hills. We had seen that name on the map long before. Like the name of the flower beside the Au Sable, The Grass of Parnassus, it had charmed us from the first. Some days later we were to see these same heights again, a little closer at hand and from the other side. That second view came near the end of a giant's swing through eastern Washington, up the river, eastward across the Idaho line, southward to Lewiston and west again through Walla Walla to the place where, at the end of its 939 tortuous miles, the Snake pours its water into the Columbia.

We started that six-hundred-mile loop with the dawn light playing over the sheen of frosted roofs and fields. We ended it, days later, in the smoky dusk with people all along the village streets burning fallen leaves. Between those two scenes stretched hours made of minutes "filled with sixty seconds' worth of distance run." And back from them come crowded memories of the western fall.

The geology of the west is a book written on giant pages. They opened before us as we drove east through a land of rimrock and buttes and mountains with their bare bones showing. High above the gorge of the Columbia we walked among petrified trees where slivers and growth rings had solidified, where knots were knots of stone and where even the chewing of prehistoric beetle grubs and ants has been preserved through thousands of years. Then rabbitbrush country. And the black dunes of Moses Lake with dusky tiger beetles running over their slopes and the initials of children formed of white stones on the black sand. East again through irrigated land and the sugar beet harvest of fall. For a time, beyond, we found ourselves among strange, rounded volcanic outcroppings that rose on all sides like the storage tanks of an oil refinery. And then once more we were in a yellow sea of wheat stubble extending over the hills to the skyline.

There are other memories: the scents of autumn, the calling of Canada geese, an all-night café where hunters in red caps drank coffee at dawn and talked of a big buck that had eluded their guns for years. We rode into Coeur d'Alene in an evening downpour with street lamps shining on pavements golden with wet fallen leaves. It was the falling leaves that so long ago gave rise to the Anglo-Saxon word "Feallan" from which our "Fall" is derived.

All down the Idaho line, after the rain, men were busy with autumn work, clearing land and burning stumps. For a time, before Potlatch, we found ourselves once more amid the yellow spires of larches. This western land is a land of golden colors in the fall—poplars and willows and larches, stubble fields and grasslands. And yellow predominated all across the vast panorama of the Snake River Valley when we saw it spread out below the 2,000-foot drop of the Spiral Grade above Lewiston. Then we were riding west again, through gray dawns and bright days and past winding, dry ravines shining with the silver of old tumbleweeds. And so back once more to the Snake, to that wild and picturesque river, seeing it for a last time at the place where its long course ends and it loses its identity in the waters of the larger stream.

At this juncture, where Lewis and Clark first glimpsed the Columbia and where they camped in mid-October a century and a half ago, there is now a state park. It is named in honor of Sacajawea, The Bird Woman, wife of the interpreter, Charbonneau, whose adventures on the trail with her infant son have made her a legendary heroine of the northwest. We passed a Sacajawea Hotel, a Sacajawea Motel, a Sacajawea Restaurant, Sacajawea monuments and plaques, a sprinkling of local Sacajawea parks, and even a Sacajawea Cocktail Lounge. Among the wild Wallowa Mountains one peak is named in her honor. In no small measure she contributed to the success of the Lewis and Clark Expedition. War parties never traveled with a squaw. Her mere presence convinced tribes along the way of the peaceful intentions of the white men.

With rapids and chasms behind it, the Snake flows in calm, almost in silence, along its final miles. The hum of bees was loud in the sunshine on its banks. Audubon's warblers, a dozen or more, flitted with flashes of yellow rump-patches among the trees beside the park's museum. And out in the Columbia seven black cormorants perched on rocks as black as themselves, drying their wings in the sun.

Beyond them, lifting in an irregular horizon blue tinted now in the midday haze, rose the heights of the Horse Heaven Hills. We gazed at them a long time. We might have crossed some bridge above or below and followed some road among them. But the current of time was pressing us downstream, hurrying us toward the falls where one of the great nature adventures of the northwest—the parade of the returning salmon—was nearing its end. So we contented ourselves with looking long at the blue hills rising to the south and west. Seen close at hand these faraway heights might have been like other hills —their magic gone. Now we would always remember them as we saw them at that moment, through haze and beyond the wide expanse of the Columbia River, a kind of Never-Never Land to recall and dream about, mysterious, enticing, far off and unattainable—the Horse Heaven Hills.

TWENTY-THREE

THE LONG WAY HOME

B ORN amid melting icefields in the Kootenay Mountains of Canada, the Columbia winds south and west in a great serpentine about 1,400 miles long. It is the largest North American river to empty into the Pacific. Once called the Oregon, long a river of mystery, described by the red men as flowing "from a mountain of shining stones to the sunset ocean," it drains some quarter of a million square miles of land. Its flow is twice that of the Nile, eight times that of the Colorado. For more than 300 of its final miles it heads almost due west, forming a natural boundary between the states of Oregon and Washington.

We were halfway down those final miles, following the "Big Medicine Road" of the Indians—the Oregon Trail—along the south bank, when we came to Celilo and the Falls of the Columbia. Over ragged, broken walls of black basalt, the river was hurling more than 100,000 cubic feet of water a second. Lewis and Clark, in the same month of the year, had portaged around these cataracts to find congregated below the falls a great herd of sea otters. Nuttall and Townsend had skirted the seething torrent at the beginning of a four-day September gale. Below The Dalles, where the Columbia "turns on its side" to squeeze into a chute between walls of basalt only 150 feet apart, they had camped while Nuttall dried out his plants.

"In this task," Townsend noted in his journal, "he exhibits a degree of patience and perseverance which is truly astonishing; sitting on the ground and steaming over an enormous fire, for hours together, drying the papers, and rearranging the whole collection, specimen by specimen, while the great drops of perspiration roll unheeded from his brow." Here, so near the end of their historic overland journey together, Townsend added: "Throughout the whole of our long journey, I have had constantly to admire the ardor and perfect indefatigability with which he has devoted himself to the grand object of his tour. No difficulty, no danger, no fatigue has ever daunted him and he finds his rich reward in the addition of nearly 1,000 new species of American plants to his already teeming flora of our vast continent."

Three thousand miles away, in the spring of the year, Nellie and I had leaned over the rail of a wooden bridge on the North Carolina coast to watch a parade of small, dark, wriggling elvers —baby eels moving upstream at the end of their incredible journey from the Sargasso Sea. Here, in another season, amid the roar of falling water in one of the great rivers of the world, we were in the presence of a different, equally famous and equally bewildering, parade, the parade of silver salmon coming home from another sea. These thundering tons of white water, this tumult of spray, the seething whirlpools and rapids below the falls, all these were part of their immemorial river road, the great barrier that for ages the fish had surmounted on their long way home.

And every fall, during uncounted centuries before the coming of Lewis and Clark and Nuttall and Townsend, Indian tribes from many parts of what is now Oregon and Washington and Idaho had come in an autumn pilgrimage to the falls to share in the bounty of the salmon run. On this day, as in years that extended back beyond tribal memory, Indians were fishing here. Many were clad in crimson shirts; many were perched on rickety-appearing plank platforms that jutted out over the foaming water along the lip of the falls. A few, here and there, braced themselves against rocks, appearing and disappearing amid sheets of drifting spray. All held dip nets with tremendously long handles. Some leaned back, resting at ease; others probed the seething turmoil of white water at the base of the falls.

Looking down from the highway, we were seeing the twilight of an age-old custom. A dozen miles downstream, the dam at The Dalles was nearing completion. Its artificial lake, backing upstream, would soon drown out these famed Cascades of the Columbia. It would inundate all the fishing sites along the lip of the falls, stations that had been handed down from father to son by the Indian tribes to whom old treaties ironically guaranteed fishing rights here "exclusively and perpetually." Government indemnity for violation of these treaties in the not distant future willy-nilly would replace the salmon caught in this annual autumn adventure with salmon in a can.

Across the river below the falls the swirling water broke from time to time where, in an arc of glittering silver, a salmon leaped. Only once in a lifetime does the salmon face the barrier of the Celilo falls. Far inland, in some mountain tributary or high-country pool, it hatches from an egg and, as a fingerling, begins the long descent, moving with the current on its way to the sea. Often in the high water of spring, when as many as 1,600,000 cubic feet a second roar over the cascades, the baby salmon ride the torrent downstream and over the falls. For all the species of the Columbia—the coho, sockeye, humpback, chum and the king or chinook salmon—life begins and ends in fresh water. The years between are spent at sea.

At the end of these years of wandering and growth—in the fifth year usually for the largest, the king or chinook—the salmon turns homeward, swimming as much as 600 miles through the ocean currents to reach the mouth of the river where it was born. Roe or milt is ripening within its body. One goal, one aim possesses it: to reach the gravelly shallows of the very pool where its egg had hatched. It never eats from the time it leaves the sea until it dies. In the long battle upstream, fighting the current—a battle that sometimes continues for two months and may carry it as far as 1,500 miles, half the span of the continent—the migrating fish literally consumes its own body. Remarkable changes take place. Its digestive tract shrinks. Its body becomes gaunt. Its reproductive organs grow swiftly. Different races of salmon return different distances upstream from the sea. Yet, in some mysterious manner, each seems provided with just the energy needed to attain its spawning ground. Life is almost over when the salmon reaches, at last, the pool where life began.

There, in hollows among the gravel, where the current scours away all sand, the female deposits as many as 5,000 eggs and the male spreads his fertilizing milt. Each egg is about three eighths of an inch in diameter, round as a pearl and salmon-red. Spawning over, with energy spent, the fish float quiescent. They are emaciated. Tails are often merely stumps of naked rays. Fungus spots spread across their bodies. They have come the long way home. They have achieved the purpose of their migration from the sea. Soon, worn-out and lifeless, they float away downstream, down a path they followed once before— only once—when they were fingerlings and life, for them, was new.

The salmon we saw at the falls that day were still in the lower reaches of the river; they all were sleek and fat beneath their plating of silver. The average chinook here weighs about twenty pounds. In a few record instances such fish have tipped the scales at more than 100 pounds. The annual salmon catch in the Columbia River, valued around $20,000,000, is sufficient, it has been calculated, to supply for the entire year the protein needs of 1,000,000 Americans.

In the early years, as the Oregonians neared the end of their journey in autumn, there were times when they seemed to be looking at a river of fish. Below the Celilo cascades the salmon sometimes congregated in such numbers they appeared to be shouldering each other out of the water. But those days are long gone. The dip nets of the six tribes that come to Celilo have taken but an insignificant fraction of the fish. It is the decades of fish wheels, of seines, of traps extending half way across the Columbia, of felled forests and diverted water, of factory wastes and dam construction that have vastly reduced their numbers. We watched, later on, salmon mounting the fish ladders at the Bonneville Dam, leaping from pool to pool, each pool a foot higher than the one below. As many as 50,000 fish have passed up these water stairways on a single early-September day. Yet only part of the homecoming salmon find the three pathways that lead around the 1,450-foot barrier of concrete. Many die below the dam. And every year, when the fingerlings go downstream, something like 15 per cent of them lose their lives in the dynamos at Bonneville. When a contemplated chain of sixty-nine dams extends up the course of the Columbia and its tributaries, the chances of salmon surviving in these waters is remote. Here their immemorial homeward journey from the sea will, in all probability, be no more.

We followed a dusty road that wound down to the edge of the falls past the unpainted temporary shacks of the Indian salmon hunters. The thunder of the plunging water mounted as we advanced. The air grew moist with flying spray. In the restaurant beside the highway overlooking the falls we had seen two or three of the less energetic Indians. They had been reading comic books, playing the pin-ball machines or dropping nickels in the jukebox. Here at the falls, we saw a different breed. The men were alert and strong, many magnificently built with shoulders like all-American fullbacks. In this natural arena they were pitting their strength and skill, risking their lives, in a dangerous game. Each year there are casualties or near escapes at Celilo. A few days after our visit an eight-year-old Indian boy slipped into the torrent and was carried over the falls. Warned by shouts from the bank, the men on their platforms swung their nets. One caught the boy like a salmon in the midst of the tumult of white water below. With the help of companions, he pulled him up, hand over hand, to safety.

Most of the men on the platforms were secured by ropes attached to the timbers. One wore a silver-colored construction worker's helmet From rock to rock, forming limber catwalks, long planks ran above the edge of the cataract. As we watched, a white Husky dog started across one of these bridges, felt the middle sag slightly beneath its weight, froze in tense uncertainty, then turned in slow motion and carefully retraced its steps. In a spiderweb, steel cables led to the more distant rocks. Below each, supported by pulleys, hung a makeshift chair fashioned from a wooden box. Riding in such chairs, Indians hauled themselves along the cables out to their isolated fishing stations. On this day only about eighty salmon came up the river. The autumn run, which reaches its peak in September, was nearly over. One man lay on his stomach peering from the edge of his platform down into the smother of spray and white water below. Another stretched out on his back, his mouth open, sound asleep.

Downstream a salmon leaped, then another. The Indian lying on his stomach got up. The sleeper awoke. Nets began going down from rocks and platforms. Fish were nearing the falls. We saw one of the men lean forward on his platform. His net dipped, scooped downstream, emerged enclosing a struggling salmon. Dragging upward on the handle the Indian slowly hauled his heavy catch onto the planks. Even after it had been killed, the magnificent fish, nearly three feet long, lying on the wet wood, was a thing of shining, streamlined and burnished beauty. The silver of its scales seemed to catch and collect the sunshine. Other fish, shining, too, came flopping onto the rocks and platforms. A quarter of an hour passed. Then the excitement began to subside. The flurry of fish in the white water below the falls eased off, then ended.

In that water, tumbling and aerated, the salmon no doubt obtain a sudden lift in energy from the increased oxygen. This is one factor in their amazing leaps up the rocks and over the cataract. Less tangible, but even more important, is the over-powering instinctive drive that holds them to their course, heading always into the current, fighting their way always up-stream no matter how raging the torrents that oppose them. No less baffling than the mechanics of bird migration is the functioning of this instinct. Each new discovery has com-pounded the wonder. The way of a salmon in the sea and in the river of its birth represents one of the incompletely solved mystery stories of science.

Only within the past half century have the details of this story been unfolded, largely through the tagging and marking of many fish. The pioneer in this work seems to have been a western representative of the U.S. Fish Commission, C. Rut-ter. In 1902 Rutter marked 150 salmon in the Sacramento River of California. Using the method employed on cattle ranches he branded the fish with a hot iron. Only three of these mutilated salmon were ever seen again. They all were taken lower down in the river before they reached the sea. Six years later, at the mouth of the Columbia, Charles Wilson Greene used sheep tags to mark fifty-nine salmon. These tags, rather large aluminum buttons normally attached to the ears of sheep, were anchored in the fins of the fish when, full grown, they returned to spawn. Seventeen of the fifty-nine sheep but-tons were recovered. In later years, employing smaller, specially designed aluminum tags, hundreds of thousands of salmon were marked and their activities and movements traced.

In 1903 Rutter was writing in a government bulletin: "It is incredible that the salmon remember their native stream and consciously seek it when they desire to return to fresh water. Probably most of them do return to the stream from which they enter the ocean, not because it is their native stream but because they do not get very far from its mouth." Incredible though it seemed to Rutter in 1903, the homing migration of salmon is today accepted as an amply proved fact. Moreover the evidence of the tags shows that the fish sometimes travel through the sea as much as 600 miles, one fortieth the circumference of the earth, away from the river to which they return.

Not only do marked fish come back to the same river from which they swam into the sea, but different tributaries of that river often have different races of salmon, each distinguishable by small but observable characteristics. For so many generations have the fish, hatching in those tributaries, been returning to them that pure strains have been produced. During the spring and autumn runs, when salmon born in many places are swimming upstream together, at the mouth of every tributary some turn off like railroad cars shunted onto a siding, while the rest, without pausing, continue up the main channel. Instinct throws the switch for those who turn. They swing into the stream that will carry them eventually to the very spot where they emerged from the egg. By notching the fins of fingerlings in the pools where they hatched, scientists have been able to recognize these identical fish when, years later, they have returned from the sea to lay their eggs in the gravel of these very same portions of the river.

This instinct of the salmon to return to an ancestral spawning ground is much like the instinct of the migrating bird to come back to its last year's nesting area. It spreads out, and thus benefits, the species. It saves time that might be lost seeking suitable sites. It utilizes all appropriate spots. And it prevents the concentration of too many fish at one place while there are too few at another. The beneficial consequences of this instinctive behavior are obvious. It is the method by which that end is achieved that has proved bafflingly obscure.

Somewhere within the fish, imprinted on its brain or nervous system, is an instinctive map or memory pattern leading it home across hundreds of miles of ocean and up hundreds of miles of river to the gravel of its birthplace. Is this homing ability the product of inherited wisdom, or of racial memory? Or is it achieved through reaction to environment, through the experiences of the individual? Scientists conducted a simple experiment to discover the answer. Taking eggs from a female salmon in one stream they deposited them to hatch in another stream. If the pattern of the salmon's return is fixed by heredity, the marked fish in this experiment would return, obviously, to the stream where the female had been caught. If, on the other hand, the homing ability results from personal experience rather than heredity, they would come back to the stream in which they hatched. And that is what they did. They returned not to the pool of their ancestors but to the place where they were born.

In another test in British Columbia, eggs from salmon in the Horsefly River were taken to a hatchery on a tributary stream, the Little Horsefly. After they were reared as fingerlings in this water they were flown back to the stream of their ancestors and released. Starting from it, they migrated to the sea. To which river would they return? Again they came back not to the water in which their ancestors had been born, although in this case the Horsefly River was the starting point of their own oceanic wanderings. They returned to the Little Horsefly. In its waters they themselves had hatched.

Apparently the water that first passes through their gills leaves an indelible impression—its fingerprint, so to speak—upon the baby fish. It is to this water that the adult salmon returns. No two streams flow through exactly the same soils, in the same proportions, or have the same water weeds, in the same quantities, growing in them. The water they carry is never, in all respects, identical. The flow of each represents a different combination of chemical elements and vegetable matter. To senses sharp enough to detect it, this combination of elements that marks the water of every stream would be as distinct and individual as a human thumbprint. It seems likely that a chain of sensory impressions leads the salmon back along the path to its journey's end.

Just offshore, in the Pacific, schools of salmon are sometimes encountered swimming close to the surface, leaping into the air, tons of fish breaking the water at the same time. Frank Dufresne, long a field naturalist with the U.S. Fish and Wildlife Service, told me of seeing such displays when I visited him one evening later on at his home by Puget Sound. His surmise is a reasonable one: Fresh water, being lighter, flows for a considerable distance out along the surface of the sea. The salmon are seeking in these upper layers some clew to the stream that is the goal of their migration.

If this is true, what sense are they using? Is it taste? Is it smell? Is it a combination of senses? Is it some capacity or ability we do not yet fully comprehend? All of these have been suggested as solutions to the mystery.

The clearest answer yet provided by scientists is one obtained at the Wisconsin Lake Laboratory of the University of Wisconsin, 2,000 miles inland from the estuary of the Columbia. There, in 1954, Arthur D. Hasler and James A. Larsen constructed an elaborate salmon tank with four miniature fish ladders branching from a central pool. Experimenting with young salmon from the Northwest, each marked with a tiny colored bead attached to a fin, they proved the fish are equipped with both a keen sense of smell and a capacity for remembering odors. The salmon demonstrated they could tell apart, by their smells, fourteen different kinds of aquatic plants. They were able to distinguish instantly between water taken from one creek and water taken from another. By associating one odor with the reward of food and another with the punishment of a mild electric shock, the Wisconsin experimenters found they could make the salmon enter or avoid whichever fish ladder they chose. By means of odor trails they could lead them to any desired destination.

Thus, though questions innumerable still remain in connection with the life of the salmon, the work of these two research biologists has put a scientific foundation beneath much that was merely surmise in the past. The fish, they conclude, identify the river of their birth and the pool of their hatching by the distinguishing odor of the water. The "fingerprint" of the river is an olfactory one. The fish that came upstream to the Celilo falls that day, as well as all the countless generations that had preceded them, were literally smelling their way home from the sea.

It was late that afternoon when, below the Falls of the Columbia, below the "Big Chute" of The Dalles, we crossed to White Salmon and the Washington side of the river. Sunset, one of the great flaming sunsets of the trip, flooded the western sky above the wide lower reaches of the stream. Shoals and swirls in the river seemed reproduced in cloud and flame in the sky. For a long time after this western fire burned low we ran between darkened woods and tinted waters. We were now on the rainy side of the Cascades. In the more humid air odors and perfumes multiplied. The smell of wet autumn leaves was strong around us. Through moist, redolent forests of the night we followed the windings of the river until at last we came within sight of the vast double glare of Portland and Vancouver blazing on opposite sides of the Columbia.

It was at Fort Vancouver, on the north side of the river, that Nuttall and Townsend had stepped ashore at eleven o'clock in the morning on the sixteenth of September in 1834. There they had come to the end of their overland travels. This was the destination of their adventurous pioneer journey. So often had we encountered their path that many times these two had seemed like companions of our own. Here we crossed their trail for a last time. Here, with regret, we parted company.

Rolling down the glaring streets of Vancouver we sought lodgings for the night. We talked, over a belated supper, of Nuttall and Townsend. We talked of the homecoming salmon. And that night we slept beside the Columbia—the goal, more than a century before, of the pioneer scientists; the goal, for aeons before that, of salmon traveling their long way home from the sea.

TWENTY-FOUR

A DAY WITH THE FERN GATHERERS

THE red jeep whirled around turns of the river road. A green pickup truck tore along at its heels. I, in my gray car, raced close after. And behind me, thundering just back of my bumper, pounded a mud-stained logging truck. For sixteen miles this automotive comet traced the serpentine of the Toutle River. We shot through Kid Valley. We rushed by a mailbox bearing the name "Rebel Stewart." We streaked in misty light past a misty pond where wild ducks were floating. Then, twenty-five miles east of Castle Rock, half way to Spirit Lake and Mt. St. Helens, the jeep slowed, the truck slowed, I slowed and the bellow of the timber truck eased away for a moment as, red and green and gray, the first three vehicles in this swift parade swung over a bridge to the left onto a rutted road that became mere wheel tracks across roots and moss and ended in the shadowed silence of a lofty forest. Thus amid speed and noise and nerve strain began my day in the hushed, green, tranquil world of the fern gatherers.

Out of the jeep climbed Donald Braun, square-set and in his twenties. Down from the pickup truck descended Orlo Stephens, slender and nearing sixty. Both men spend their days wandering over the forest floor, picking fronds among the dense green fountains of the sword ferns. All across the western edge of Washington and down the Oregon coast, over thousands of square miles that day, the fern harvest was in full swing. For the free-lance frond gatherers of the Northwest the peak of the year's activity comes in the fall. Daily now they were busy along remote streams, deep in rain forests, up mountainsides almost to timberline. In back-packs and horse-packs the fronds were coming out of the woods to lonely roads. Then by jeep and truck and ancient flivver many of them were rolling toward Castle Rock and the great gray Fern Barn at its eastern edge.

The day before, Nellie and I had driven fifty-three miles north from Vancouver to this community of 900 inhabitants. It was at Castle Rock, in 1906, that Sam Roake started the fern picking business in the forests of western Washington. His first shipments were trundled to the railroad station in a wheelbarrow. Today in the region there are eight major companies dealing in forest ferns. Their annual shipments to florists throughout the United States total about 20,000,000 bunches or approximately 1,000,000,000 fronds.

Ray Chapman, who manages the Fern Barn and operates the company Roake originally started, showed us the towering piles of fronds that had come in during the day. They are tied in bunches of fifty with two added to provide for breakage. First soaked in water, sometimes up to twelve hours, the ferns are kept under refrigeration, occasionally as long as ninety days. In wood or fiber or cardboard containers they go out to every state in the Union by truck, by train, by boat, even by plane. Because of their large size, the grace of their fronds, their keeping quality and the strength of their stems, the sword ferns of the West are in special demand among florists.

As we talked three men from Cougar, Washington (population 43) arrived in a battered sedan crammed with fronds. Partners—one young, one middle-aged, one old—they pick along timberline until snowfall, sometimes carrying pocket warmers or lighting chunks of pitch from time to time to keep their hands from growing numb. High on mountainsides the ferns tend to be of better quality than in the lowlands. From all sources as many as a quarter of a million fronds may come to the Fern Barn during a single autumn day. Yet, because the pickers take only part of the fronds and leave the massed roots or stools uninjured, the ferns continue to grow year after year as luxuriantly as before.

Orlo Stephens, as he and Braun shouldered their empty back-packs, recalled one stool that has remained virtually unchanged for a quarter of a century. He has been picking over the same area, along the side of the seven-mile ridge up which our trail ascended, ever since the end of the First World War. And he has noticed no lessening in the number of sword ferns growing there.

The forest closed around us, a forest of giants such as I had never entered before. We paused beside a stump, furry with moss and moldering away. It seemed, in the dim forest light, as big as a cabin. I gazed at the massive trunks of spruce and fir and hemlock. Soaring up and up, they appeared to lean together in their great height. The tops of some of them were 150 feet above us. We stole with noiseless footfalls along the mossy trail beneath these giants, three small Gullivers in an arboreal land of Brobdingnag.

Thus we advanced into the green silent depths. The air was cool and humid. It was rich with earth scents. All the leaves of the bushes were shining with a film of moisture. Our feet, at every step, sank into the deep plush of the moss. And extending away among the decayed trunks of fallen trees, lifting from the humus of the forest floor, rose the fountainlike clumps of the sword fern or dagger fern, *Polystichum mumitum.* This western relative of the eastern Christmas fern sometimes rises almost shoulder high. Its curving fronds at times reach a length of more than four feet. And as many as 200 may be rooted in a single stool. In the mild climate of the coastal Northwest the leaves stay green the year around. A new crop in the form of fiddleheads appears each spring in March. Even while the new leaves are unrolling the harvest of the old fronds continues. About ninety days are required for the spring fiddleheads to unroll, reach their full length and harden. It is mainly this supply of new fronds that is gathered in the autumn.

One of the remarkable features of the sword fern is the variety of its habitats. It grows in swamps. It clings to canyon walls. It crowds together along stream banks near sea level. It ranges as high as trees extend on mountainsides. But it is found only where it is sheltered from sun and wind. In deep, wet, misty woods, such as the one we had entered, it attains its greatest size. Most often it is associated with the vine maple, both the tree and the fern seeming to thrive under the same conditions.

For a time our trail skirted a swampy stretch where the ferns grew densely. They ran on and on, crowded together, their fountains overlapping. In this rank growth the tips of the ferns tend to be damaged and imperfect.

"We pick these alder swales last of all," Braun explained.

I gazed around. Thinking of the low alder bushes of the East, I inquired:

"Why are they called alder swales? I don't see any alders."

"You are leaning against one right now!" Stephens told me.

I looked up. The alder was a tree more than fifty feet high. Touched by that strain of giantism we saw everywhere in the forests of the Northwest, the red alder sometimes attains a height of more than 100 feet and lives for a century.

Leaving the swale behind we climbed steeply upward, at times stooping under curtains of delicate tree moss, at other times skirting or clambering over fallen trees. Braun's cream-colored Husky dog scouted ahead, first on one side of the trail, then on the other, frequently popping from the bushes, his fur wet, his red tongue lolling out beneath his black, pointed nose. Fern hunters often take dogs into the woods with them. They are company. They warn of bears. In case of a broken leg or other serious accident they would go home and thus bring help. For the dog in the woods the days are filled with fun and adventure. Once as we rounded a turn in the trail Braun's dog made a sudden rush. There was a scuttle and airy roar of wings.

Three dark ruffed grouse shot upward in a high, steep climb among hemlock branches.

We had followed the trail into the forest almost two miles before the harvest of ferns began. The men separated about an eighth of a mile and set to work. Some fern gatherers use a sharp jackknife to clip off the stems of the fronds. Others fashion a triangular cutter from a tablespoon. But most often they use a ring-knife, such as is used for cutting twine, wearing it on the middle finger of the right hand. Stephens showed me how, almost in one motion, the frond is selected and the stem clipped off within the little sickle-like curve of the cutting blade.

Only the last two feet of the fronds are harvested. The tips must be perfect, not brown or bug-eaten or curled over into a spider nest. As soon as he had clipped off twenty-six fronds, Stephens tucked them under one arm while he picked twenty-six more. Then, holding the fifty-two between his legs, he pulled a short length of white string from a bunch tied to a button of his overalls and, with a swift whirl of his practiced hand, tied the butts together. In turn each bunch was added to a green stack that began rising on the moss carpet of a small open space.

Some years ago a national magazine published an article that depicted fern picking in the Northwest as a smooth and easy road to riches. Letters poured into Castle Rock from all parts of the country. People asked for more details. They wrote they were coming from as far away as the Atlantic seaboard. Local pickers, foreseeing an invasion and a reduction in their incomes, were up in arms. Actually most fern gatherers make around forty dollars a week. But many of them spend only part of the day in the woods. About 100 bunches a day is the average harvest of a fern picker. The record, so far, was set one October a few years ago when a family of three brought in 1,700 bunches that had been collected in three days.

Families not infrequently pick together. In one instance five boys in the same family put themselves through school with spare-time fern gathering. When a husband is ill, a wife will often pick ferns to tide things over. Again, when the woods are too dry for lumbering and loggers are laid off temporarily, they may turn to harvesting ferns. Those who go to the woods during spare time, usually in summer, are known as "sunshine pickers." A comparatively recent innovation has been the leasing of exclusive picking rights in certain areas by lumber companies that own extensive forest holdings. Stephens and Braun, for example, rented each year the fern rights to 16,000 acres along the flank of the ridge where they were working.

Beginning early in October, for several weeks on dry days the fern hunters work in moving clouds as though surrounded by fine smoke. For then, in untold billions, the spores of the sword ferns are being shed. On this day, after a shower in the night, little of this living dust was in the air. But all autumn long, after every comparatively dry day, the fern gatherer goes home from the forest embrowned from head to foot with the fine powder of the spores.

By afternoon the overcast had broken. When I looked up, as through a long tunnel, to some small opening in the treetops, I could see the brilliant blue of the sky. There was no wind that day and all the moss-clad forest lay in a kind of charmed silence. I wandered alone down side trails, endlessly fascinated by the unknown mosses and the unknown plants and the unknown frothlike formations of the fungi. There is, in Washington and Oregon, a remarkable specialist fungus, *Cordyceps myrmicophila*. Its tiny yellow ribbons develop only in one place—on dead ants. Another related fungus, *Cordyceps sphecocephala* of the Southeastern United States, it is interesting to note, has been found growing nowhere else except on the bodies of dead wasps.

So many were the unknown plants, the strange bushes, the unfamiliar trees around me that at times I felt as though I were traversing Alice's wonderland forest behind the looking glass.

" 'This must be the wood,' she said thoughtfully to herself, 'where things have no names.' "

Before we left, late that afternoon, however, I had become acquainted with a good many of the unknown trees and plants and bushes. Orlo Stephens knew them all. He pointed out the smooth bark of the cascara tree. He pulled a licorice fern from among the thick moss sheathing a vine maple. He initiated me into the ways of the largest member of the ginseng family, the devil's-club. Each of its immense rounded leaves was greater in expanse than my two hands laid side by side. Now golden yellow, they formed the biggest splashes of color in the forest. But it is not its huge leaves that draw special attention to the devil's-club. It is the rows of slender, needle-sharp spines that thrust out from the trunk, the branches, even from the underside of the leaf stems.

Rising to a height of a dozen feet or more, the plant bristles with hundreds of these spines. I ran a forefinger cautiously across them and found they were stiff as wires. When they puncture the flesh they sting like nettles and, unless removed at once, seem to work inward in the manner of porcupine quills. Once that day I accidentally brushed the tip of a spine against my thumb. The small wound bothered me for days afterwards. No doubt the botanist who bestowed the scientific name on this plant had had first-hand experience with it. For he called it *Fatsia horrida*. Yet in the spring when the leaves are soft and juicy, elk and other forest animals browse on the devil's-club. For this reason one of its colloquial names is elk's-briar.

Aside from the spines of this plant and the smaller needles of an occasional nettle, the fern gatherer has little to avoid in the forest. There is no poison oak here. He can reach down into the masses of the ferns without fear of snakes, for there are no venomous species in the region. Less than a dozen times has Stephens encountered bears in the woods. Once, some years ago, he and his wife were picking huckleberries on a mountain-side when they discovered a large brown bear a couple of hundred yards away, equally busy harvesting the fruit. Using both forepaws it was raking in the berries. All that afternoon, keeping their distance, the three continued working within sight of one another. So far as is known, no fern gatherer has ever been seriously injured by a bear in the woods. Probably the nearest approach came when a woman on the Olympic Peninsula reached over a log and surprised a bear and two cubs. With a raking swipe of a forepaw the mother ripped a piece from the jeans the picker was wearing. But fortunately both cubs, squealing with fright, ran off in the opposite direction and the large bear turned and followed them.

The real danger for the fern picker in the woods comes not from bears but from men. Both Stephens and Braun that day wore bright red hats. This was the deer-hunting season and there was always a chance of being shot by mistake. This is especially true because the men are bent over as they work among the clumps with a swishing and crackling of fronds. Moreover, they frequently enter tangles of vine maples and ferns where the deer are commonly found. Some protection is afforded by having a dog ranging about in the vicinity. It is likely to give warning both to the hunters and to the fern harvesters.

When the hunting season is over and the wild creatures of the forest are less fearful, Stephens sometimes will look up from his picking and see a deer peeking at him from behind a tree or bush. Again, when he is entering the woods in the still of the morning, walking on the plush carpet of the moss, he occasionally surprises two or three deer browsing beyond a turn of the trail. And when, at noon, he is sitting alone, eating his lunch at the foot of a tree, a camp-robber jay is likely to fly down and hop all around him, almost perching on his knee if he feeds it crumbs.

On this day we saw but few birds in the forest. Once near the alder swale we found ourselves in the midst of a flitting, calling flock of juncos. Three or four times during the morning the stirring clamor of Canada geese reached us faintly from flocks flying high over the treetops. About mid-afternoon, when I had wandered some distance away from the fern gatherers, I came to a small opening beneath the giant trees. There I stopped suddenly. A whistle, clear and vibrant, rich and musical, filled the dusky forest. The call of a bird unknown, it brought to mind the voice of Rima amid the shadowed treetops of W. H. Hudson's *Green Mansions*. I stood listening for a time. But the invisible singer remained mute. Only that once did I hear its voice. I was on the point of turning away when a flash of movement caught my eye. A robin-sized bird dashed across the opening. That momentary glimpse, seen from a front-quartering view, revealed a deep orange breast with a black collar extending across it. The secretive singer was identified. It was that lover of the deep, dark coniferous forests of the West, the varied thrush.

The two piles of ferns, where Stephens and Braun were working, mounted as the day progressed. Each bunch of fifty-two fronds weighs about a pound and a quarter. In lots of eighty bunches, weighing about 100 pounds, they are packed out of the woods. I watched Braun load his pack, placing the successive layers of bunches with the butts pointing in opposite directions. Two miles through the forest is about as far as the ferns are transported by back-pack. Beyond that distance a horse or burro is used.

As we followed the outward trail for a last time that day, the two men ahead of me half hidden beneath their bulging packs, a dark little squirrel stole silently down a trunk and onto a branch to watch us pass. It was the only squirrel I saw during that whole day. I remember once we halted beside a tilted maple where three branches, one above the other like the spreading ribs of a fan, leaned out over the path. Each branch was dripping with a filmy curtain of tree moss shot through with golden splashes of the autumn leaves.

Watching those fronds bobbing up and down in the packs

ahead I wondered what their final destination would be. Where would they be seen for a last time? Who would see them? They might, as part of floral decorations, reach even the far side of the continent. As for myself, I knew that wherever I should see them the rest of my life, the graceful fronds would bring back vivid memories of this day—memories of towering trees and of the green fountains of the sword ferns extending away, seemingly without end, beneath them.

TWENTY-FIVE

MYSTERIOUS MOUNDS

THE cats of Zanzibar.

I lay in bed thinking of them while the watered-milk light of that foggy dawn slowly paled. Thoreau, in a famous line in *Walden*, observes that it is not worth our while to go round the world to count the cats in Zanzibar. To this H. M. Tomlinson adds a postcript in *A Mingled Yarn*. Thoreau is right, he says, but: "We wish he had tried it. He would have counted more than cats. We miss the book he would have made." It was Thoreau, himself, I think, who remarked that today you can write a chapter on the advantages of traveling and tomorrow another chapter on the advantages of staying at home. On this morning, as on every morning of our trip, we were torn between the two advantages. Here was much we regretted to leave, much that would have absorbed our delighted attention for weeks. But always ahead lay something new.

On this morning of fog it proved to be mystery mounds. We had gone another fifty miles northward into this twenty-fifth state of the trip. We had followed what geologists call the Puget Trough extending north and south between the Cascades on the east and the Willapa Hills, below the Olympics, on the west. Twelve thousand miles of autumn wandering lay behind us when, in mid-morning, we found ourselves among innumerable small, rounded knolls. On either side of the road they stretched away until their forms grew dim and they disappeared entirely behind obscuring vapor. This multitude of small hillocks presented one of the great riddles of western geology. The famous Mima mounds of Tenino, they were the subject of a century of speculation. We saw them that morning enveloped in veils of mist as, for so long, they had been shrouded in mystery.

For nearly twenty miles we drove, with frequent stops, surrounded by the mounds. They were uniform in shape, roughly round and from three to six feet in height. At times they ran in irregular or curving lines. And they stood so close together that the skirts of their gradual slopes met in the depressions between them. It is estimated that here in Thurston County, south of Puget Sound in southwestern Washington, there are 1,000,000 Mima mounds. The hillocks get their name from the Mima Prairie where they first were studied.

Several times we walked out among the knolls. The ground was springy with mosses and lichens, wiry grass and bearberry vines. Bracken, rusty-brown from the autumn frosts, ran among the mounds, gathering into a thicker growth, a kind of topknot, at the summit of many of the little hills. Wild strawberry plants grew here and there and small glacial stones, most of the ones we saw a dark blue, lay scattered among the vegetation. We seemed walking on tundra land. This impression was heightened by the fact there were no trees growing among the mounds. In the distance we caught sight of a few trees—gray, looming shapes in the mist; but here the bracken was the highest growth in sight. Nowhere did we see a stump or come across a seedling tree. Perhaps the thick mossy carpet prevents the roots of sprouting tree seeds from reaching the soil. In early days the Indians are said to have burned over the area annually and this prevented encroachment by the forest. Recently, in checking over old lines, surveyors have found that the trees have been gradually advancing out onto the edges of the mounded prairies.

Gazing around us in what an ancient writer once called "the greate beauty of mistes," we puzzled over the origin of these thousands upon thousands of mounds. They stretched away like an infinite number of low haycocks or some collection of giant anthills or some vast prairie-dog metropolis. And, in truth, both ants and gophers have been seriously suggested as the source of the knolls. So have many other things during the hundred years and more that explorers, scientists and tourists alike have been bewildered by the Mima mounds.

Gas pressure, oil pressure, volcanic action—all these have been suggested. And all these easily have been disproved. Some pioneers maintained that the mysterious areas represented "buffalo wallows." A variation of this belief, even more fantastic, held that the mounds were constructed by the Indians to simulate a herd of sleeping animals as a decoy for buffalo! Beaver also had their adherents. The mounds, this group suggested, were the remains of the platforms on which the houses of an extensive beaver colony had been built at a time when the whole area lay at the bottom of a pond. Another imagined solution rested on a wind-and-tree relationship. The roots of the trees, now long dead, were supposed to have held together the soil in heaps at a time when a great gale blew away all the earth between the trees. There was, at one time, a wayside lunchroom in the vicinity where the proprietor offered to tell tourists, at fifty cents apiece, the true story of the origin of the mounds. His explanation: They were made by Chinese miners digging for gold!

The first man, apparently, to examine the mounds closely was Captain Charles Wilkes, of the United States Navy. In the fourth volume of his *Narrative of the United States Exploring Expedition, 1838–1842,* published in 1845, he recounts his first sight of the mounds during a trip from the Nisqually River south to the Columbia in the spring of 1840: "We soon reached the Bute Prairies which are extensive and covered with tumuli or small mounds, at regular distances asunder. As far as I could learn, there is no tradition among the natives relative to them. They are conical mounds, thirty feet in diameter, about six or seven feet high above the level, and many thousands in number. Being anxious to ascertain if they contained any relics, I subsequently visited these prairies and opened three of the mounds but nothing was found in them but a pavement of stones."

The belief that they are burial mounds has persisted to recent years. I talked to a young filling-station attendant in Tenino who recalled digging into several of them as a boy after finding Indian beads—where they apparently had been dropped years before—on the outside of one of the knolls. But within he had found only gravel, black dirt and scattered stones. In several places along the road grading had exposed the interior of the mounds. Not far from the Scatter Creek Pentecostal Tabernacle, below Tenino, we rode for nearly half a mile between the cross sections of mounds, the surface of the ground rising and falling as though reproducing the profile of waves on water. I stopped to examine one of the exposed knolls. The material was not stratified. The proportion of soil was no greater at the top than at the bottom. Although this soil looks like black loam, it had a hard feel between my fingers. It is, in fact, a fine mixture of clay and sand. There is almost no humus in it. Its only resemblance to rich black loam is its color.

Curiously enough, of all the solutions proposed for the riddle of the Washington mounds one of the widest of the mark was that offered by the great Louis Agassiz of Harvard. In 1873 a friend returning from the Northwest described the mounds and exhibited a sketch of them. Agassiz unhesitatingly pronounced them the work of fish. They were, he believed, made by a western relative of the suckers that constructed their moundlike nests on pond bottoms near Boston. In that same year another famed scientist, Joseph LeConte, suggested a different theory. Writing in the *Proceedings of the California Academy of Sciences,* he reasoned that the mounds were formed of sediment deposited at some time when the area had been covered by the waters of Puget Sound. Later, after these waters receded, erosion began. Massed vegetation held down the soil in certain places while the earth around was washed away and thus, he thought, the knolls came into being.

Over the years—as I discovered later when I looked up the literature in libraries on the other side of the continent—the debate continued on the manner in which the Mima mounds were created. Walking among them that day we were sure that one of the proposed answers—that the wind produced them as dunes are formed—was obviously unsound. Wind-formed dunes have a longer slope on one side and a more abrupt descent on the other. All of the mounds, on the other hand, were rounded. Their slopes on all sides were almost equal both in length and in angle of descent.

An important step toward a solution of the long mystery came in 1913 when the University of Chicago published *Glaciation in the Puget Sound Region* by J. Harlen Bretz. This book turned the spotlight on the probable glacial origin of the Mima mounds. Summarizing the various speculations and theories that had been advanced, Bretz concluded: "The agencies which might have produced the mounds are practically limited to ice and water." For several decades a hypothesis that he advanced was widely accepted. This was that silt, blowing across the ice sheet covering the area during the last glacial period, had collected in depressions. When the ice had finally melted, these pockets of silt had been deposited in the form of mounds on the gravel below.

Twenty-seven years after Bretz's book appeared, in the November 10, 1940, issue of the small *Geological News-Letter*, published by the Geographical Society of the Oregon Country, R. C. Newcomb of the U.S. Geological Survey proposed an entirely different explanation involving glaciation. On the outwash plains formed behind the retreating ice sheet, he suggested, it was the cracking of frozen silt that was the originating force in producing the mounds. Studies in the far north have revealed that under certain conditions an extremely cold period in winter will cause the ground to shrink and cracks to appear as on a drying mud flat. Aerial photographs of the arctic tundra sometimes reveal a curious honeycomb effect in which polygons of earth are surrounded by ice. Forming in the cracks, the ice acts as a wedge. During successive thawing and freezing, it exerts increasing pressure. Newcomb concluded that eventually this pressure had bowed up the centers of the enclosed polygons of earth on the outwash plains and later, after the complete melting of the ice, this silt had "slumped down into mounds." He was, in 1940, very close to what is now the accepted theory.

Thirteen more years went by. Then in 1953, in *The Journal of Geology*, Arthur M. Ritchie, geologist of the Washington State Highway Commission, detailed what is believed to be the correct answer to the century-old riddle of the mysterious mounds. Ice and water—just as Bretz forty years before had concluded—are the two forces involved. The action of first one and then the other, Ritchie believes, created the million mounds of the Tenino region.

Severe freezing, as Newcomb suggested, caused the salt and gravel of the outwash plain to break up into flat-topped polygons surrounded by walls or wedges of ice. According to Ritchie's reconstruction of these long-ago events, the ice wedges melted before the ground between them. Just as these blocks, still flat-topped rather than bowed up, were thawing out, the water of an ice-choked flood river flowed across the plain. It cleaned out the trenches where the ice had surrounded the polygons and it stripped away the thawed ground from the solidly frozen, rounded central cores. For the polygons thaw out in the manner of a melting ice cube which is reduced to a rounded central portion that disappears last of all. This eroding flood was of short duration. When its water subsided only the igloo-like cores of still-frozen earth remained. Thawing out eventually, these cores dotted the plain and formed the mounds that have bewildered and baffled generations of visitors.

The flooding, Ritchie believes, came at just the right time. If it had been delayed until the polygons were completely thawed out all the material composing them would have been carried away by the running water. Because the polygonal cracking occurs only where the soil has a high percentage of fine sediment in it, the effect was limited to the areas where Mima mounds are found. In these places just the right combination of soil and just the right timing of the prehistoric floodwaters joined to produce a geological enigma.

Ritchie's so-called "frozen ground erosional theory" was unknown to me that day. For us this riddle veiled in vapor was completely baffling. As we walked about the mist grew denser. From beneath a bit of wood sunk in the vegetation we heard the low music of a cricket. And from somewhere in the mist beyond the bracken-topped knolls a meadowlark sang. Then rain splashed down, first a drop, then scattered drops, then a steady drumming. Looking back as we drove away, seeing the mounds wavering in the mist and the rain, we were thinking of another riddle in connection with their long endurance.

Erosion was all-important in the original formation of the mounds. Why has erosion produced so little effect in the years since? The character of the fine clay soil may be a factor. The clothing of low, mossy vegetation, water-absorbing, a botanical balance-wheel, a buffer to wind and rain, may be another. No doubt the stratum of loose gravel which descends as much as thirty or forty feet below the mounds and into which water quickly sinks, plays an important part. But even so, in this land of ample rain, the changelessness of the mounds seems touched with the miraculous.

For the violence of wind-driven rain such as we met that day must be an old, old story to the Mima mounds. The pavements streamed. Our windshield wiper swung endlessly with a steady "ker-*foot!* ker-*foot!* ker-*foot!*" Headlight reflections ran along the wet concrete and speeding cars passed us with a great "swoosh!" of spray. So tumultuous was the downpour that we

SEA LIONS in their cavern on the Oregon coast. Here great combers enter and shatter, filling the interior with foam.

SUNSET CALM and wet, shining sand surround the towering rocks that are a feature of the picturesque Oregon coast.

saw ducks sitting on farmhouse porches out of the rain. Yet such storms, storms without number through aeons of time, have swept across the mounds. Their permanence, their endurance, their immunity to erosion—the secret of these things seemed to us a riddle almost as great as the mystery of their origin as we drove north through the storm.

TWENTY-SIX

THE GOLDEN SQUIRREL

DURING autumn the earth advances nearly 150,000,000 miles on its elliptical course around the sun. Throughout all the changes of the season its unslackened speed carries it ahead nearly 1,600,000 miles each day, more than 65,000 miles each hour, more than 1,000 miles each minute, eighteen and a half miles each second. It traveled more than 100,000 miles on this November night while we wandered alone in chill and silence and moonlight in a dead forest with the glacier-clad upper slopes of Mount Rainier far above us gleaming in cold alabaster white against the depths of the night.

The Hunter's Moon of October had given way to the Mad Moon of November. The fern forests of Castle Rock and the mystery mounds of Tenino lay to the west behind us. Along the slope above us, down the slope below us, rose gaunt tree trunks, dark with shadow on one side, lighted by the nearly full moon on the other. In the fall of 1947, on the night of October 1, melt-water from the Kautz Glacier had suddenly broken free. Carrying 50,000,000 cubic yards of debris into the valley below, the avalanche of water and rocks and rolling tree trunks had plunged down the steep descent. Falling trees had been shredded and pounded to pulp by the boulders. Those that remained had been killed by grinding rocks and smothering silt. Now, half a dozen years later, sparse new growth had taken root—fireweed and pearly everlasting and red alder first of all. Only after unhurried decades of healing would this long wound on the mountainside fill in and disappear.

The trails we followed among the lifeless trees led over debris twenty or thirty feet deep. And always towering far above us rose the shining mountain. Its cap of snow and glacier ice, framed by the gaunt tree trunks, at times gleamed with such brilliance in the frosty air that the whole peak seemed formed of cold and flameless light. No other mountain we have ever seen was as beautiful as Rainier appeared under that November moon.

We were looking up for a last time beside the road when, in the intense silence, I became aware of a slight scratching, scrambling sound. My ear traced it to a metal drum that park officials had placed beside a tree as a trash container. I ran the beam of a flashlight around the interior. Motionless now, staring up at me transfixed by the rays was another of those mammal mileposts of our trip, a white-footed mouse —this time the Washington white-footed mouse. I tilted down the drum and it scurried away. In Mount Rainier National Park no other animal is so numerous. One of these little rodents was even found at the very top of the peak, 14,408 feet above sea level.

Beyond the edge of the dead forest, among living trees that had escaped in the disaster of 1947, we paused that night near one of the largest Douglas firs growing on the slopes of the mountain. By its girth scientists judge that it was already towering high in the air when Christopher Columbus reached the New World. Here the shadows beneath the lofty trees were dense and inky black. A little way off, amid such shadows, a pool of moonlight lay beneath a small opening in the canopy of the forest. In this space—some thirty or forty feet across—the carpeting moss, the curving ferns, the great instep of one of the immense trees all appeared as though on a spotlighted stage. And as we watched, out from the shadows and into the light stepped two sleek and exquisite does. They moved among the ferns as graceful as the fronds. They paused. They browsed. They turned in our direction only once, their great ears uplifted, their dark, liquid eyes watching us where we stood. Then unafraid they moved out of the light and into the shadows again.

One of the annual signs of autumn on this mountainside is the movement of the Columbian black-tailed deer down from the higher levels. In spring they climb the slopes after the retreating snow. They spend the summer among the high mountain meadows free from the multitude of flies that infest the lowland woods. Some, particularly the older bucks, range even above the timberline. Then with the first heavy snows of autumn the deer move down to the valleys again. Year after year, following the same trails each time, they engage in this definite seasonal and altitudinal migration.

On the map and on the globe up is north and down is south. We speak colloquially of "up north" and "down south." With justice we might use the same terms on a mountainside. For any creature that ascends a lofty peak enters a succession of environments that progressively parallel conditions farther and farther north. Coming down, the reverse is true.

Although most of the 130 species of birds that have been recorded in the Mount Rainier National Park fly down the map in a long horizontal migration that carries them in autumn beyond the boundaries of the continent, a few, instead, fly down the mountain in a short vertical migration that leaves them still within sight of the peak. Each fall, about the time the deer move down, the Clark's nutcrackers, the Oregon jays, the Hepburn's rosy finches descend in an aerial toboggan to the lower levels where they find their winter food.

A few jays and nutcrackers were still haunting Paradise Valley when we climbed the twisting road that carried us to its 5,400-foot elevation the following afternoon. There, beneath our tires and under our feet, was the first snow of the trip. It lay three or four inches deep on the ground, prelude to the towering drifts that would form in this mile-high valley before the winter ended. Over it came flying a dozen jays and nutcrackers, unafraid after a summer-long contact with friendly visitors. They perched on the hood of the car and on its open door. When I bent over, a nut-cracker alighted on my back. One jay hopped about inside the car looking for food. I rummaged in the trunk and found a box of crackers. The birds ate at our feet. They retrieved crumbs from the snow. They ate from our fingers. An Oregon jay landed on Nellie's arm and when there was a delay in the appearance of the next cracker crumb it would tug at her sleeve with its bill.

Into the midst of this activity there darted from a snow-covered jumble of rocks an alert, beautiful creature we had thought we were too late to see. It was an animal about ten inches long from nose to tail-tip. Down its side ran a wide white stripe bordered with black. At first glance we seemed looking at a large and brightly colored chipmunk. But here were none of the face stripings that we had seen on the little seed gatherers that had scampered along the stone walls of New England. Here the whole head, the little upright rounded ears, the forelegs were all tinged with a coppery-golden hue. This creature, darting across the snow of this far-western mountain height, was one we had long wished to know, one we had dreamed of meeting, one that by this November day we had despaired of seeing. Like the grass-of-Parnassus that we had come upon beside the warbler river, it had been an object of special interest since first we saw its name in a guidebook. Here at last was the golden squirrel. Here in Paradise Valley, close to timberline, dashing among late-lingering jays and nutcrackers, was our first mantled ground squirrel, *Citellus saturatus*, the famous mountaineer rodent of the high Cascades.

Fourteen subspecies of the mantled ground squirrel—of which *saturatus* is one—live in upper reaches in the mountains of eleven western states. Sometimes they even make their homes above timberline amid the same wind-swept rock slides where the pikas live. In the Sierra Nevada mountains of California, one of these ground squirrels was observed at an elevation of 10,700 feet. During summer, fruits and seeds, grasshoppers and beetles, provide most of their nourishment. Returning to their burrows from foraging expeditions they, like the eastern chipmunks, carry harvested food in bulging cheek pouches.

Perhaps it was the harsh grating calls of the nutcrackers that drew our ground squirrel from its burrow among the rocks. That call no doubt had been associated with food all during the tourist season now ending. At any rate it had left a snug little nest at the bottom of its tunnel, where it would soon fall into the deep sleep of hibernation. Such nests are usually lined with soft plant fibers or hair. In different surroundings additional material is added. One golden mantled ground squirrel was observed tearing up a brown paper bag with its feet and stuffing the fragments into its cheek pouches to carry underground. Where sheep are pastured on mountain meadows the ground squirrels of the region often collect bits of wool and carry them underground as winter lining for their nests. There they literally sleep through the months of cold tucked in a woolen blanket.

For only a short time did the squirrel stay out. Then in a sudden rush back across the snow it disappeared among the rocks again. Usually these "mantled chipmunks" remain active until the first heavy storms of autumn snow them in. Then, snug in their nests under the high-piled drifts, they sleep the winter away. This was one of our golden squirrel's last appearances above ground. Ours was a late-autumn view. And that was the only view we had. Close to the park museum at the Longmire headquarters I thought I saw a second mantled squirrel whisk into the mouth of a burrow. But I could not be sure.

It was another animal that attracted our attention at Longmire. Unlike the ground squirrels, the Pacific raccoons of Rainier make no attempt to hibernate. We spent some time watching two that took their stand under the wooden steps leading into the park store. They had learned, apparently, that there was no food to be obtained from people going in the store and they wasted little time on them. It was the sound of feet moving in only one direction over the boards above their heads—going out of the store, down the steps, along the route newly bought groceries traveled—that brought them ambling into the open to beg for handouts.

During the 1890's, in these western mountains, the American naturalist C. Hart Merriam studied the manner in which the increasing altitudes on an ascent produced more and more northern environments. He originated the concept of life zones. At Longmire, at an altitude of 2,761 feet, we were in Merriam's Transition Zone. At the beginning of our climb to Yakima Park, on the opposite side of the mountain from Longmire, we were at an altitude of 3,500 feet and in the Canadian Zone. At Yakima Park, at 6,400 feet, we were in the Hudsonian Zone. Above us towered bleak slopes that represented the Arctic Zone. There conditions were similar to those beyond tree line in the far north. Climbing upward thus we were, in effect, rushing northward into the advancing autumn. Each successive zone—with its own particular brilliance or special manifestation—was recording the arrival of fall.

At the 3,500-foot level we stopped below one long rise sheeted from top to bottom in the flame of the vine maples. At other times we saw their foliage, crimson and brilliant orange-red, in great streaks or splashes or strewn through the forest on some steep ridgeside beyond a valley. At 5,000 feet we had almost entirely left the vine maples behind. But here, running across the open spaces, was the rich wine-red of the huckleberries. Once we looked back as we made a turn late in the afternoon. Long slender shadows of evergreens extended away across acre after acre of mountain huckleberries flowing down the slope in a solid carpet of autumn brilliance.

On the alpine meadows—where spring comes late and autumn early and the blooming season of the wildflowers is short but intense—we wandered among plants long since gone to seed. Here yellows and russets predominated. But in the wake of the melting snow the following year sudden growth and sudden blooming would be the rule. Across these high openings wildflowers would open swiftly with reds and blues and oranges and purples intermingling. From the waxy-white avalanche lily and the rose-colored mimulus through the gold of the alpine buttercup, the lavender of the anemone, the purple of the lupine to the creamy white masses of the beargrass—which is not a grass at all but a lily—the plants of these heights would seem to bloom overnight. And the brightest of all, scarlet and magenta and yellow and purple and blood-red, would be the Indian paintbrushes. All this flood of color, this tapestry of high-country blooms that reaches its peak in July and August, all now was contained in the dry perennials, in the seeds of the annuals that were falling everywhere across the meadows in these latter days of autumn.

Wherever we went those days, above the flaming maples, above the rich red of the huckleberries, above the tan and russet of the upper meadows, in sunlight or moonlight, there towered above us the shining mountain. Against its immaculate whiteness the drifting clouds appeared gray as though composed of smoke. The wind at times drew into the sky from the tip of the peak long curling banners of snow. And we saw it all through the world's finest breathing space, through clear mountain air, sparkling, perfumed by ever-greens, stretching away mile after mile untainted by smoke, undimmed by fog.

No other peak in America, no other peak in the world it is said, carries so great an expanse of glaciers as Mount Rainier. With an area of forty-eight square miles, its twenty-eight glaciers wind in all directions downward from its peak. Seen from the sky the ice-clad mountain resembles a multi-armed starfish or octopus, each curving arm formed by a glacier. Now in a warming climatic cycle, this ice is melting back at the rate of about seventy feet a year. Over rocks of gray granodiorite I clambered close to the snout of the Nisqually Glacier. There the water of the melting ice gushed forth to tumble down a steep valley over boulders and gravel in the foaming first mile of the Nisqually River.

Some days later we saw the last mile of this same river close to Puget Sound. Then it was moving deliberately, a wide, placid, lowland stream. And then Mount Rainier, with its gleaming ice, its snow banners, its rosy finches and its golden squirrels, lay off to the east and we were well on our way toward the Olympic Peninsula.

LAND OF THE WINDY RAIN

A CIRCLE within a square—that roughly represents the Olympic Mountains. Their jagged peaks cluster around Mount Olympus and form the enduring heart of the peninsula that comprises the far northwestern corner of the United States. Rising from sea level to 5,000, 6,000, 7,000 and almost 8,000 feet in the space of less than fifty miles, the mountains lift in a great stone wall against which blows the prevailing wind from the sea. That wind has one of the highest average velocities for the entire country, more than fourteen miles an hour the year around. Like a rapidly moving conveyor belt it brings in moisture from the sea. The mountains drive it steeply upward, cool it suddenly, condense its moisture into precipitation. In effect they quickly wring the water from this ocean wind.

As a consequence the western side of the Olympics receives a greater amount of rainfall each year than any other place in America. The average is about 140 inches, approximately 2,000,000,000 gallons or 9,000,000 tons of falling rain for each square mile of land. By far the greater part of this precipitation comes between November 1 and May 1; the heaviest rains begin in autumn; the three wettest months are November, December and January. Yet during the November days we spent wandering in this land of the windy rain the silver cord that, according to Greek mythology, held gales and storms prisoner within a leather bag remained securely tied. The sun shone. The breeze only occasionally freshened into a wind. The showers were short and infrequent or the rains came in the night. Under favoring skies in this prolonged and unusually dry autumn we roamed through the green, mossy world of a northern rain forest.

We had come up the east side of the peninsula, past red-barked, red-berried madrone trees, over the Hama Hama River, past Lilliwaup—which reminded us how often in this rainy land place-names had a wet, squashy sound, like Satsop, Lilliwaup and Tumwater. Then, based at Port Angeles, we had explored the northern coast along the Strait of Juan de Fuca. We followed roads where a rat trap dangled from a pole in front of every farmhouse to hold the brown canvas bag set out for the country postman. We continued as far as Cape Flattery and the Indian village of Neah Bay where gulls and fish crows fed in the street like sparrows. Along this wild coast we had seen our first surf birds and our first black turnstones. Then we had swung south down the outside of the peninsula, down to the Hoh River and the nineteen-mile dirt road that winds into the rain forest as far as the Hoh Ranger Station and the beginning of the path that climbs eventually up to the high meadows and the glaciers of Mount Olympus. During the two succeeding days we wandered along the lower miles of this rain-forest trail.

All around us the vine maples, the towering hemlocks, the firs and the spruces were draped and bearded with moss. Great trunks rose above us green and furry as far as we could see. Branches spread over us shaggy with the primitive spikemoss, *Selaginella*. Under our feet the plush of the forest carpet grew so dense and deep we sank at times above our shoetops. In the misty light we saw it roll on and on, wave after wave, over the moldering logs, across the uneven floor of the forest. Scientists believe 100 kinds of moss grow on the Olympic Peninsula. The green carpet that covers the forest floor is formed of many species, many strands; its warp and woof are made up of a multitude of mosses.

Here and there along the path streamers of sunshine probed between the giant trees. Drawn in glowing silver lines they slanted down through the humid air. And above each spot where they reached the saturated carpet of the moss, mist curled up like smoke from a fire being started with a burning glass. And all the while the long fingers of the spikemoss, hanging from the branches like gray-green stalactites forming under the roof of a cavern, dripped endlessly. As each drop fell it entered the plush of the living carpet without a sound. It was absorbed without a trace. Moss is nature's great silencer. This was a forest soundproofed by moss.

We stopped beside a tree where the trunk had split a third of the way down from the top and half had fallen to the ground. All down the divided tree the sheathing of moss had parted as though it were a thicker shell of bark. On some trunks the coating is so dense it has the appearance of a shaggy pelt. I was told that when natives are caught in the forest overnight in the dryer summer months they sometimes strip off great sections of this moss with their hunting knives and use them as soft, thick blankets. In rare periods of comparative drought it is the tree-moss that dries out most quickly. At such times a conflagration will race ahead through the forest faster than fire-fighters can keep up with it.

An astonishing paradox in connection with the moisture of the Olympic Peninsula is the fact that less than thirty miles from the saturated forest through which we walked irrigation farming is practiced. Around Sequim, in the northeastern corner of the peninsula, rainfall is sometimes only fourteen inches a year, one-tenth that on the other side of the Olympics. There we saw troughs and ditches carrying water to dry fields lying in the rain shadow of the mountains. Coming west we had run through a succession of such areas of dryness. Prevailing winds from the west vault over the Olympics, over the Cascades, over the Rockies. Each time they leave most of their moisture on the western side of the range and little remains to water the land lying on the lee side to the east. Oregon and Washington are lush and green west of the Cascades, so dry they are often almost deserts east of the mountains. But nowhere else did we see so dramatic a demonstration of the effect of mountains on moisture as here within the narrow confines of the Olympic Peninsula.

Along our path beside the Hoh the evidences of abundant rainfall were everywhere. Combined with a mild climate and a long growing season it had produced a tropical luxuriance of growth. Immense tree trunks lifted from the moss and ferns, soared upward, towered above us, disappearing at last among the maze of the upper branches. In some cases the lowest branch was 100 feet in the air. Here in the rain forest of the Olympic Peninsula numerous trees attain their record size.

The world's largest Cascade fir grows in the wild country between the Hoh and the Bogachiel rivers and, near the mouth of the Hoh, the western red cedar reaches its maximum size in a seamed and twisted giant. On the east fork of the Quinault River the biggest known western hemlock has a girth of twenty-seven feet, two inches. Among the Douglas firs—that race of giants that with the single exception of the sequoias are the hugest trees in America—the largest of them all grows in the valley of the Queets River, south of the Hoh. Four and a half feet from the ground its circumference is fifty-three feet, four inches. And along the trail we followed, some four miles in from the ranger station on the Hoh, one of the most beautiful trees in the world, the Sitka spruce with frosted needles and silvery bark tinged with lavender and purple, reaches its maximum dimensions with a circumference of forty-one feet, six inches.

These are virgin trees in a virgin forest. Protected within the glorious living museum of this national park are some of the arboreal patriarchs of the world. Many times during our trip we felt that America's great national park system is one of its finest achievements, action by the people for the people on a high plane. Yet those who think of any national park as something permanent make a grave mistake. It can always be changed if not abolished. Its boundaries can be altered, permitting the finest of its timber to be cut. Its rules can be modified, allowing grazing here, mining there, dams destroying areas supposed to be inviolate. And because of the wonder of its trees the Olympic National Park, more than most, will always be in danger.

Decades ago John Muir declared that the Olympic Park would be attacked again and again. His prediction has been amply vindicated. Men who see no more in a tree than board feet, elected officials who refer to the nation's public lands as being "locked-up resources"—as they might refer to songbirds as being "locked-up light meat and dark"—these men we will have with us always and always they will pose a threat to our national parks. Only the vigilance of conservationists over the long haul, only an alertness to attack in a thousand guises, can prevent raids and invasions and destructions within these areas that the people believe have been permanently saved.

On June 17, 1853, Henry Thoreau noted in his journal: "If a man walks in the woods for love of them for half his days, he is esteemed a loafer; but if he spends his whole day as a speculator, shearing off those woods, he is esteemed industrious and enterprising—making earth bald before its time." That attitude is not one that disappeared when the Walden Woods were felled. It is current in every generation. It is ranged against every effort to save wild places. Those to whom the trees, the birds, the wildflowers represent only "locked-up dollars" have never known or really seen these things. They have never experienced an interest in nature for it-self. Whoever stimulates a wider appreciation of nature, a wider understanding of nature, a wider love of nature for its own sake accomplishes no small thing. For from these is formed the enduring component of the conservation move-ment. Many people are attracted to a fight who drift away when the excitement dies down. It is only those who are deeply and fundamentally interested in nature itself who, in the long haul, the all-important continuity of effort, carry on.

Nellie and I talked of such matters under the great trees beside the Hoh and again that evening in a cabin overlooking a curving beach piled high with the flotsam of tremendous timbers. White surf thundered on the sand, swirling, seething, ripped by the offshore rocks. The sunset died beyond bleak Destruction Island while we dined on the only food we could find in a country store, crackers and corned beef and apples —saving for breakfast the sardines and oatmeal cookies and instant chocolate. Each time we awoke in our cabin we heard the roaring of the white surf in the moonlight and saw the spearheads of the spruces rising black against a starry sky. Thus passed our first night on the shore of the open Pacific.

When we left the sea and entered the forest again next morning the autumn mist was heavy among the trees. Fall is proverbially the season of ground fog and mists. The lengthen-ing nights permit the earth to lose more of its heat, the waning strength of the sun slows down the process of warming up the ground in the morning, the lighter winds then prevailing disperse the accumulated mist less quickly. For these reasons autumn and mist are linked together in most parts of the country. Here in the moistness of the rain forest it was late in the morning before the temperature of ground and air be-came more nearly uniform and the heavier mist among the trees thinned away.

All along the trail winter wrens, like flitting winged mice, appeared and disappeared among the jumbles of the fallen trees. In these mossy woods they live the year around. Douglas squirrels, the chickarees with tufted ears and birdlike voices, darted off at our approach leaving behind on stump tops the kitchen middens of their cone scales. Ferns were everywhere, licorice ferns drooping like green feathers from the shaggy branches of the vine maples, deer ferns with dry fronds like antlers, oak ferns, western bracken, delicate maidenhair ferns clinging to moist, dripping embankments, lady ferns believed by generations of European peasants to produce magic seed that made the possessor invisible, clumps of sword ferns like green vases filled with fallen leaves. And here and there we came upon splashes of brilliant red and orange where slime mold, that mysterious substance that dwells on the borderline between plant and animal life, spread away across decaying wood.

All through the forest life was rising from death. Along the length of every moldering, fallen tree seedlings were rooted, young trees were growing. Often we would see four or five giant spruces rising in a perfectly straight line as though—like peas in a garden plot—their seeds had been planted along a taut string. In their case the string was six feet thick, a log perhaps 200 feet long. Many seedlings sprout on these fallen "nurse trees" but only a few survive the first years of competition. We came upon roots that extended five feet or more down the sides of moldering logs and once, where a tree had begun growing at the top of a massive stub, roots dropped fully a dozen feet to reach the mold of the forest floor.

On this day we continued farther on the trail. For eleven of its eighteen miles it threads among the trees of the rain forest following the course of the Hoh. On old maps this river appears as the Hooch, the Huch, the Hook, the Holes and the Ohahlat. It is the largest stream on the Olympic Peninsula, carrying away 85 per cent of the melt-water from the glaciers of Mount Olympus. Now in the autumn its flow had lessened greatly. The stream ran shallow, glinting and sparkling among water-smoothed stones in its wide gravel bed.

We were looking across a stretch of rapids where the river tumbled with a swifter current when Nellie caught sight of a bird balancing itself on a boulder amid the flying spray. Slaty-blue, short-tailed and chunky, it was about the size of a starling. As we watched it bobbed rapidly several times. Then it slipped down the side of the rock and plunged head-first into the rushing torrent. It seemed inconceivable that it could escape being drowned or dashed to death against the rocks. Yet a few moments later it popped up as buoyant as a cork and mounted another rock a yard from the first. It was not only safe and sound, it was even dry. The bird we watched was the famed dipper of the West, the water ouzel of swift mountain streams. This relative of the wrens, without benefit of webbed feet or any of the other special adaptations of the water bird, is able to walk on the bed of the stream or, with the aid of its wings, swim in the swiftest current.

Time and again it disappeared in the foaming, tumbling water along the edge of a gravel bar. Once it dived into a tiny pool while on the wing. Another time it alighted on a little rug of moss between two stones. Here it turned around and around, facing first this way then that, shifting its direction a dozen times before it flitted with a rapid flutter, almost a whirring, of its wings to another perch. Not infrequently while clinging to some low stone it would thrust its head under the surface and peer about beneath the water. At last it climbed onto a rock at the end of one of its dives clutching in its bill the prize it had sought, the white larva of some aquatic insect. Tilting back its head it gulped it down. Then began one of the wonderful moments of the trip. For the first time in our lives we heard the song of the water ouzel.

It went on and on like the music of the stream. The song was clear and ringing; it was sweet and varied. On a perfectly still morning it is said the voice of the ouzel can be heard a mile away across a mountain lake. It progressed with trills and warbles, whistled notes, long cadences and flutelike phrases. It suggested the song of the mockingbird or the brown thrasher or the catbird, rich with improvising and imitating. Some notes were liquid like the gurgling of the stream, others were short and harsh like the grating together of stones. At moments we were reminded of the song of an oriole, at other moments that of a warbling vireo. Yet in its entirety it was unlike any of these. For fully ten minutes, stopping and beginning again, the bird sang to itself, and to us, as it wandered alone along the edge of the gravel bar.

The water ouzel is one of the few birds that sing the year around. Wishing the song would go on for hours, we listened entranced. But at last the music stopped and the singer darted away downstream, flying low, only inches above the tumbling water of the rapids. At Yellowstone, and again at Rainier, we had glimpsed ouzels in the mountain streams but only here, we felt, had we really come to know the bird. And only here, beside this rain-forest river, had we heard its song.

Beyond Mount Tom Creek the trail became more and more a cowpath followed by the wild cattle of the forest. Its moist earth was imprinted with a lacework of heart-shaped tracks left by the black-tailed deer. One time when we looked back we saw the antlered head of a buck lifted above distant underbrush as the animal watched us going away down the trail. And again, at the edge of an open space, we came upon two does nibbling on bright yellow fungus. Occasionally among the deer tracks in our path we discovered more oval hoof marks, suggesting the two halves of a coffee bean. These were the tracks of the Roosevelt elk.

Only once did we catch a fleeting glimpse of one of these great animals—the dark head and huge dark ears of a female gazing at us among bushes and disappearing almost as soon as we turned that way. The hunting season had already begun. Pitched in the forest around the edges of the park were the tents of the elk hunters. One herd of sixty-nine animals, fortunately still within the park, had been sighted early that morning. But the main bulk of the elk had remained on the higher slopes of the mountains. Like the Columbian blacktails of Mount Rainier, in fall these animals migrate down to the lowlands. In the mild autumn of this year the early snowstorms that start the movement had been delayed, thus, no doubt, saving the lives of many an elk. For although the total number of these animals—native only to this northwestern peninsula—is estimated to be only about 6,000, as many as 5,000 special elk-hunting licenses are issued in one season to men who roam the fringes of the forest just outside the boundaries of the park. Without the protection of this sanctuary these noble animals would face quick and certain extinction.

There were times later on when our trail swung away from the river and the sound of its running water was inaudible. Then the stillness of the forest became intense. In such a silence we rested once beside a mossy stub starred from top to bottom with oxalis. Down the trail a falling leaf, huge and yellow, descended from the lower branch of a big-leaf or Oregon maple. It rode the air in a wide serpentine, stem-first, sliding to a stop like a landing airplane. Although it was fully 100 feet away our ears caught the faint scraping of its stem along the ground and among the already fallen leaves. In that profound silence we could even hear the lisping, sibilant whisper of the dry needles sifting down from the Sitka spruces.

In one of his books W. H. Hudson speaks of what he calls "forgotten memories"—recollections of experiences in the past, long buried in the mind, unthought of for years, perhaps, that some small thing, a sound, a scent, a turn of the road will bring to vivid life. Standing there I found myself reliving an odd adventure of the past, seeing again in suddenly sharpened focus a white-bearded man who looked like a

Biblical prophet, a man I met but once under curious circumstances, long ago. And in its way this memory was linked intimately with falling leaf and sifting needle, with Oregon maple and Sitka spruce.

An editor had sent me from New York to a chicken farm on the edge of a small New Jersey village. One of the men who fed poultry there was reported to have the oddest collection of musical instruments on earth. I found him, a patriarchal old gentleman with mild blue eyes. He explained quite simply that he saw visions and that once, years before, he had watched 126 angels, each playing a different musical instrument. He had set out to reproduce on earth all the instruments he had seen. We examined a score or more he had completed: fiddles with three necks instead of one, a harp so huge it could be played from a second-story window, violins with crook necks and extra strings, harps and fiddles combined. All of his instruments had been turned out with no special training and with the use of ordinary carpenter tools. Yet one of his smaller violins, he told me, because of the sweetness of its tone had sold for $500. Afterwards I checked with the owner and found this was true. The wood that went into all these instruments came from a common lumber yard. But the instrument maker believed that he was guided to certain boards, ones that rang like a bell when he thumped them. All the resonance and beauty of tone in the finished product, he maintained, was inherent in the fibers of the wood.

Years later I talked with one of the leading manufacturers of fine violins in America. I remembered this idea and asked him if it was true—if certain boards are selected because their wood gives a finer tone or a greater resonance. He said no. But he added something that meant less to me then than it did on this day beside the mossy stump amid the silence of the rain forest. Most of the wood going into the construction of violins in America, he explained, comes from the West, from two trees, from the Oregon maple and the Sitka spruce.

On the outward trail later that afternoon we found ourselves in a small opening covered with the brown of autumn
bracken. Golden-crowned kinglets darted among the surrounding trees, their wiry, lisping little calls coming from here, from
there, from everywhere around us. It was while we were
watching them that a small black-capped bird with a rufous
back caught our attention—our first chestnut-backed chickadee.

In the depths of the forest, in the twilight of its shadows,
birds are comparatively few. Here the varied thrush sings
and here the sooty grouse makes its home. Most dwellers
in dusky forests are, like this grouse, particularly dark in color.
Once on our way out we saw a sparrow, with plumage almost
black, flitting among the bushes. It was the sooty song sparrow
of the rain forest. Pelts of the now extinct Olympic wolf
show that it, too, was so dark it was almost black. If you know
the rainfall of a region you can make a pretty accurate guess
as to the density of color of its wildlife inhabitants. For evolution favors dark-hued creatures in the deep woods just as it
favors light-colored creatures on the open desert.

It was after sunset that day when we rounded a turn on the
endlessly winding road that leads down the west side of the
peninsula and came upon another dark tenant of the rain
forest. A dusky cottontail bolted from the shadowed roadside. Even in the distance its actions appeared peculiar. It
hopped first this way, then that, as though unable to make
up its mind. It would stop, then hurry on in aimless zigzag
fashion, then pause again irresolute. As we drew close what
appeared to be a squirrel came bounding from the roadside
bushes a hundred feet or so behind the rabbit. It halted,
seemed to break in two, the front half reared up, light beneath,
flat-headed like a cobra, teeth showing in a weasel grin.

This was the bloodthirsty cause of the rabbit's distraction.
So terrified was the cottontail it seemed literally out of its

mind. In a matter of minutes it could have leaped away in a straight line and outdistanced its short-legged pursuer completely. But it appeared incapable of effective action, bereft of all powers of decision. Many times I have remembered that silent nightmare in the dusk. It was a terrible thing to see a living creature with nerves unstrung and wits departed, stupefied by terror and delivered by fear into the hands of its enemy. We were almost abreast of the rabbit before the spell was broken. Then the weasel whirled and darted into the bushes. The cottontail, in a sudden awakening to sanity, bolted away down the road in swift, effective flight.

During the days that followed we left the rain forest behind—in its quiet, subdued way the most beautiful woods we had ever seen. We wandered north into a land of birches and willows and aspens. We crossed the Fraser River, ran the gantlet of bone-china stores and Cheerio Motels, and entered Vancouver, B.C. Here, at the farthest-north point of our trip, we turned back. From now on, during the remaining weeks of fall, we would be working southward down the coast, moving in the direction that autumn moved.

TWENTY-EIGHT

TIDEPOOLS

WE peered through a gray curtain of falling rain. Beside the road the leaves of a wonderful poplar tree, all gold above and silver beneath, fluttered in the wind. They were washed by the downpour, gyrated by the gusts. Even in the hooded light of the overcast they shone with metallic brilliance. And at every blast waves of gold and silver intermingling ran along the boughs. Behind the tree extended the width of a drowned river, gray under the gray sky and crawling slowly toward the sea. Here the Columbia was nearing its mouth. Not many miles ahead lay Astoria.

Out on the river near this spot, almost a century and a half before, a man in a dugout canoe had rested a travel-worn notebook on his knee and had written these words:

"Ocian in view! O! the joy!"

In that simple entry, dramatically eloquent in its understatement, Captain William Clark had recorded the goal attained in that long, laborious, heroic, pioneer westward trek "over the Shining Mountains to Everywhere-Salt-Water."

On the coast south of Astoria, next day, where the Necanicum River curves in a shallow flow across the sands to the sea, we paused again, this time at the last spot we would meet associated with Lewis and Clark. Here they had found the stranded whale—the one thing among all her adventures that Sacajawea talked about in later years—and near here the men had boiled sea water in iron kettles to obtain salt during that "wet and stormy" winter at Fort Clatsop.

When we started on again there stretched away to the south before us nearly 400 miles of Oregon coast—its great black rocks and creamy surf, its towering headlands, its tide-pools and wave-cut caverns making it one of the world's most picturesque meeting places of land and sea. Day after day we moved leisurely southward along the shore or cut inland where robins swarmed among the berries of the madrone trees, where wild roses bent beneath a load of crimson hips and where whole hillsides now were covered with fallen leaves overlapping like shingles on a slanting roof.

Near Roseburg we advanced amid denuded hills—earth made bald before its time. It was here, in primeval forest, that David Douglas had first found the giant cones of the sugar pine. At the top of one inland pass we came to a forest of frozen fog. Every tree and twig was plated with the congealed breath of the autumn mist that streamed on the wind up the slope. Another time, as we passed a run-down valley farm in morning fog, we glimpsed for a moment the tableau of a humble drama: a white horse lay on its side in a dooryard, a blanket over it, a bonfire near it, a man and woman bending above it, a child running with a pail of steaming water from the house—a sick horse, a major tragedy on a small farm.

But always after cutting inland in those days we swung back to the coast again. There we moved south past Falcon Cove and Arch Rock and the wind-swept height of Neah-kahnie Mountain. Offshore, all along the way, white islands of foam marked the hidden rocks. We came to Tillamook, famous for its cheese, set among green lowland pastures where, when the morning fog lifts, placid herds feed all across the fields surrounded by the sparkle of mist-dew on the grassblades. We reached Cape Foulweather and Otter Crest with its tremendous view of the coast ahead.

Down that coast, off and on for a hundred miles, we wandered in succeeding days over the sands beachcombing amid the autumn flotsam. Here, for the naturalist, the helpings are larger. Bigness is on the beach as well as in the forests of the Northwest. Like great bullwhips the ribbon kelp, *Nereocystis lutkeana*, stretched across the wet sand, sometimes more than fifty feet long. In some instances these seaweeds reach a length of 150 feet. We saw their thick yellow-green cables intertwining in great tangles on the upper beach. Even greater lengths are attained by a related seaweed, the giant kelp that ranges down the Pacific Coast from Alaska to California. It is without doubt the longest plant in the world. Specimens have been reported 1,500 feet from one end to the other—a single plant more than a quarter of a mile long.

The sands were many-colored when we approached Agate Beach. Metallic blues and browns and reds were woven by the waves into intricate patterns on the shore. These lines of color intersected endlessly. At times their mingled hues produced an effect that suggested the blended coloring of a moth's wing. Again for long stretches bluish sand ran before us in wavering lines like oil stains on the shore. At other times we walked as though on fine emery dust or amid specks that glittered in the sun like disintegrated mica.

Tides run high on the Oregon coast. The water had fallen away a full nine feet to its low point when we went beachcombing before breakfast near Newport. Foam clung to the wet sand in anchored clouds, trembling in the breeze, shimmering at times with iridescent colors as though formed of innumerable soap bubbles. Everywhere along this western coast the sea foam is abundant, dense and creamy. We saw it piled high in airy windrows on the shore. We saw it extending like a thick blanket of whipped cream across quiet bays. We saw it filling long corridors at Seal Rock and churning and tossing on the mighty seas of Boiler Bay. A scientist I talked to later on in California explained the more creamy foam of the Pacific as the result of the emulsifying effect produced by the breaking up of swarming plankton among the great rocks, each microscopic animal contributing by its death a tiny droplet of oil to the water.

This dense foam of the Pacific swirled all around the submerged ledges and black volcanic rocks at Yachats Beach when, on an ebbing tide, we moved through the emerging gardens of those animal-flowers, the sea anemones. Great combers cannonaded on the lower ledges and exploded over the upper tidepools. Between waves the sea anemones appeared all down the dripping rocks. Then they were blotted out by foam and rushing water. Over and over again tidepools would be filled with a solid lid of foam. Then, growing thin, it would part like clouds, revealing the starfish and the sea anemones adhering to the rock. With the gradual descent and retreat of the sea the upper tidepools became quiet.

Here, surrounded by the crashing of great waves on a rocky shore, my mind went back to another sea anemone in a vastly different habitat on the other side of the continent— the burrowing species I had glimpsed on the quiet, muddy bottom of Shinnecock Bay when the autumn trip began. It had been a glowing pinkish hue in the backlighting. In these Oregon tidepools most of the blossomlike creatures, with their spreading rosettes of tentacles, exhibited a beautiful pastel shade of green. Other species are tinted orange and rose and coral pink and white and blue and yellow and purple. In color as well as in form the sea anemones resemble flowers. Yet some of these bright-hued creatures live where bright sunlight never penetrates, as much as 300 feet below the surface of the ocean.

With the tip of a forefinger I touched the orifice of one of the green sea anemones. With surprising suddenness all the petals of the tentacles turned inward, closing on my finger. The sensation was similar to one I experienced long ago when, as a boy, I let a calf suck my finger. The grip of the sea anemone was a solid, sucking pressure. I slowly pulled my finger free. A small fish or other tidepool creature would have scant chance of freedom once it became enmeshed within that circle of tentacles, each bearing on its surface a host of small but effective organs of suction.

The astonishing gripping power of these tubercles was revealed in 1917 when G. H. Parker reported in the *Journal of Experimental Zoology* the results of a series of experiments on the California coast. In his tests he used the common greenish sea anemone of the western coast of North America, *Cribrina xanthogrammica*, in all probability the same we were seeing in the Oregon tidepools. Ten times Parker measured the force required to pull a smooth piece of seashell away from one tentacle. The average of the results showed that the suction possessed by such a tentacle is equal to 15.6 pounds to the square inch.

In the region of Carmel Bay, on the northern California coast, *Cribrina xanthogrammica* attains a size that is said to be exceeded only by the giant sea anemones of the Great Barrier Reef, off Australia. More than one of the specimens found growing on a small rocky islet in this bay measured sixteen inches across their extended tentacles. Always when the tentacles are outstretched the sea anemone is hungry. It remains tightly closed, with tentacles folded in, when it is digesting captured prey. In some of the greenest of the green sea anemones scientists have found an unexpected pigment. It is chlorophyll. Unicellular algae live in the tissues of the sea creatures, plant and animal apparently existing in a state of symbiosis, much as the two plants, fungus and alga, live together in lichens.

One of the oddest paradoxes of longevity is the fact that the frail-appearing, almost protoplasmic sea anemone has a life span that may exceed that of the great leviathans, the whales that each fall, in November and December, migrate south, often within sight of these very tidepools. Even the greatest

of all the whales, the blue or sulphur-bottom, a creature that
is the largest animal that ever lived on earth—exceeding in
bulk the prehistoric dinosaurs—is believed to have a life span
of less than thirty years. Yet in at least one instance a sea
anemone lived more than twice that long in an aquarium,
remaining active for a period of sixty-nine years.

Over many of the headlands of this part of the coast there
is thrown a dense blanket of salal, rhododendron and huckleberry. Sheared off and pressed down by the wind, it forms
the famed marine gardens of the region. With infinitely varied
shadings of autumn reds and browns and greens, it rolled
away up and down all the slopes around us as we neared
Heceta Head. When we examined closely this wiry blanket it
was the salal that interested us most. A spreading shrub with
glossy leaves, olive-green and leathery, it is a western relative
of the wintergreen. The tiny bells of its flowers are white,
tinged with a flush of pink. Oregon Indians highly valued its
black, aromatic berries. We were bending down, feeling the
thick, tough leaves and fingering the sturdy twigs, when we
heard a clear trilling. It was the voice of an unfamiliar bird.
At first we thought it might be the Oregon junco. Then we
saw the singer, red and black and white—a spotted towhee.

A mile or so beyond, at the top of a towering precipice of
black basalt that plunged in a sheer drop to the white surf
below, we stopped at the sound of a far different voice.
Strangely exciting, it came up the face of the rock, the mingled
barking of many sea lions. Looking down we saw them littering the rocks, clustered together on the ledges, sunning themselves just out of reach of the breakers. A great surf-filled
cavern extending back into the cliff at its base is the home of
hundreds of these marine cousins of the bear.

This cave is unique. It is the only rookery of its kind along
the western coast. When we descended wooden stairs to the
interior of the 1,500-foot cavern, a little later on, we found it
echoing with the thunder of the surf. Great combers would

shadow the two doorways leading to the sea. Then a white tumult of water would roar in, tossing the swimming sea lions, tumbling the animals from the lower rocks, carrying them in a long rush toward the outer openings.

As our eyes became accustomed to the dim illumination, we could see the animals, big and little, light and dark, lying on the rocks all around the edge of the cavern. They barked incessantly, bawling in a confused clamor that rose and sank away amid the cannonading of the waves. At moments the sound suggested the calling of cattle in a barnyard; at other times it swelled around us hoarse and guttural and foreign. One sea lion lay stretched out on its stomach on a small black island that lifted just above the water in the middle of the cavern. Over and over again it was washed away by the rush of the surf. Always it scrambled back and laid itself down to rest only to be carried away again. Twice it clung to its place while weaker waves rushed over it, each time as soon as the water receded shaking itself like a puppy coming out of the rain.

More than once we saw one of the swimming animals slammed against a rock by the violence of the water. Yet they never showed any signs of injury or even of discomfort. Tough hides and a padding of fat no doubt protected them. They also protected other sea lions from even greater poundings outside the cavern where waves from the open ocean shattered against the headland. Each wave as it met the wall of rock climbed upward stories high, spent itself and fell back in a lacework of foaming waterfalls into the sea. We stopped many times as we climbed the stairs on our return to watch sea lions riding these soaring combers up and up along the rock face of the cliff in an effort to reach a slanting resting place just above the farthest reach of the waves.

Sometimes the first attempt was successful, the sea lion reaching a small, rough ledge where it could cling with its flippers while the water rushed back, then hunch itself upward, a few inches at a time, before the next wave came. But more often it had to try and try again, each time being dragged back before it could get a flipper-hold, skittering down the rocky slide in a long bumping zigzag from waterfall to waterfall as the wave fell away.

A hundred or more of the sea lions had succeeded in reaching the resting place. They stretched out, basking in the sun, some pale yellow, others so dark a brown they seemed almost black. The former were the northern, or Steller's, sea lion, the latter the California sea lion. Here the two species meet. A sign of fall, as surely as the changing color of the leaves, is the presence of the southern animals at the sea lion cave. A few come north each autumn, spend the winter at the cavern, and move south again in the spring. Another indication of the season was the absence of the pigeon guillemot. These black-and-white oceanic birds, with their brilliant red feet at breeding time, nest near the cave in summer. But each year, around Labor Day, they leave to spend the winter at sea.

Where low black rocks appeared and disappeared in the white welter of the surf we noticed what looked like miniature palm trees, each a foot or so high, scattered across the basalt. As each wave struck, they all heeled far over like trees in a hurricane. Yet always when the force of the wave had spent itself they rose upright again. These submarine palms were the remarkable seaweed, *Postelsia palmaeformis*. All down the coast as far as we went with the autumn we saw these treelike algae. And our amazement never lessened at the untiring endurance of these marine plants that, in tumultuous seas, bend and rise again, all day and all night, all the span of their surf-engulfed lives.

Threading their way among these rocks swam a shifting parade of sea lions. Often two would move side by side with noses almost touching for as much as a quarter of a mile. Others would turn over and over in the surf like children at

play. Because these creatures, like the dark-eyed, trustful
harbor seals, are fitted by the economy of nature to be eaters
of fish—usually fish of little commercial importance, at that
—they are persecuted all along the coast. The great cavern
in the Oregon cliff might well have been a slaughter pen
for these animals except for the incorporation of the whole
headland within the boundaries of the Siuslaw National
Forest.

One of the glories of this wonderful coast is the chain of
public parks and sanctuaries that extends down the whole
length of the Oregon shore. We came, the next morning, to
what is probably the oddest link in that chain. This is the
Darlingtonia State Park. It is dedicated to the preservation of
a pitcher plant. When we came north with the spring we
had wandered among a host of insect-catching pitchers in
the open pine woods and savannas of the Cape Fear region
of North Carolina. Here, on the other side of the continent
such carnivorous plants are represented by a single species,
Darlingtonia californica. So restricted is its range that it is
found nowhere else in the world except on this small part of
the Oregon coast and in a few scattered stands over the line
in northern California.

We came to this pitcher-plant sanctuary just north of the
great sand dunes that rise at the mouth of the Siuslaw River.
Only a few acres in extent, it is a low swampy stretch where
the green, hooded pitchers grow densely. In places hundreds
were massed together in almost solid stands. Commonly
called cobra plants because the shape of the hood suggests the
raised head of that serpent, they have been offered for sale
by nurserymen as "cobra orchids." Scattered over these cowl-
like hoods we noticed numerous small translucent spots or
windows. If the insect that once enters the tube of the pitcher
tries to fly out again, it is attracted to these lighter spots,
bumps against the windows and is knocked back into the
tube below. There enzymes secreted by the plant digest the

captured prey. Scientists who have studied these plants have noted an interesting thing—the insects that fertilize their blooms almost never lose their lives in the pitchers. These species rarely seem impelled to enter the tubes.

When we climbed the high dunes to the south we saw between us and the sea a score or more of smaller dunes all elongated, all shaped in smooth, flowing lines, all pointing in the same direction, the direction from which the prevailing winds come from the sea. A few hours later, below Bandon with its hills of spiny Irish furze, we turned west and came out on the wind-swept height of Cape Blanco and saw this same molding effect of the sea gales recorded in a different medium.

For half a mile across the top of this promontory ran a multitude of streamlined masses of the evergreen huckleberry, *Vaccinium ovatum*. They varied in size. Usually they were two feet or so in height near the front. But they all tapered away to the rear like the cockpits of racing planes. Each elongated mound was a solid mass of wiry twigs, twisted and intertwining. Set only a few feet apart, these hundreds of low, wind-molded huckleberry clumps were all streamlined in exactly the same way. They all pointed in exactly the same direction. They all recorded, like a multitude of wild weather vanes, the line of movement of prevailing gales from the sea.

Road menders were burning brush beside the highway that afternoon when we neared Port Orford. And all the air was filled with a strange and wonderful incense. It was the perfume of one of the rarest and most beautiful trees in America. Like the Kirtland's warbler and the *Darlingtonia* pitcher plant, the Port Orford cedar is remarkable for its restricted range. It is almost entirely concentrated in a narrow strip along the coast about thirty miles wide and no more than 200 miles long. We stopped a little farther down the road to spend an hour enjoying the delicate beauty of these

OTTER SURF at the foot of a headland on the Pacific coast. Amid such foaming, seething water the sea otters once lived along much of the western edge of America. The animals sleep offshore entwined in ribbons of kelp.

MONARCH butterflies, above. Below, entrance to the famous
Butterfly Park at Pacific Grove where monarchs overwinter.

aromatic conifers. Each upward-slanting branch was clothed in the golden-green lace of its feathery foliage. In virgin stands these trees sometimes reach a height of 200 feet, the smooth columns of the trunks rising for a hundred feet or more devoid of branches. But here, in second growth, the fernlike fronds of the foliage descended almost to the ground.

I crushed a twig tip between my fingers and for a long time my hand was redolent with the fragrance of the tree's perfume. When we had passed a rambling gray building on Coalbank Slough at Coos Bay, earlier in the day, we had found the air all around it delightfully scented. Later we had learned that this was the sweet smell of the white, satiny, pungently perfumed wood of the Port Orford cedar. There it was being cut and processed for market. Because of its remarkable properties it is always in demand. It is light, strong, durable and resistant to acids. It rides in every automobile as separators in the battery. Sir Thomas Lipton specified that Port Orford cedar be used in the construction of all the yachts he entered in the races for the America's Cup. At one time this fragrant wood was widely used in China for making caskets. And because it takes a high polish and stains beautifully it is employed in cabinet making. Thus the cutting of this rare, restricted tree continues unabated. Unless active steps are taken for their preservation, it is estimated the last of the virgin trees will disappear in less than a quarter of a century.

Another endangered species in this region of beautiful trees is the Oregon myrtle. Ironically the same pamphlet that stressed its scarcity and the need for its protection carried at the end a directory of all the places where products made from the wood of the felled trees might be purchased. Although no two trees could be more different, the myrtle is, in its way, almost as handsome as the cedar. Instead of rising to a spire, as the cedar does, it is solid and rounded. Instead of the filmy lace of the cedar's foliage, its limbs are densely clothed with heavy, glossy leaves. At times the trees seem so solid they might have been carved from wood and painted dark, rich green. We saw them dotting the hillsides and running down the zigzags of the gullies. Where they clustered together the shadows beneath, even at midday, seemed as dark as night. Each of the heavy leaves shone as though coated with a beautiful lacquer. And so it would shine on through the months ahead. For the Oregon myrtle is evergreen. To its glossy foliage autumn brings no change.

But elsewhere as we neared the California line—even in the prolonged Indian summer of this mild climate, even with pink wild roses still blooming beside the road—the changes of the season were apparent. On every breeze rode the cottony drift of the groundsel tree, *Baccharis*. Its early-autumn blooming was over; its late-autumn seeds were on the wind. Although we were now on the fourth great flyway of the continent the birds were few; they had traveled this way long before us. But at once the most beautiful and the most evanescent sign of the altering season was one we saw when, with the sun high in the sky behind us, we looked back up the coast where great spray-crowned combers were parading to shore. As each wave reached a certain point the fragment of a rainbow burst into brilliance low above it and moved slowly down its length to fade and vanish. Once a white gull, soaring on rigid wings, advanced along a wave in pace with the moving colors as though, in a moment of magic, it rode on a rainbow. Seen from our particular vantage point, this vision of fleeting beauty was, in itself, an evidence of the lateness of the season. It indicated how far to the south the sun had traveled.

TWENTY-NINE

THE REDWOODS

THE next afternoon we crossed the line into California.
Twenty miles north of Crescent City, on U.S. Highway 101, at 3:55 P.M., we entered this final state of the trip,
the twenty-sixth, the one in which we would see the most
eventful autumn of our lives come to its end.

California, with a coastline of 1,200 miles, sweeps southward from Oregon to Mexico. Its area is second only to that
of Texas. It contains both the highest and the lowest points
in the United States. Forty-one of its peaks rise above 10,000
feet. For the naturalist, this land of deserts and glaciers, forests and headlands, sequoias and sea otters, the rare white-
tailed kite and the rarer condor, provides, in its limitless
variety, fascination enough for a score of lifetimes.

Hardly had we entered the state when we found ourselves
in the midst of one of its most impressive attractions. All
down the fog belt of the coastal mountains, in a chain 450
miles long, the groves of the redwoods rise, each with the
lofty columns, the filtered light, the still serenity of a living
cathedral. When John Masefield, the Poet Laureate of England, first saw the redwoods he set down the observation
that the trees rose up with dignity and power and majesty,
as though they had been there forever. Even if we knew nothing of their great antiquity we would sense in their presence a
calm aloofness to the cares of the minute. As many as fifty

human generations—each with its labors, its adventures, its achievements and disasters—had come and gone during the span of life of some of the immense trees we looked upon and touched.

Once a native of Europe, of China, even of the arctic regions, the sequoia is now indigenous only to California and a small portion of the southwestern corner of Oregon. The big tree, *Sequoia gigantea,* is confined to the high Sierra Nevadas; the redwood, *Sequoia sempervirens,* to the coast. Rarely does the redwood grow more than thirty miles inland or at an elevation of as much as 3,000 feet above sea level. The big tree exceeds the redwood in bulk but the latter is higher. It towers above all other trees on earth. It is the tallest living thing.

Over the line in Oregon, up Grants Pass way, we visited the most northern of the redwoods. Then working from grove to grove we moved south. We crossed Rough and Ready Creek. We crossed Rowdy Creek. We came to Smith River and the Jedediah Smith State Park, northeast of Crescent City—both named in honor of that remarkable Bible-carrying pioneer trapper, crackshot and explorer who, although comparatively unknown, ranks with Lewis and Clark in his contributions toward the opening of the West.

We originally crossed his trail on the Great Salt Lake Desert of Utah. He was the first white man to span that desert. He was the first to cross the Sierra Nevadas. He was the first to reach California by the overland route. He was the discoverer of the Great South Pass in the Rockies through which the main tide of the westward movement flowed. In ten adventurous years he roamed the western wilderness from the Missouri to California and from Canada to Mexico. He was only thirty-three when he met his lonely death at the hands of Comanches somewhere between the Arkansas and Cimarron rivers on the old Santa Fe Trail. Three years before, on

June 2c, 1828, he had stood beside the California river and among the California redwoods that now commemorate his name.

Every scenic route, we have decided, should be traveled at least twice—once in each direction. So not infrequently in those days of wonderful trees we turned around and back-tracked to see some grove from a new angle or in a different lighting. At times Highway 101—which for long stretches later on would trace the path of El Camino Real, that ancient Royal Road of the Spanish padres—carried us close to the sea and almost 1,000 feet above the surf. At other times it wound inland and the forest of the giants closed around us. Once, I remember, when the great trees stood some distance from the highway early in the morning, the shadows of their thin, topmost spires barred the concrete as the dark lines of the cornstalks had ribbed the road in Illinois, now so many miles behind us.

Thus down the long chain of more than forty groves we wandered. We came to the valley of the Eel River with its virgin stands. We came to the Avenue of the Giants. We came to the Dyerville Flats and the Founders' Tree, the high-est in the world, its spire-tip 364 feet above the ground. We stayed overnight at Laytonville and found our car shining with a thick rime of fog-frost in the morning. We wound among the hills near Santa Rosa where Luther Burbank had used his shoelaces and strips of his necktie to mark special wild plants for subsequent transplanting in the early days. We came to a sign in the middle of one magnificent redwood grove: "Dump No Garbage." We passed a gigantic stump that had been turned into a railed-in observation platform, with stairs leading up to it, and a roadside giant with an arch cut in its trunk big enough for automobiles to drive through. And, later on, in a narrow canyon threaded by a creek, we valked amid the redwoods that have been seen by more people than any others, the trees of the Muir Woods National Monument, only ten miles from the Golden Gate Bridge, north of San Francisco.

Enveloping each grove we came to was the same cathedral hush, the same air of profound peace and unhurried calm. It was an atmosphere as remote from the clang and whir of city life as it was from the crash and seethe of headland surf. The trees seemed living in the world of Swinburne's line where "all winds are quiet as the sun, all waters as the shore." They held something of the calm of the stars, something of the tranquillity of the placid sunset sea.

Deeply furrowed or vertically fluted, the great trunks rose from among the ferns and oxalis like prototypes of the classic Greek column. Many were bare of branches for a hundred feet or more. The spongy layer of the outer bark, encasing them sometimes to the depth of a foot, is one of the secrets of the redwoods' longevity. It resists fire and it cushions abrasions. At one turn of the road in a grove of giants we saw the bark near the base of a tree gnawed by passing cars that had swung too close. They had bitten and gouged grooves in the bark without reaching the wood below. Other factors in the long life of the redwood are its immunity to the attacks of fungi and insects and the resistance of the heartwood to rot. Fallen trees that have been buried for more than two centuries have been found to have heartwood that is still hard and perfectly sound.

Although it is largely immune to insect and fungus and fire, the redwood is not immune to the saw. Any fine morning a power saw can fell a tree that took a thousand years to grow. It can destroy a redwood that was alive when the Normans invaded England. All down the coastal belt for more than half a century lumbermen have been reaping where they have not sowed. Red sawdust blew across our road from busy mills and we often met what looked in the distance to be a milk truck coming down the road—a lumber truck loaded with a single great tanklike section of a giant log. Three hundred sawmills were operating in the redwood counties of Del Norte, Humboldt and Mendocino when we went through. A single mill in Humboldt County occupies 400 acres, almost the total extent of the Muir Woods National Monument. Even the bark of these noble trees is in demand. Because it is resistant to moisture, insects and decay and does not absorb odors, it is shredded and baled and sold for use in insulating and air conditioning.

When Jedediah Smith wandered north among the redwoods, a century and a quarter ago, these towering trees covered at least 2,000,000 acres. The intervening years have seen fully half this stand destroyed. Since 1918 one of the most effective friends a tree ever had, the Save-the-Redwoods League, has been working for the establishment of sanctuaries. Through its efforts more than 50,000 acres of virgin trees have been set aside. Gifts from private individuals throughout the country have resulted in the establishment of more than 125 small memorial groves, each providing protection for its redwood inhabitants.

For a tree that may be higher than the Statue of Liberty, that may weigh more than 2,000,000 pounds, that may contain enough wood to build several houses or a complete church, the redwood has a comparatively shallow root system. The leaves that clothe its branches are also unexpectedly small. All the vast cumulus clouds of green feathery foliage that fill the upper spaces of the tree are formed of tiny scalelike leaves that are only a quarter of an inch long. But even more paradoxical than its roots and its leaves are the cones of the redwood.

At the California Academy of Sciences, in San Francisco, we later examined an exhibit of the cones of twenty-three western evergreens. The tiniest of them all, less than an inch long, came from this world's highest tree. The actual seed from which the lofty spire of a redwood springs is hardly larger than the head of a pin. All the vast trunk, all the towering height of the tree, all the long span of its life that may extend over a period of 2,000 years, all these have their beginning in a seed that seems trifling and inconsequential compared to a lima bean or a garden pea.

In the forest only a small fraction—some estimates place it as low as 2 per cent—of the redwoods grow from these seeds. Most come from sprouts that emerge from the knobby, boulderlike burls that form around the base of the trunk. Oftentimes a ring of such sprouts will encircle the stump of a felled tree.

Along paths that led us through the eerie, gray-green half-light of the redwood glades, we found slight evidence of the changing season. A few yellow leaves on lower bushes, a drying of the foliage of the tan oaks, the acorn-shaped fallen fruit of the myrtle or laurel—these were evident. But in the long life of the ancient trees, the changing seasons—was this the five-hundredth or the thousandth autumn?—passed almost invisibly, leaving almost no mark that caught the eye.

"You need a calendar," one of the park rangers at the Muir Woods declared, "to tell the Fourth of July from Christmas."

In fact, here in the redwood belt, the seasons are mainly two instead of four: the dry season of summer and the wet season of winter. Comparatively few plants bloom in the deep shade of the forest floor. But those that do begin flowering as early as February. Trillium and adder's-tongue and clintonia appear. However their blooming season—like that of the redwood rose—is comparatively short. The last flowers of all are provided by the azaleas. Along Redwood Creek in the Muir Woods they unfold in June and July. When their petals drop, the blooming season of the year is over.

Along some of the trails through the twilight of the redwood floor the air was filled with the rich smell of fallen laurel leaves. Each pungently aromatic leaf that was broken underfoot released its fragrance into the air. The scent brought to mind barber shops and bay rum. It explained another name sometimes given to the California laurel: the bay tree. We were following one such perfumed path when we heard far up in the sky above us, invisible behind the clouds of the redwood foliage, a jet plane passing by. A new sound had been added to the ancient noise of wind and rain so long associated with these age-old trees.

I had first seen the redwoods at their southern fringe, seen them briefly one winter day years before. Beyond a small mountain brook, spanned by a bridge of planks, they had risen in a clustering grove of giants. As I had walked among them, out of the half-light under the trees a gray-and-white kitten suddenly appeared. Apparently coming from some house in the region, it walked toward me unafraid. It waved its tail. It rubbed against my legs and purred. Then it wandered off again. That was thirty years ago—close to the thirty-three the dictionary gives as the definition of a human generation. Yet the scene is still vivid. I have remembered that kitten among the great trees, remembered it many times in many places. I remembered it now near the end of our days of roaming down the chain of groves. In its appearance and disappearance there seemed something symbolic, as though it were a performer in some masque of time—this wandering, transitory speck of life set against the great span of the redwoods.

THIRTY

VALLEY OF THE WEST

INLAND from the sea, 100 miles from the redwoods, somewhere between the Bear and the Yuba rivers in northern California, we came to a plowed field as brilliant as a flower. All its furrows stretched away in the morning sunshine a deep, rich apricot hue. Nowhere else in nearly 17,000 miles of traveling had we encountered such soil. It added another shade to the innumerable earth colors we had enjoyed. Anyone who crosses the continent by a wandering course sees not only the power and glory and wealth of America but also the exhaustless variety of its beauty—even such simple, endlessly changing beauty as the color of its soil.

During these days we meandered widely amid new, inland signs of the season. We met trucks hurrying down from mountain forests piled high with Christmas trees. We caught glimpses of the brilliant holly-red of the toyon berries. We went past boys clambering among roadside walnut trees, shaking the branches.

Here we were in the upper part of California's Great Central Valley. This titanic bowl, elliptical in shape, is about fifty miles wide and 400 miles long. Its area is greater than that of New Hampshire and Vermont combined. It stretches from near Redding, just below Mt. Shasta, to the country beyond the Kern River, south of Bakersfield. Like the Great Valley of the Appalachians, it runs north and south. Western geologists call it the California Trough.

Parallel to the length of its lower half extends the San Andreas Fault, one of the most famous lines of weakness in the earth's crust. For millions of years the area has been geologically unstable. The trough itself came into being during the formation of the Sierra Nevada mountains in Pleistocene times. Then, under inconceivable pressures, a great slab of the earth's surface tilted slowly upward like one-half of a rising drawbridge. When the movement stopped the lofty range of mountains lifted in a serrated skyline to the east. During the ages since it was formed the California Trough has been gradually filling with detritus brought down by streams from the surrounding highlands. In this valley wells have been drilled 3,000 feet deep without striking bedrock.

In all its 400-mile length there is only one break through which rivers can escape to the sea. The Sacramento—carrying the waters of Grindstone Creek and Antelope Creek and Cottonwood Creek, of the Bear and Feather and Yuba rivers— flows down from the north. The San Joaquin, almost as silt-filled as the Mississippi, moves up from the south. They join near Stockton. Their united flow pours into San Pablo Bay and passes out through the Golden Gate into the Pacific. All the water draining from the length and breadth of the valley emerges through this one break almost at the exact center of the western wall.

To the pioneers, weary of mountains and canyons, this wide central valley of California was a boulevard, a land of easy traveling. Where we advanced with the aid of road maps and highway numbers, a hundred years later, they had guided themselves by the lay of the land. Still other travelers, then moving across the valley floor in an annual autumn journey, were obtaining their bearings in a different way, in a manner that is still a mystery. These were the ladybird beetles that each year take wing in uncounted millions to converge on certain mountain canyons where they mass together among the rocks in winter hibernation.

We drove for fifty miles into the wildly beautiful Feather River Canyon, north of Oroville, searching for these spectacular beetle concentrations. We stopped near red madrone trees to scan the walls of the gorge. We peered down the rocky river banks. But only once did we see what may have been a massing of the beetles, a dark-red splash of color among the higher rocks of the canyon wall. Each winter "ladybug" prospectors search this area for pockets and veins of beetles. Sometimes the insects form solid masses several feet thick. Scooped like grain into gunny sacks, they are carried down to the valley and sold by the gallon to farmers and orchardists who distribute them over their land to consume aphids and other agricultural pests. We sought to find one of these ladybug hunters —a man with the storybook name of Golden Land who lived at Feather Falls—but without success. Customers from as far away as Texas send to Oroville for consignments of ladybird beetles. One gallon—about 135,000 ladybugs—is prescribed for five acres. More than 100,000,000 of the spotted beetles are shipped from the region in the course of a year.

Nobody knows from how large an area these concentrations are drawn. Nobody knows how far the insects travel to reach their hibernation grounds. Nobody knows whether, when winter ends, they migrate back to the places where they were born. But it is known that year after year they congregate in the same parts of the same canyons. It has been suggested that the winds that blow over wide areas of the valley into the canyon mouths may guide the flying insects. Once inside the passages they may recognize by scent the location of their ancestral wintering grounds.

That night, near Sutter Buttes north of Yuba City, our old friend of the moonlit badlands, a burrowing owl, fluttered up in the glare of our headlights. The next day we saw half a dozen more of these same owls when we rode north and west across rolling rangeland to visit still another wonderful tree, the venerable Hooker Oak of Chico. In the fall of 1877, John

Muir had brought Asa Gray, the leading American botanist, and Sir Joseph Hooker, Director of the Royal Gardens at Kew, England, to see the oak. The tree was later named in honor of Hooker by its owner, John Bidwell. Justly rated as one of the greatest of the California pioneers, Bidwell had come west before the gold rush, at the age of twenty-one, a member of the first overland wagon train to reach the coast. His vast Rancho Chico was famed for its fertile land, its experimental orchards and its native trees. Oregonians and Washingtonians, amid their towering firs and spruces, are wont to refer to the hillside oaks of northern California as "deer grass." But even in their eyes the Hooker Oak, largest of all the valley white oaks, must appear a magnificent tree.

We came to it at sunset. Later we saw it at dawn, at midday, in many subtle variations of lighting. Always it gave the same impression of symmetry, of strength, of long endurance. The outstretched arms of its lowest branches cover a span of 153 feet. Eight feet from the ground its trunk has a girth of more than 28 feet. Its massive rounded crown rises more than 100 feet in the air. And the circumference of the circle of shade it casts when the sun is directly overhead is 481 feet. Allowing two square feet to a person it has been calculated that this single widespread tree could provide shelter for a throng of nearly 8,000 people.

A ton of acorns—each cartridge-shaped and more than two inches long—will sometimes carpet the ground beneath the Hooker Oak during autumns of special abundance. To the Indians of the Great Central Valley acorns were the staple food. They held the same place in their lives that pine nuts occupied among the tribes of Utah. Separating the good acorns from the bad by the simple expedient of dropping them in water and discarding the lighter, wormy ones that floated on the surface, they roasted them, ground them up, made cakes and gruel of them. But always the Indians had competition from other acorn-gatherers—the squirrels, the jays, the woodpeckers. When we looked up along the trunk of the massive oak we saw the bark peppered with acorns. Each was wedged tightly into a small hole. This was the work of that famed acorn-hoarder, the California woodpecker.

Later we saw telephone poles, cottonwood trees and even the gables of houses decorated with these stores of acorns. William Leon Dawson, in his *The Birds of California*, tells of a telephone pole in the Sacramento Valley that held 1,500 acorns. He recalls a large sycamore, growing near Santa Barbara, that had 20,000 embedded in its trunk. And he notes that a towering ponderosa pine in Strawberry Valley, in the San Jacinto Mountains, was studded from base to crown. It contained, as near as he could calculate, at least 50,000 acorns. The California woodpeckers are extremely sociable, and such large stores of food are the work of many birds. Occasionally an almond will be added to the hoard and in rare instances instinct will go astray and a woodpecker will carefully tamp into place a pebble instead of a nut.

Each time we stood beneath the Hooker Oak we heard, far and near around us, the loud cackling, up-and-down laughter of this woodpecker's call. We saw the birds flying away with black backs and white rump patches. We saw their faces through our binoculars, faces with spots of black and red and white and yellow that give them the appearance of clowns in a circus. Other birds were everywhere—in the open spaces around the big tree, along the overgrown banks of near-by Big Chico Creek, amid the branches of twin cottonwoods that rose side by side sheathed almost from top to bottom with the russet-red of wild grape vines. We traced the lazy drawling sweetness of a song we had never heard before to the golden-crowned sparrow. We saw the brown towhee with plumage as soft as the waxwing's. Once 100 western robins alighted around the great oak when the sun was hidden behind clouds. The clouds parted, the sun came out, and a great chorus of robin music filled the air.

For a tree as huge as the Hooker Oak the leaves that clothe its story on story of outstretched limbs are surprisingly small. Only a few lay scattered over the ground. Leaf-fall for the valley oaks of this region comes late in December. But for many neighboring trees the drifting autumn descent of foliage was in full progress or had already taken place. Just north of Chico we watched a small flock of pine siskins swoop down like striped goldfinches and alight in an almond tree. Instantly a shower of leaves fell to the ground. In these late-autumn days they were set on a hair trigger. Even so light a touch as a small bird's foot upon a branch was sufficient to send them raining down. Laboratory experiments in recent years have led scientists to believe that the falling of leaves may be controlled to a considerable extent by the hormone auxin, created within the leaf. As long as it continues to be made in sufficient quantities the stem remains attached to the twig. But when the foliage is damaged or when changes in the season slow down the production of the hormone, then leaf-fall occurs.

A dozen miles to the west of Chico, the next day, we crossed a lonely stretch of the Sacramento River. As far as we could see its winding banks were lined with yellow-leaved cottonwoods lumpy with mistletoe. For miles on the way to Orland we ran through almond groves. Then for other miles, heading south toward Williams, we were amid dikes and rice fields and level land stretching away to a low horizon. We passed a leafless tree filled with western bluebirds. We went by a dozen American egrets scattered among sheep feeding in a creekside pasture. This was the beginning of one of the great bird days of our lives.

For between Willows and Williams we came to the teeming Sacramento National Wildlife Refuge. This sanctuary is to the fourth great flyway of the continent what Bear River is to the third. Its 10,000 acres of marshes, ponds and flat lands provide a haven for vast numbers of migrants each fall. During the peak of the autumn concentration it may contain as many as 1,115,000 pintail at one time. The rare little Ross's goose, coming south from its nesting grounds along the arctic shore east of the Mackenzie Delta, spends the winter here. As we followed the winding trail of the dike tops the rest of that day, hundreds of thousands of ducks and geese were scattered across the sanctuary, and the sky around us was continually filled with the moving skeins and clouds of flying waterfowl.

Wherever we went the roar of waterfowl wings preceded us as mallard and pintail and baldpate and green-winged teal —perhaps some of the very birds we saw at Bear River—shot into the air from behind the curtain of the tule rushes. Coot, like thousands of dark chickens, wandered along the dike tops or strummed their odd, metallic calls amid the cattails. At times we came out on openings where, in a long white drift across yellow fields, 10,000 snow geese fed together. In other openings these birds were mixed with Canada geese, white-fronted geese and the mallard-sized cackling geese that, with their short bills, resembled snub-nosed Canadas in miniature. In these mixed flocks we noticed it was always the Canada geese that took off first of all. Here in the Great Central Valley of California, as on the sandbar opposite Farm Island in the Missouri River, they were the wary, the cautious breed.

The continuous calling of the multitudinous waterfowl came to us from all sides—from across the tannish masses of the cattails, from behind the dark green and brown stands of the tule rushes, from over the yellow plains of the rice fields. There were times when this wild chorus mingled together into a confused murmur like bees humming or water rushing over rapids in the distance. Toward the end of the afternoon, while we were still walking in brilliant sunshine, the sky to the north grew sullen. Storm clouds, swollen and slaty-blue, rose above the horizon. For a time, later on, we saw everything touched by that peculiar enchanted light that sometimes invests a countryside before a storm. Once more than 1,000 snow geese peeled from the ground together and trailed in a long procession, gleaming white and spotlighted by the sun, across the backdrop of this dark northern sky.

It was before the windstorm struck that evening that we witnessed the homecoming of the blackbirds, the event that stands out most vividly of all in our memories of that day. As early as three o'clock they began leaving the rice fields and returning to the cattail and tule marshes where they roost. At first they approached flying low and in small flocks. Then the concentrations swelled. Flock joined flock. The numbers pyramided. We were in the midst of swirling swarms of birds, flowing rivers of birds, deafened by their clamor.

We had seen huge concentrations of redwings in Florida and along the Gulf Coast in Louisiana. But nowhere had we experienced anything comparable to this. And here we had four kinds of blackbirds roosting together. We identified them all that afternoon—the common redwing with yellow bordering its scarlet epaulets; the tricolored redwing with white replacing the yellow; the bicolored redwing with red patches alone; and the Brewer's blackbird with dark plumage, white eyes and no wing patches at all.

At first we tried to estimate the numbers of the homecoming birds. But soon we lost all count. They poured over us in ever-increasing flocks. They came faster and faster. We were overwhelmed by numbers. At the very least we saw 500,000 blackbirds coming home that day. The number may well have been twice that total. Experts have calculated that there are often more than 1,000,000 individuals in these autumn concentrations. Nowhere else in America can more blackbirds be seen at one time than at the Sacramento refuge in the fall.

Before settling down for the night, the great clouds of birds —tens and hundreds of thousands of birds—turned and swooped in aerial evolutions, diving toward the marsh, zooming up again, whirling and dancing, flying in unison, seeming to enjoy the playtime after the work of the day. We saw everything around us, the skeins of white waterfowl, the horizon

line of misty mountains to the west, through this storm of
flying blackbirds. Flock after flock, hundreds and thousands
at a time, they dropped into the marsh, blackening the cattails and sinking into the acres of crisscrossing tules. We
could see them working their way downward among the
rushes. And always fresh flocks whirled above them ready to
descend in turn.

The sun set that day with little color, a red ball disappearing behind a low wall of slate-covered clouds. And still the
blackbirds came. In the deepening dusk we could hear the
rushing sound of their wings as flock succeeded flock. There
were literally acres of blackbirds around us when, with the
lights switched on and the storm close at hand, we started
away at last. We talked about how that scene would look on
a calm evening silvered by moonlight. And we planned to
return next day when the storm had passed and see it all
again.

But the storm did not pass. We awoke in Williams the
next morning in the midst of slashing rain and a fifty-mile-an-
hour gale. I switched on the radio. The weather report predicted continued gales with the wind rising to as much as
eighty-five miles an hour by night. We decided to move 100
miles on down the valley away from the storm.

In that wide level land the gusts at times caught us in
smashing sidewise blows that sent the car veering half across
the pavement. Walnuts rolled along the road where trees had
been stripped in the night, and long zigzag gashes were opening on slopes as fertile soil washed away in boiling, swirling
rivers of runoff water. We passed bedraggled livestock feeding
tail to the wind. And once, under the ragged, dirty-skirted
clouds that swept low over the land, we saw a flock of snow
and Canada geese struggling to descend in an open field. Time
after time gusts caught them and tossed them aloft before
they finally touched the ground. What was happening, we
wondered, to the blackbirds and the teeming waterfowl at

the Sacramento sanctuary? This was a great emergency. But it was also a natural emergency, the kind birds have endured for ages. Wind and rain, weather at its worst, these they were equipped to meet. It was the unnatural emergencies, the pressure of shooting, the draining of nesting grounds, the destruction of wintering areas, that endangered them more.

In the calm of another evening, more than 100 miles south of the sanctuary, we climbed out of the Great Central Valley into the foothills of the Sierra Nevada mountains. Our road reared, dived, wound, wriggled upward, twisted downward to bring us, long after sunset, to a narrow valley threaded by a river that seemed half lost in the rocky maze of its floodtime bed. Coming west we had crossed many tributary streams. Some were called brooks, some creeks, some branches, some prongs, some runs. Here they were known as forks. One California stream goes by the name of the West Fork of the South Fork of the North Fork of the San Joaquin River. The stream beside which we stopped was the South Fork of the American River. And the spot where we walked along its bank was the exact site where, on January 24, 1848, James W. Marshall had glimpsed in the tailrace of Sutter's mill the yellow specks that had started the California gold rush with all its world-encircling reverberations.

A century before our visit this lonely valley had teemed with frenzied activity. But long since the fever had died away. The quiet of that evening was as profound as it had been all through the ages before Marshall's discovery. We wandered among low willows beside the stream. The dark forms of small birds flitted before us in the deeper shadows. Then one lifted its voice in a wonderful song, a minor melody, simple, plaintive, infinitely moving. In the tranquil, windless silence of that hour when it was no longer day and still not yet night, this frail and haunting strain was repeated again and again, now here, now there, perhaps always the same voice, perhaps the song of several singers.

Over the rocks, through the weeds, in deep sand, among brown mulleins, across flood debris, under the digger pines with their great fallen cones, we followed the siren song of the unknown bird. But it remained mysterious and undiscovered. We glimpsed only flitting shapes that disappeared as soon as seen. The dusk became chill, the shadows deepened, and the moon grew bright above the valley before we gave up the quest. But now, whenever we think of Sutter's mill or the gold rush or the river or the valley at twilight, we are reminded of that simple, strangely affecting song heard at the end of a late-autumn day.

We drove away in the moonlight and the silence of the night. And I remembered John Burroughs on his second visit to the Grand Canyon. After remarking how beautiful it all was, he turned away with the added words:

"But there can be only one first time."

Perhaps someday we would discover the name of our unknown singer. Perhaps sometime we would hear its minor melody once more. But never again would it be quite so affecting. For here we had heard it—as we had experienced so many things in our autumn journey now so close to its end—as a fresh, memorable, deeply moving first time.

THIRTY-ONE

OTTER SURF

THE hundredth day of our trip—the day of the cinnamon teal and the thirteen magpie trees—came at Los Banos. Here we were 120 miles south of Sutter's mill, at the western rim of the Great Central Valley, facing the passes that lead over the coastal mountains to Monterey. Thanksgiving was now well behind us. Christmas lights and Christmas music and Christmas decorations were a feature of every town we passed through. The end of our carefree autumn wandering seemed rushing toward us at breakneck speed.

"The weeks," Nellie said that morning, "are going by like days!"

Ever since Bear River we had been looking for the cinnamon teal. This was the only species of those swift, colorful little waterfowl—for which I have always hoped some remote ancestor of mine was named—that we had never seen. We were familiar with the green-wings and the blue-wings, even with the European teal. But at Bear River the cinnamon teal had already gone west to the Sacramento refuge. When we reached the Sacramento they had just left for the third great stepping-stone in their southward movement, the sanctuary at Los Banos. We had been behind them all the way. And here at the ponds and tule marshes of Los Banos we found that only the week before they had been the commonest duck of all; now, we were told, only a few stragglers remained.

All that day we searched in a land filled with the life and

beauty of unnumbered migrants. Once more clouds of snow geese twinkled in the sky. Ducks, thousands at a time, shot up from behind the tule, the windy roaring of their wings like long gusts rushing through the treetops. Here, in smaller form, were Bear River and the Sacramento refuge all over again. We watched whistling swans and cackling geese and little brown cranes. Along the miles of roads and trails we saw black phoebes and long-billed curlews, violet-green swallows and Florida gallinules. But in all that vast, wonderful concentration of bird life we failed to find the cinnamon-colored waterfowl we sought. It was nearly sunset when a small dark duck flashed by, pitching down onto a little stretch of glowing water walled in by rushes. For a moment we had it clear in our glasses—the reddish plumage, the pale blue patches on the wings, the head with no white crescent before the eye. This was our long-sought bird—the last of the teal.

Driving back to Los Banos that evening we came to a row of thirteen eucalyptus trees on the edge of a pasture. All around them the air was heavy with the scent of their medicinal oils. So shaggy were the trunks of several with strips and sheets of hanging bark that the trees looked as though they had been struck by lightning. Each year this shedding of the bark increases in the winds and rains of autumn. At the same time the latter days of fall bring the beginning of the flowering period for the eucalyptus. Its season of blooming extends from December through May.

Darting among the gray-green foliage of the trees, scattered across the level ground of the pasture, brilliant in their contrasting black and white, more than 100 magpies had gathered for the night. This was their roost. To it they had come from a wide area. As we watched the birds constantly changing position, screaming raucously all the while, we saw others arriving to join the flock. Every bird has a bright-yellow bill. Only in California, mainly in the Great Central Valley, are these yellow-billed magpies found. Although the eastern edge of their range is as close as fifty miles to that of the more widespread black-billed American magpie, nowhere do the two ranges overlap. In the dusk we drove away from these thirteen magpie trees puzzling over why two species of birds, almost identical otherwise, should evolve bills of a different color. Within their respective ranges what possible contribution to survival was provided by the color of the bill? Yet every single magpie east of the Sierra has a black bill; every single magpie west of the Sierra a yellow bill.

With the sun behind us next morning we climbed into the foothills of the Diablo Range. A faint flush of green was already spreading across these tawny-yellow slopes in the wake of the first autumn rains. Mist closed in around us on Pacheco Pass, then disappeared again as we dropped down among the sycamores and vineyards of the valley beyond, then enveloped us once more on Hecker Pass at the top of the Santa Cruz Mountains before we rode down the last slope of the coastal range to Watsonville and the edge of Monterey Bay with its mild climate, its sea figs, its bush lupines and its California poppies still in bloom.

Around this famous bay the year resembles one long Indian summer. There is hardly more than ten degrees difference between the temperatures of midsummer and midwinter, between the mean for August and that for January. The weather is more uniform along this part of the California coast than at any other place in the United States. Thunderstorms are so rare they average only one or two a year. In San Francisco, where virtually the same conditions prevail, summers are actually slightly cooler than autumns. The frequent fogs that shield the land from the sun, and the sea breezes that pass over the cool California Current before reaching the coast, both help moderate the summer heat.

We turned south from Watsonville, following the curve of the bay. We stopped at Moss Landing and at Elkhorn Slough, famous for their shorebirds. We traversed a wide.

flat land below Castroville where tens of thousands of acres of artichokes spread away around us. It was over such fields, a few days later, that Charles and Viola Anderson, of Salinas, showed us one of the rare forms of wildlife on the North American continent, a beautiful, beneficial creature that persecution has pushed close to extinction. In Audubon's time the white-tailed kite ranged eastward through Texas to Florida. Before it received belated legal protection, however, it had almost entirely disappeared throughout its range except for comparatively small areas near the California coast. In 1927 when Ralph Hoffman published his *Birds of the Pacific States,* he estimated that there were no more than fifty pairs of white-tailed kites in all of California.

On the day we hunted for this rare bird the wind blew heavily across the miles of thistlelike artichokes. All around the mouth of the Salinas River the autumn harvest was in progress. Truck after truck passed us loaded with the edible flower-heads of the plants. Toward midafternoon Anderson pointed into the wind. A bird about the size of a small duck hawk, but more light and buoyant in its flight, was coming toward us, turning, hovering, scudding before the gusts, sweeping with the grace of a skilled skater on ice, its long, pointed wings delicately adjusted to the play of the air currents. As it drew nearer we saw its white head and white tail and the black patches at the bend of its wings that give it the colloquial name of the black-shouldered kite. Writing of a smaller South American form of this bird which he remembered from his youth on the pampas of Argentina, W. H. Hudson recalled how "it delights to soar during a high wind, and will spend hours in the sport, rising and falling alternately, and at times, seeming to abandon itself to the fury of the gale, is blown away like thistledown, until, suddenly recovering itself, it shoots back to its original position."

Toward sunset that day we were driving home when we saw another of these airy, graceful kites hovering on the wind close to the Salinas River. It was not more than 100 yards from the road and only fifty feet above the rows of artichokes. It paid no attention to us. Facing the wind, its slender wings rising high as it fluttered, it turned its beautiful sleek white head this way and that as it peered intently at the ground below. Rats, mice, gophers, grasshoppers, small snakes and shrews are its usual fare. Sometimes 90 per cent of its food consists of meadow mice, prolific creatures that begin to breed when only three weeks old. In spite of its constant aid to man, the kite often has been killed, its habit of hovering over one spot, absorbed in its hunting, making it an easy target. Another factor in the reduction of its numbers has been the beauty of its eggs. Creamy white and overlaid with blotches of rich and varied shadings of brown, they are the most striking eggs laid by any hawk. In former times they were much prized and sought after by the avid egg-collector, a species of bird enemy now happily almost extinct.

Three times the kite we watched swept in swift circles, its snow-white tail spreading wide as it turned. But each time it curved back to hang with beating wings above almost the exact spot where first we saw it. For nearly five minutes it concentrated on the ground below. Then it ceased hovering, swung off in a great arc to the south and went racing away downwind. In an amazingly short time it grew small in the distance. At leisure, close at hand, we had seen, beyond our hopes, this rare and beautiful bird.

A continent-span away from the low dunes of Monomoy, the next day we wandered among other low dunes edging the shore just north of Monterey. We sat in the warm sand and ate our lunch of French bread and bits of cheese. Around us rose bush-lupines, silvery-leaved, and sand verbenas, yellow-flowered in December. In the distance, clustered on a curve of the shore, the colorful buildings of the old Spanish capital of California crowded down to the edge of the bay. Rich in beauty and rich in history, the whole region of the

Monterey Peninsula forms one of the most attractive parts of all America.

It was at Monterey that Thomas Nuttall landed on the North American mainland again after his voyage to Hawaii. It was at Monterey that Richard Henry Dana came ashore from the brig *Pilgrim* during his *Two Years Before the Mast*. It was at Monterey, in 1831, that two great pioneer botanists —David Douglas, the Scotsman, returning from his lonely wanderings through the Northwest, and Thomas Coulter, the Irishman, the first scientist to cross the Colorado Desert in search of plants—met and compared their experiences. It is easy to understand the emotion with which Douglas wrote home at the time: "And I assure you, from my heart, it is a terrible pleasure to me thus to meet a really good man, and one with whom I can talk plants."

Along the very beach that curved away below our dunes, Robert Louis Stevenson had walked in 1879. He had noted that it would be hard to find a more solitary path or one more exciting to the mind. In his chapter on "The Old Pacific Capital" in *Across the Plains* he recalled: "Strange sea-tangles, new to the European eye, the bones of whales, or sometimes a whole whale's carcase white with carrion-gulls and poisoning the wind, lie scattered here and there along the sands." At the same season of the year, three-quarters of a century later, we followed the same miles of bay-shore. The whales were gone. Monterey had grown. But long stretches of the beach were still solitary, still exciting to the mind.

The hoarse barking of sea lions reached us from far across the intense blue waters of the bay. Close at hand that most beautiful of western gulls—the Heermann's, with its red bill and snowy head, its dusky wings bordered at the rear with white, its black tail ending in a shining white band—paraded by, riding updrafts above the breaking waves. And all along the bayward side of the dunes sea figs spread their dense mats, the fleshy fingers of the succulent leaves upthrust like myriad small bananas. Some of these masses were a dozen feet across. Others extended runners outward from their rims like the points of a star. All originally had been green; now gaudy autumn coloring, flame and coral red, was running across the masses. Another sign of fall, the fruit with its innumerable tiny figlike seeds, was maturing on the vines. When Stevenson picked his way among the whale skeletons of this shore, just such fruit no doubt was ripening and the mats of the sea figs, then, as now, were touched with the same flame of autumn red.

So, too, across the peninsula at Point Lobos—where Whaler's Knoll was the inspiration for Spyglass Hill in *Treasure Island*—ferns in all probability were unrolling their fiddleheads at the time of Stevenson's autumn visit just as they were at the time of ours. For here there is a spring-in-autumn. Ken Legg, the enthusiastic naturalist at the Point Lobos state park, told us he sees the first signs of spring each year in mid-November. In the following weeks buds swell, ferns unroll; events that usually take place at the end of winter here take place at the end of fall.

But, year around, the unique beauty of this 354-acre preserve is provided by the green, flaring, wind-formed Monterey cypresses along the edge of the headland. Once widely distributed these trees are now confined to the rocky coast of the Monterey Peninsula region. Many, particularly those in saddles or draws, stream inland, flattened and elongated like flames in the wind. They represent the spirit of the gale-swept headlands as the gaunt Saguaro cactus represents the spirit of the dry Sonoran desert.

Wherever the trails led us along the edge of the cliffs, the wild, sculptured beauty of these trees formed the most impressive feature of the landscape. Once where a score of cypresses huddled together at the brink of a cliff, all the ends of the dead twigs were plated with brilliant red. They seemed to have been dipped in sealing wax. This coating was the alga, *Trentapohlia aurea*. And darting among these colorful twigs were colorful birds, little warblers with brilliant black-and-yellow faces, the Townsend's warbler, named for Nuttall's young companion. Sometimes the tiny gray bush-tits of Point Lobos coat their nests with the red alga. Always such nests are in the midst of twigs of the same flaunting color. Thus, gaudy in gaudy surroundings, they are made inconspicuous.

All around the base of the cliffs, all around the offshore rocks where sea lions basked, all around the bird islands black with roosting cormorants, all around the coves where red phalaropes were swimming, the blue of the water was hidden beneath tossing ridges and blankets of creamy foam. But farther out the water was unflecked and brilliantly clear. One of the profound impressions left by all this part of the coast is the blue of the sea. Richly, wonderfully blue, with infinitely varied shadings blending together, the water rolls in from the deep. On this rocky coast there is no silt to muddy the colors. Here we look into a clearer medium. We see the sky reflected to greater depths. And the glorious richness and variety of the blues results.

Beneath another and higher headland some miles south of Point Lobos, on a later day, great seas were running. Roller after roller swept in to shatter in a thunder of water and exploding spray against jagged rocks far below us. The blanket of foam that extended out for a hundred yards or more was continually ripped and hurled together again by the pounding waters. It was in the midst of this maelstrom of surf that we first glimpsed the swift, lithe form of a creature that only a few years before was thought to have disappeared forever from this coast.

The sea otter, nearly five feet long and often weighing more than fifty pounds, has a head round like a bowling ball, eyes dark and piercing, ears hardly an inch high and almost invisible. With a scraggly moustache, grizzled hair

on its head and shoulders, forepaws like mittens, it is to
northern natives the "Old Man of the Sea." Only the pika,
of all the creatures we have met, exceeds the sea otter in
instant charm.

Two centuries ago, Steller, the great naturalist of the north,
set down the first and one of the best descriptions of the
home life of the sea otter: "They prefer to lie together in
families, the male and his mate, the half-grown young and
the very young sucklings all together. The male caresses the
female by stroking her, using the forefeet as hands; she,
however, often pushes him away from her for fun and in
simulated coyness, as it were, and plays with her offspring
like the fondest mother. Their love for their young is so
intense that when their young are taken away they cry
bitterly, and grieve so much that after ten or fourteen days
they grow as lean as skeletons and become sick and feeble
and will not leave the shore."

That was written in 1742. Since then innumerable observations have confirmed Steller's impression of the human-
like traits of these sea animals. They have a single mate.
They are said to pair for life. Mating takes place at all times
of the year. A single offspring, rarely twins, is born after a
period of gestation that is almost exactly the same as among
humans. Although born at sea, the young have to learn to
swim and dive like human children. While suckling her
offspring at her twin breasts, the female utters a soft plaintive
cry that led early hunters to believe she was singing her
baby to sleep. On land, where she can flounder along almost
as fast as a man can walk, she carries her offspring in her
mouth as a cat carries a kitten; in the water, she floats or
swims on her back with her pup cradled on her breast or held
up in her forepaws. Sometimes she will toss the baby sea
otter aloft and catch it. When she dives for food she leaves
the infant entangled in strands of kelp, tethered to seaweed,
on the surface.

At times sea-otter families will play together, flipping water into one another's eyes or tossing a ball of seaweed back and forth as they frolic amid the waves. Treading water, they will rear up and look around them with one forepaw held up like a hand to shade their eyes. And when they lie on their backs asleep they sometimes place both paws over their eyes to keep out the sunshine. Almost always the sea otters are peaceful and affectionate. Although they are closely related to the weasels they have none of the bloodthirsty intentness and high-strung irritability of some of their relatives. They are the gentle weasels.

Sea otters, like humans, eat three meals a day. A few individuals take snacks between times but the main feeding of the herd corresponds to our breakfast, lunch and supper. They dive for their food, usually in comparatively shallow water but occasionally as deep as 150 feet. Slanting down obliquely, they descend with forelegs folded over their breasts and their webbed hind feet, twelve inches long and four inches wide, driving them forward with powerful thrusts. They can stay under water for as long as six minutes at a time. When they come to the surface, they bring shellfish, crustaceans, cuttlefish, sea urchins and similar creatures of the sea bottom. Turning over on their backs they eat at leisure, using the whole ventral surface of their bodies as a table. On a number of occasions one of these animals has been observed bringing a flat stone to the surface along with its shellfish. Carefully balancing the stone on its chest it uses it as an anvil on which it pounds the shell to break it open.

Edna M. Fisher, who reported in the *Journal of Mammalogy*, in 1939, the results of four months of intensive observation of one herd of sea otters, found that along the California headlands the animals fed mainly on the red abalone, *Haliotis rufescens*. These flattened sea snails are often so firmly attached to submerged rocks that a man requires a crowbar to pry them free. Yet the animals, by use of either their strong canine teeth or their powerful forepaws, are able to dislodge large abalones. One that was brought to the surface measured 8¾ by 6¾ inches.

At the end of its meal the sea otter licks its "fingers" to get the last of the taste and then washes vigorously. It rolls over and over. It scrubs the fur tablecloth of its chest and stomach. It rubs its forepaws together like a man using soap and water. It washes its face, even going behind its tiny ears. It splashes water over its head, chest and shoulders. Finally it smooths down its moustaches. This done it stretches out on its back for a long siesta. Before dozing off it usually wraps a strand of kelp about its body to keep it from drifting away from the herd. Similarly through the night the otters sleep on the waves anchored to the seaweed of the kelp beds.

In 1741, when Vitus Bering was sailing back to Kamchatka from his last pioneer voyage of discovery, his ship, the *St. Peter*, was wrecked on one of the desolate islands of the foggy Bering Sea. For seven months his men lived largely on the meat of the sea otters. They made tents of their skins. And when they reached Kamchatka the following year in the forty-foot craft they improvised from the timbers of the wrecked vessel, they carried with them more than 700 otter pelts. Thus was the remarkable fur of these animals introduced to the commercial world.

That fur, the softest imaginable, shining like satin, is so fine and so dense that oftentimes fingers cannot reach the skin below even when the pelt is stretched. In spite of its delicate texture it is particularly durable. In color it ranges from light brown to brown-black with a frosting of silvery guard hairs. Unlike many other pelts, the fur of the sea otter is prime the year around. Once it reached the markets of Europe and China it quickly took its place as one of the world's most prized and luxurious furs. Because of this rich splendor of its pelt the gentle sea otter was hunted, speared, shot, clubbed and netted year after year until it was hardly more than a step away from extinction.

Russian fur-hunters, in pursuit of these "beavers of the sea," pushed from island to island along the Aleutian chain. They roamed down the coast of Alaska. They established posts as far south as Fort Ross, less than 100 miles above San Francisco. It was the sea otter rather than gold that drew the first pioneers to this part of the country. The sea otter helped shape the course of Western history. All up and down the coast it fanned the rivalry between "Boston Men" and "King George's Men"—the American and British fur-seekers of the early nineteenth century. And it was the depletion of the otter supply in northern waters that played an important part in inducing Russia to sell Alaska to the United States so cheaply.

During the century and more the slaughter of the otters continued, old and young were hunted down. Even the hardened hunters who pushed forward the massacre were amazed at the way these gentle creatures sometimes approached and even nuzzled against the men whose clubs were poised to take their lives. For ages the only danger the otters had known had come from the sea; their only enemy had been the killer whale. When man appeared they showed merely friendly curiosity and so fell easy prey to the butchers that arrived in ever-increasing numbers. Mother otters, with their pups in their mouths, were pursued as they dived again and again seeking escape from an enemy that was always waiting when they rose for air. Because the animals sank when they were shot, natives of Hawaii, famed for their swimming prowess, were kidnapped and carried north to dive in the cold seas as short-lived human retrievers. After the purchase of Alaska, Americans used long-range rifles while standing on the shore, killing the otters at sea and trusting to luck that their bodies would be carried in by the waves.

A single vessel, in 1804, sailed back to Russia with a cargo of 15,000 otter skins. Between 1881 and 1890, one company

ANCIENT bishop pines crown this hilltop on the road
to Point Reyes. The scene spreading away below formed
one of the final views of the long journey across autumn.

HEADLAND rocks provide a lookout for the author on the sea-otter coast. Below, Point Reyes and the last sunset of fall.

averaged nearly 5,000 pelts a year. As early as 1818, Baron von Wrangel, manager of the Russian-American Company, predicted the extermination of the sea otter unless the killing was restricted. As the animals decreased the hunters advanced the same fallacious argument that has accompanied the decline of every persecuted species. "The sea otters have gone to other grounds," they said. In 1911, a fleet of thirty-one schooners scoured the formerly rich breeding grounds of the Bering Sea and returned with only a dozen skins. In that year the last commercial pelt was sold in London for $1,990. Also in that year, when the sea otter seemed doomed, England, Russia, Japan and the United States signed an international agreement giving it complete protection. The possession of any part of a sea-otter pelt is a federal offense in the United States.

Along the California coast, state laws passed in 1913 give the persecuted creature special local safeguards. But even as the laws were passed they seemed to have come too late. For a quarter of a century afterwards no one saw a sea otter on the California coast. Scientists concluded the species had been entirely wiped out in the region. Then in the spring of 1938, a filling-station attendant near Bixby Creek, about fifteen miles below Carmel, began noticing strange animals sporting in the kelp bed just offshore below a precipitous cliff. Charles E. Mayfield, game warden for the region, checked the story. The dramatic news spread. The sea otter, given up for lost, had been rediscovered just south of the Monterey Peninsula.

In spite of the hundreds of thousands of these great fur-bearers that were killed and stripped of their pelts, only a few museums have mounted specimens or even skeletons. The hosts were slaughtered by ignorant men and so little was known about the sea otter that, one story has it, the specimen in a famous eastern institution was found to have its hind legs reversed. One of the finest mounted sea otters in the country is on exhibition, appropriately, in the superb little museum at Pacific Grove. This animal died of natural causes and was found by Fish and Game Department men at the entrance of Bixby Creek.

With the Curator, Merton E. Hinshaw, and Assistant Curator Grace B. Selzer—two of the most cordially helpful people we met anywhere along the way—we started one afternoon for the high cliffs south of Point Lobos in search of sea otters. Here and there, as we walked across one lofty eyrie overlooking a wide stretch of the sea, our feet crushed low clumps of California sage. Each time the air was filled with a richly pungent smell. Here the hen-and-chickens masses of the gray-green stonecrop reflected the coming of fall. Their fleshy leaves were swelling. This is an annual occurrence as the moister autumn succeeds the more arid summer.

A quarter of a mile from shore a wide island of kelp spread out on the surface of the ocean. All around it the water was quiet. For kelp beds, like oil, still the waves. It is around such beds, from Monterey Peninsula south to Morro Bay, that the sea otters have been seen. Nobody knows their total numbers; estimates run from 65 to 300. But for them all, the kelp is an important element in their lives from birth to death. The pups are brought forth on the kelp beds. The adults spend their nights and part of their days sleeping entwined in the strands. The kelp screens them from their ancient enemy, the killer whale. Moreover the round bladders of the seaweed, colloquially known as "sea-otter cabbage," are in shape and size almost exactly like the round heads of the resting animals. They provide wonderfully effective camouflage.

Back and forth over the seaweed island we swept our field-glasses. Hinshaw was the first to recognize an otter. Like a dark little log, it lay on its back, its feet rising stiffly in the air, floating amid the kelp. It was motionless, apparently sound asleep. Then we saw other little logs, four of them, five, six, seven. A few moved or changed position as we watched. But most lay quiescent, rising and falling gently on the smoothed-out swells. Theirs was a scene of peace under the sunset sky.

We walked to the edge of the precipice and looked over the lip down at the black rocks and tumult of torn surf below. Among broken islands the white water formed a seething caldron. And there, just below us, as though sporting in a millpond, two magnificent sea otters played in the storm of waters. They rolled over and over, twining and intertwining, diving and being tossed aloft, floating on their backs with head and feet in the air, swimming side by side with noses touching. They seemed unaware of the towering breakers that were thundering on the rocks and exploding all around them. In mating the otters often choose the wildest surf; they appear to be stimulated by stormy waters.

No creature of air or land or sea we had ever met seemed more a master of its element than these dark, lithe swimmers. At times they spun in a fast sidewise roll. At other times they shot into view in curving, porpoiselike leaps. Some observers have reported seeing the otters grab their blunt ten-inch tails and whirl around in the water like rolling hoops. For fully five minutes we watched the supple grace of the otters, their speed and joyous abandon. Then they swam, side by side, out beyond the white water, toward the kelp bed and their sleeping companions.

When Harold E. Anthony, in 1928, published his *Field Book of North American Mammals*, he wrote: "The sea otter is such a rare mammal today, so nearly extinct, that there is very little likelihood any of the readers of this handbook will ever see one alive." Here, at least, we had come on a story of wildlife with a happy ending. Across the continent, most of the days of our trip, we were forced to remember Thoreau's comparison of nature to a book from which many of the pages had been torn by preceding generations. So much was gone that once had been. So much was going even as we watched. "The beautiful is vanished and returns not." Yet here, on a magic headland in an hour of sunset, beauty that along these shores had almost vanished lived again.

THIRTY-TWO

BUTTERFLY TREES

IN the year of the sea otter's return, on November 16, 1938, the City Council of Pacific Grove passed Ordinance 352. "Inasmuch," it reads, "as the Monarch Butterflies are a distinct asset to the City of Pacific Grove, and cause innumerable people to visit said city to see the said Butterflies, it is the duty of the citizens of said city to protect the Butterflies in every way possible from serious harm and possible extinction by brutal and heartless people." A fine up to $500 and a jail sentence up to six months are provided for those who, "within the corporate limits of said city," intentionally molest or harm the overwintering insects. Street signs direct visitors to the butterfly trees and every year the schoolchildren march down the main street in a butterfly parade. The monarch is on the seal of the Chamber of Commerce. "Follow the Butterflies to Pacific Grove" is the slogan of the municipality. It represents one of the few insect sanctuaries on the face of the earth.

All across the American autumn we had encountered that sign of the season, the migration of the monarchs. We had seen them winging their way south over the dunes of Monomoy, above the ridges of the Great Valley, across the flat lands of Ohio, from the end of Point Pelee, along the banks of the Mississippi, even far out over the shimmering white waste of the Great Salt Lake Desert. Always they had been working south, moving toward some remote destination.

Here the black and orange-brown insects had arrived. Here among the butterfly trees of Pacific Grove, at Point Pinos, at the far southern end of Monterey Bay, monarchs in numbers beyond counting had come home to an ancient ancestral wintering ground.

We first walked through a grove of these butterfly trees in the sunshine of early morning. They rose high above us. All were of the same species, that rare and restricted tree, the Monterey pine, *Pinus radiata*. The needles were long and richly green; the bark, the darkest of any California pine, was almost black. It is this species of tree, and this species alone, that these western monarchs choose for their winter homes. Looking up we saw the branches were shaggy and gray with what appeared to be Spanish moss. It was the pendant lichen, *Ramalina reticulata*. Over the beards of the lichen, over the outer ends of the higher branches, over the sprays of the needles, in clusters and festoons, clung thousands and tens of thousands of monarch butterflies. Their wings were tightly closed. They hung motionless, touched by the morning sun, packed together like masses of gray-brown leaves.

In hardly more than three acres of these pines—at the famed Butterfly Park, at near-by Milnar's Motel and at Washington Park—it is estimated that as many as 2,000,000 butterflies clothe the branches of the trees. Some come from as far away as British Columbia and Southern Alaska. The monarchs from more than 1,000,000 square miles are believed to spend the winter in the Pacific Grove pines. They stay about five months. They arrive usually in mid-October and leave in mid-March. The rest of the year there is not a monarch butterfly in the region.

First as a trickle out of the far north, then as a rivulet, then as a swelling stream continually enlarged by new flocks along the way, the great river of monarchs builds up and flows southward during the early days of autumn. This drainage of butterflies, almost comparable to the drainage of water, follows the lay of the land. Tributary streams pour out of the valleys, down the canyons, over the passes to join the main flight moving down the coast. Flocks so immense they have taken more than two days to go by a given point have been reported from a pass in the Siskiyou Mountains of northern California and from another near Broken Top in the Cascades of southwestern Oregon.

The monarch is a strong flier. Heading straightaway it can easily outdistance a walking or running man, maintaining a steady pace of from twelve to fifteen miles an hour. Its wings are lightly loaded. Unlike those of a bird they contain no muscles. All their movements are produced by muscles within the insect's body. Only occasionally does the butterfly pause for food or rest. During a favorable day in autumn it may advance as many as fifty miles along the path of its migration. Observations made over the years indicate the insects follow the same route each year and probably stop at the same places along the way. Yet each butterfly is a pioneer. It is traveling through country it has never seen before. In spite of this, it often follows a compass-straight course. One monarch was seen flying through the open doors of an empty freight car that stood in its way and on another occasion a whole parade of butterflies rose higher and higher in the sky in order to pass in a direct line over a widespread forest fire.

By mid-October this southward-flowing stream of monarchs has usually reached the redwoods of the Santa Cruz Mountains above the northern end of Monterey Bay. Surprisingly the insects never follow the easy path around the shore of the bay. Instead they always launch out on a straight course across more than twenty-five miles of open water toward an invisible goal, Point Pinos and its lichen-draped butterfly trees. It is this habit that, during certain years of prolonged autumn fog, produces one of the most spectacular sights of the region. Ordinarily the butterflies cross the bay in scattered flocks, taking about three weeks. in these years, however, their path is blocked by the mist day after day. The migrants are fog-bound. The flowing river of butterflies is dammed. In pyramiding numbers the monarchs pile up around the northern end of the bay. Then comes an autumn rain, clearing weather and brilliant sunshine. All at once, in one vast cloud, the insects leave the land behind. Fishermen far out on the water find their boats suddenly surrounded by tens of thousands of fluttering, glinting wings. Usually the monarchs fly low, only a few feet above the water. In a colorful, orange-brown carpet of butterflies, undulating and miles in length, they move across the bay.

It is usually about four o'clock in the afternoon when such an approaching multitude is sighted from Point Pinos. Near the old lighthouse at the end of the point the living cloud swings inshore. There is no hesitation, no searching, no uncertainty. Passing over hundreds of other pines, no different in appearance, they flutter directly to the identical trees their ancestors used. There the cloud descends, the boughs are covered, tree after tree is enveloped in butterflies.

Instinct replaces experience among these small creatures. Instinct provides the foreknowledge that brings them down the long flyway from the places of their birth. Now, amid these seaside pines, instinct reverses their mood, changes their wanderlust to quiescence. After days and weeks of striving they fall into the sedentary routine that will occupy almost half a year.

Lucia Shepardson, who first called modern attention to the trees and who began watching the butterflies as a schoolgirl in 1907, has noted that as each new flock descends the already-alighted mass gives a quick flutter of its wings. The effect is "like twinkling lights all over the tree." She has also noticed that at this period the insects sometimes produce a rustling sound like crumpling paper. For several days after their arrival the monarchs are restless. They feed heavily. They are easily alarmed. They frequently take off, circle high in the air, drop swiftly to the treetops. But little by little they quiet down.

Only a handful of butterflies were in the air around the trees we first visited. But on later days, in the warmth of afternoon, we sometimes saw hundreds circling and gliding and fluttering about the lichen-draped pines where the monarchs were massed. Looking up, minute after minute, we found there was something hypnotic about this continual circling, this slow swirling of butterflies against the sunny sky. Once, in Washington Park, behind the butterfly drift we saw the shining white apparition of what appeared to be a whistling swan passing high overhead.

A few of the monarchs take wing each day to feed. We saw some of these butterflies visiting the golden flowers of the acacia trees and others finding nectar in the bunched blooms of the sand verbenas. But the vast bulk of the insects remain on the trees without movement. So well camouflaged are they that black-and-white photographs of the upper branches fail to distinguish lichen from butterflies. In the leaden light of an overcast day the resting insects are difficult to make out even with fieldglasses. Many visitors, at such times, go away convinced there are no monarchs there at all. During periods of bad weather the insects may remain unmoving for two or three weeks at a time. Throughout the winter they are semidormant. They are not, in the true sense of the word, hibernating. Nor are they, as a local belief has it, clinging in a drunken stupor after imbibing the oozing sap of the pine tree.

While a barber cut my hair in Monterey one morning, he assured me that the butterflies came to Point Pinos only on a certain day in June—he thought it was June 25 but he could never remember the exact date and so had never seen the event himself. They arrived on this one morning only. They alighted in one tree, no other. They stayed twenty-four hours, no longer. Then they disappeared. It was a great miracle, he said. For thirty-three of his fifty years, he told me, he had lived in Monterey hardly more than a mile from the trees themselves. Yet during all these three decades and more his mind was stocked with nonexistent miracles when all the while the truth and the real miracle lay but a quarter of an hour's walk away—and he had never seen it.

One superstition of the region apparently has some basis in fact. This is the belief that an early arrival of the butterflies presages a long and stormy winter. Premature cold in the north, ushering in the longer winter, may well start the migration moving south ahead of time and thus bring the monarchs to Pacific Grove at an earlier date than usual. The number of butterflies varies from year to year. For some reason the peaks coincide with particularly dry summers. Old-timers, whose memories of the trees extend back to the 1880's, recall that the butterflies were always particularly numerous in periods of drought.

Beneath the pines we found only a few dead monarchs, never many. These migrants have an unusually long life span. Some of the overwintering insects may live for eight months as compared to the few weeks of most American butterflies. Combined with this longevity is their relative immunity to the attack of birds. Robert G. Wind, in charge of the Butterfly Park, told us he has seen only one bird molest the clinging insects. This was a jay that began to eat a monarch but quickly spit it out again.

On rare occasions a hungry bird will consume one of these butterflies in spite of the acid bitterness of its blood. John W. Aldrich, U. S. Fish and Wildlife Service research biologist, once told me of seeing a red-tailed hawk along the Kittatinny Ridge reach out with one foot, grasp a migrating monarch, strip off the wings and eat the insect as it soared along. In 1949 a member of the Linnaean Society of New York saw an immature herring gull off Jones Beach catch a monarch in the air, alight on the water and devour it. And in West

Virginia Maurice Brooks observed a starling feeding on one of these butterflies. As a rule, however, both birds and animals avoid them. No predators follow the migrating hosts southward to Pacific Grove. No bird or animal preys on the massed insects at their overwintering trees. We saw squirrels running up the trunks, jays hopping along the branches, pigmy nuthatches working close to the butterfly clusters, all paying scant attention to the dormant insects.

Near Milnar's Motel, one chilly morning, we came upon scores of the butterflies resting on the ground. Apparently in the night they had become chilled and had lost their hold. Later, warmed by the sun, they took wing and rose among the higher branches of the tree once more. Frost is rare on the Monterey Peninsula. But Robert Wind recalled one night in which thousands of monarchs were killed by a sudden drop in the temperature. Under some of the trees of the Butterfly Park, the next morning, he found a carpet of dead insects four inches thick. Rain bothers the monarchs but little. Their wings shed water like the feathers of a mallard. But strong winds that tear away masses of the lichen will sometimes send clusters and clouds of butterflies streaming away from the trees. Following a gale the insects come straggling back for days afterwards. When blown to the ground, the monarchs hide behind rocks, in crevices and under bushes. Among the trees they move nearer the trunk on the lee side. Several times at the Butterfly Park they have exhibited a kind of "storm sense," moving in from the branch tips or changing to the downwind side of the tree well in advance of a gale.

Two or three times when I was taking close-up photographs of the monarchs I noticed them give a jerk or twitch at the metallic click of my shutter. Among the butterfly trees the insects appeared to be sensitive to both noise and vibration. Years ago, Lucia Shepardson informs me, dynamite was set off near the trees during blasting operations for a new street. The frightened insects rose in a body. They disappeared from the whole Monterey Peninsula. It was two years before monarchs were seen again at Point Pinos.

Toward spring the butterflies grow increasingly restless. They move lower in the trees. They feed heavily. They are wilder and more active in flight. Most of them by now are faded and some are frayed. For all, life is nearly over. As the March days grow warm mating takes place all over the butterfly trees. After that, singly or in small groups, in a scattered movement that is hardly noticed, the monarchs move north. Among the pines of Pacific Grove they become fewer day by day until at the end of two or three weeks all are gone.

As the females lay their eggs not long after mating, it is believed the next generation starts on the milkweed plants within 100 miles or so of Point Pinos. Apparently it is this generation that, in a kind of relay race, carries the advance up the map. The females are the first to leave the trees; the males are the last to go. But for all, their departure is a flight of no return. It is their descendants that, seven months later, stream southward toward these same pine trees, repeating once more that ancient, still-mystifying movement of fall.

Why do the monarchs overwinter on this particular point? Why do they come to these particular trees? Why do they choose only Monterey pines? Were their ancestors in ages past associated with these trees before the range of the pines became so restricted? How do they recognize the exact boughs on which preceding generations rested? Are these branches, as some think, impregnated with the perfume of the male monarchs? At times visitors have reported noticing a special scent around the trees, but we were unable to detect it. How did the long autumn journey originate? Was it, as has been suggested, a product of a descending Ice Age that pushed the butterflies gradually farther and farther south out of a once-warm northland? And how do the autumn travelers find their way? What guides them over vast stretches of country to this small pine grove beside the sea?

Looking up at the dense masses of insects clothing the upper branches, we puzzled over these things as innumerable other visitors to these trees had puzzled before us. More and more the riddles in the monarch's life are attracting attention. In numerous places the butterflies are being marked with aniline dye, with stamps employing indelible ink, with tiny labels glued to the wings, in order to trace their movements. More than 30,000 were marked in 1955 under the direction of Fred A. Urquhart, of the Royal Ontario Museum of Zoology and Paleontology, at Toronto, Canada. Because the monarchs are so many, the areas they traverse so vast, the individuals that can be marked so comparatively few, the chances of their being seen among all the hosts of the journeying migrants so slight, only such large-scale and persistent efforts hold much promise of success. But through such research alone can we obtain a clearer understanding of the distances traveled by the migrants, the time consumed, the routes employed—information that is basic in considering the central riddle of how the monarch finds its way.

It might be reasoned that the western butterflies merely follow the coast south to Point Pinos. But what of the monarchs of Point Pelee setting their compass course across Lake Erie with its miles of featureless water? And what of the monarchs spanning the dead white plain of the Great Salt Lake Desert? They had no landmarks to guide them—unless there are landmarks in the sky.

And that, possibly, may be. As in the case of birds, it has been suggested in the past that the insects might follow the invisible pathways of electromagnetic lines of force running north and south on the earth. But no experiments have ever produced any evidence to support this hypothesis. Recently, however, another possibility has been opened up by the researches of Karl von Frisch, the famous discoverer of "the language of the bees." When I talked to him in 1949, during his visit to America, he was already planning a series of experiments employing Polaroid screens. They have since proved that honeybees orient themselves by means of polarized light, which varies in different parts of the sky. Their eyes have the ability to see and analyze such light, in which the rays are all vibrating in the same plane. More recent studies by other experimenters have revealed that certain species of ants find their way in a similar manner. May not the monarchs, too, on their long flights north and south, use polarized light to guide them?

They migrate only by day, by sunlight, when the sky is strongly reflecting polarized rays to the earth. Just as some insects are attracted to light at one time and repelled by it at another, may not the butterflies be so adjusted that in fall they are drawn by the polarized light coming from the southern sky and in spring by that coming from the northern sky? Each spring and fall, moreover, the sun, in effect, makes its own migration north and south across the heavens.

The eyesight of the butterfly provides a promising field for research. Much yet remains to be discovered. Only in very recent years, for example, have the experiments of Dora Ilse, in Germany, revealed a characteristic that seems unique. Honeybees can see short-wave ultraviolet rays. But they cannot see long-wave red light. Only butterflies among all the insects, so far as we can know, can do this. Other distinctive abilities, particularly those in connection with polarized light, may be disclosed in further studies. Out of such researches may come at last explanations for many of the unanswered questions that now surround the travels of the monarch.

More than once as Nellie and I wandered beneath the butterfly trees of Pacific Grove, gazing silently at the enigmatic clusters of the insects, I longed for the magic gift of Melampus. He, according to old mythology, was the first human endowed with the ability to understand the language of the animals and birds and insects. Once in the night he heard the wood-worms talking and learned that the timbers of the house were almost eaten through and so was able to escape unharmed. If only I, like Melampus, could understand the language of the butterflies! How soon then would understanding replace conjecture and surmise!

THIRTY-THREE

MOUNTAIN SNOW

NOW all the days of the autumn had dwindled down to a single week. All our wandering had narrowed to one last inland swing. Then—ending as we had begun on a cape outthrust from a far edge of the continent—we would come to winter's eve. We would meet the final moment of the fall.

On the cliffs above the sea otters, we had attained the point farthest south along the coast. Now, leaving the headlands and the windblown cypresses, the white-tailed kites and the butterfly trees, the long Indian summer and all the fascinations of the Monterey region behind us, we climbed over the coastal ranges once more. We crossed the Great Central Valley with its rusty-red vineyards and its persimmon trees laden with fruit as gay as Christmas decorations. Beyond Merced, the following day, we began climbing the long uplifted block of the Sierra range.

In 1868 John Muir gained his first indelible impression of the Sierra Nevadas from the summit of Pacheco Pass. It chanced that near this same spot we, too, saw their snow-clad beauty appear under extraordinary circumstances like a revelation in the sky. The mountains had been veiled in mist when first we had come down the valley. On this afternoon near Pacheco Pass they were once more hidden, this time behind swollen, rolling clouds that sealed in the whole length and breadth of a stormy sky. We were still in dark shadow with fine rain falling around us when far out across the valley the lid of the sky began to tear apart. Streamers of sunshine slanted down through widening rents. Then in one continuous movement along the eastern horizon the clouds rolled back, the heavens opened and the "range of light" stood revealed, every high, jagged, snow-covered peak alabaster-white in the sunshine. In the center of this breathtaking vista, vertical bands of color, the foot of a rainbow, rose above the mountains and faded in the sky. For several minutes this stupendous spectacle lay spread before us across the valley. Then the sky darkened, the sun-streamers were pinched off, the clouds tumbled together, the mountains and the rainbow were gone. It was thus that we first beheld the famed central portion of the Sierra Nevada range.

When we left Merced the next morning, the mountains toward which we drove were blotted out by valley mist. At this time of year, with more moisture in the ground and with chill air descending the mountainsides at night, many California valleys are great mixing bowls of fog. In the vague, milky light of that morning we saw California quail running as though with shoulders hunched. We passed a side road, dimly seen, that led into the Cathay Valley where the Bible Tree grew. This pine enveloped and preserved a small leather-covered Bible that had been left in a recess in its trunk. Similar trees—the Maryland oak with a gold ring in its heart, the Michigan tree that swallowed a millwheel, the Washington tree that grew around a rifle, the tree in a Connecticut cemetery that embraced a Colonial gravestone—all these arboreal prodigies have been a source of astonishment and folklore across the country.

Out of the mist into the sunshine, out of the great valley into the small valley, out of the warmth of the lowland into the frosty air and mountain snow and crystalline beauty of Yosemite in December we climbed that day. Once before we had tried to reach this famous hanging valley but a blizzard had blocked us out. Now, at an elevation of 4,000 feet, we found ourselves in a frosted fairyland glittering in the sunshine. Here was that final aspect of fall, the autumn of December, that we had missed in the mild climate of the western coast.

Yet all along our trail from Monomoy almost to the Pacific this was the aspect of these last days of the third season. Snow lay white on the Kittatinny Ridge, ice locked in Lake Itasca and the warbler river, freezing winds swept over the badlands, drifts choked the high passes of the Rockies. Everywhere along the way we had come west, this tail-end of autumn was a time of winter weather. We read of elk hunters lost in drifts, of telephone lines down in sleet storms, of trains delayed and buses stalled by snow. In a time of changing foliage we had seen the green miles turn to red and gold miles; now all had become white miles. Harvest and fulfillment were over. The affairs of the year had been wound up. Now—with the burrows of the long sleepers hidden from view, with migrants far away—the hazy, drifting hours of Indian summer had been replaced by nights of starlit frost and days of sparkling snow.

Scattered all across the roadside drifts, under Arch Rock and El Capitan and Half Dome, near the long filmy veils of the waterfalls, amid the incense cedars and ponderosa pines, frost crystals, the largest, the most complex, the most beautiful I had ever seen, glittered in the sun. Often they were massed together as dense and luxuriant as ferns on a rain-forest floor. By midafternoon these delicate frost-ferns were shrinking and fading in the slow warming up of the valley. But in the piercingly chill air of the next morning they were back again. Wherever tires had left their tread patterns in the soft snow every embossed portion of the design was richly overlaid with the shining crystalline jewels of the frost formations. Along the winding banks of the Merced River the tree trunks seemed whitewashed. To the height of ten or a dozen feet the bark of each was plated with frost.

During our days in Yosemite the sun was close to its farthest-south point in the sky. The shadow of the high southern wall, even at midday, extended far out over the floor of the valley. Sometimes the snow in this shaded portion of the park lies four feet deep when it has almost completely melted from the ground below the northern wall. At this time of year the slanting rays of the sun strike this wall more directly than they do in midsummer when the sun is overhead. They warm the rock which in turn warms the air, and this moderates the winter climate of this particular part of the valley. Wayne W. Bryant, ranger-naturalist at the park, told us of a study he once made of a cross section of the valley. Taking a strip about a mile wide, he began at the top of one wall, worked down it and across the floor of the valley to the other wall and up it. This ecological survey revealed that the vegetation of the warmer northern side varies considerably from that of the colder southern side.

We slept that night in a log cabin among incense cedars. Darkness comes early in the depths of the valley. When we walked down icy roads in the evening the black, towering trees around us ascended up and up until they appeared supporting all the spangled canopy of stars and constellations above. We breathed deeply the evergreen air, spicy and invigorating. We listened, in the stillness of the night, to the faint liquid lisping of waterfalls. Back at the cabin, the last thing we saw before we turned out the lights was a deer looking in our window.

The first thing we saw next morning was another California mule deer nibbling on a yellow-green spray of incense cedar. A little later we came upon a doe standing in a snowdrift. It was consuming the cellophane wrapper from a package of cigarettes. The curious craving of deer for tobacco is so well known that the old-time meat hunters used to lure the animals to their death by tying a bag of Bull Durham out of reach on a limb above a trail. In rainy weather drippings from the bag would draw deer to the spot as to a salt lick.

Although it was perfectly still that morning on the floor of the valley, a wind rushing along the upper portion of the northern cliffs flared the white veil of Yosemite Falls far to the west. At the time, the falling water, only about one-tenth its maximum flow, was even more filmy than usual. From the icy road that climbed to the sequoias of Wawona Grove we looked back. The sun had just edged above the southeastern wall of the valley and all across the windblown vapors of the waterfall ran glowing bands of rainbow color.

Wawona Grove, the first and most famous of the sequoia sanctuaries, was waist-deep in snow when we reached it. But the road had been plowed out as far as the Grizzly Giant. This 3,700-ton patriarch, with a trunk that has a circumference of forty-six feet 90 feet above the ground, is believed to be at least 3,800 years old. All the arts that make this printed page possible, even to the invention of paper, occurred within its lifetime. With 100 or 150 feet of its top gone, the Grizzly Giant still towers to a height of 209 feet. Six times in a single storm this tree was struck by lightning. Yet it has endured, in spite of fire and thunderbolt, for nearly forty centuries.

While the coastal redwoods were seen by the Spaniards as early as 1769, these mountain redwoods, *Sequoia gigantea*, were not discovered until 1833 when the exploring party led by Joseph Walker crossed the Sierra Nevada in the region of Yosemite. As compared to the 2,000,000 acres originally covered by the coastal trees, the total for all the high-country groves of *Sequoia gigantea* is only about 30,000 acres. Unlike the taller redwoods, the more massive and older sequoias do not grow in pure stands. They are mixed with other trees such as the great sugar pines we saw dangling their eighteen-inch cones from the tips of their upper branches. A sequoia is several hundred years old before it begins to reproduce. This it does with cones hardly two inches long. So numerous are they that two small branches were once found to hold 480. Each cone is packed with from 150 to 300 seeds so small they range from an eighth to a quarter of an inch in length. The little western chickaree with its finely tufted ears never seems to get enough sequoia seeds. In a single day one of these squirrels may cut down as much as a bushel of cones.

When we first came to the grove it was enveloped in the age-old calm of these greater redwoods, a hush that was almost complete. Blue-tinted shadows ran across the snow of open spaces, the oldest tree shadows we had ever seen, cast by the same trunks on this same portion of the earth for ten or twenty centuries before the *Golden Hinde* carried Sir Francis Drake to the Pacific. Under the snow the spreading roots of some of the titan trees extended through an acre of soil. In one place where the sun's rays descended between two shadow paths we saw a shining mote, the form of an amazingly hardy gnat, dancing in the light surrounded by the blur of its wings. Here side by side in nature's vast machine were the largest and one of the smallest of its cogs—the long, slowly revolving life cycle of the sequoia and the swiftly completed existence of the gnat.

Looking up along the grooved, cinnamon-red trunks of the many-autumned trees we saw the brilliant green of western lichen running in lines up the ridgetops of the bark. This same growth mantled the upper branches of the Grizzly Giant and here and there green blotches stood out on the snow where tufts of the lichen had fallen. At times we heard the far-away surf-sound of wind coming toward us through the treetops. In the changeable mountain weather it approached in single, isolated waves with a recognizable front. Each time we would hear the sound grow in volume, pass high overhead with "a rushing like the rushing of mighty waters," then sweep on and become faint in the distance, leaving the great trees once more wrapped in stillness.

Only three times during our two afternoons in this snow-covered sequoia grove did other visitors appear. Once it was a couple from British Columbia, another time a farm family from Nebraska and the third time an elderly man bundled in robes and sitting alone in the back of a limousine driven by a liveried chauffeur. Occasionally the profound hush of the forest was broken by the calling of a white-headed woodpecker, the voice of a Steller's jay or the small clinking sounds of feeding nuthatches. Whenever we remained motionless for any length of time we became aware of a slow, almost imperceptible drift of tiny bark fragments raining down from the trees. Where these particles collect in depressions on the trunks, mountain chickadees and thin-billed nuthatches sometimes take dust baths high above the ground. Woodpeckers, on occasion, excavate their nest holes entirely within the bark of the sequoias. For no other tree has so heavy an outer layer; on large trunks it may be as much as two feet thick.

One of the secrets of the sequoia's longevity is the protection against fire and injury provided by this bark. The wood of the big tree is particularly brittle. It fractures across the grain. In consequence the trunk of a felled sequoia breaks into such small sections that nearly 80 per cent of the wood is unsuitable for lumber. This characteristic, together with the remote and mountainous location of its groves, has played a major role in saving it from the axe and saw. And the abundant supply of tannin it contains brings it immunity from the attacks of insects and fungus. Wherever the trunk of a sequoia is cut the wood turns jet black as the tannin oxidizes on contact with the air. John Muir, in this very grove, used to make the ink he used by dissolving in water flakes of reddish gum obtained from the cones of the big trees. Letters he wrote with this tannin-rich sequoia ink are still legible more than seventy years later.

All through the Yosemite country, wherever you go, you cross the trail of this remarkable man and hear echoes of the days he spent there. With a sack of bread over his shoulder and a notebook tied to his belt, Muir roamed alone among the mountains making the pioneer studies on which his early books were based. It was in Wawona Grove, then known as Mariposa Grove, that Muir camped with Theodore Roosevelt in 1903. Thirty-two years earlier he had shown the same sequoias to Ralph Waldo Emerson.

"The wonder is," Emerson had remarked, "that we can see these trees and not wonder more."

When, after only a few hours' visit, the Emerson party prepared to leave the grove, Muir remonstrated:

"It is as though a photographer should remove his plate before the impression was fully made."

Always he was amazed by the rich and distinguished visitors who came to Yosemite and then rushed away again, so "time-poor" they could spare no more than a day or so to see the glories of the mountains.

"I have not yet in all my wanderings," he wrote to his sister, "found a single person so free as myself. When in the woods I sit at times for hours watching birds or squirrels or looking down into the faces of flowers without suffering any feeling of haste."

Since Muir's day the margin of time in the average man's life has widened as working hours have become shorter. Yet the demands on that time have been ever increasing. Hazlitt's wish for "a little breathing space to muse on indifferent matters" is a desire that seems each year harder to fulfill. When the famous Sierra Club was formed, one of the early members told me, a primary purpose was to induce people to come to Yosemite. Now in summer the cars move bumper to bumper and the problem is what to do with all the people who come. Time and space—time to be alone, space to move about—these may well become the great scarcities of to-morrow. Freedom as John Muir knew it, with its wealth cf time, its unregimented days, its latitude of choice, such freedom seems more rare, more difficult to attain, more remote with each new generation.

We were thinking of John Muir and of space and time that day when we left the sequoias—those trees so full of years, so independent of the clock. The last of the autumn days were slipping away. In the life of the sequoia those days represented but an infinitesimal flicker of time. But to us they would round out the season. They would bring to a close our long westward pilgrimage through the fall. During this journey we had wandered as we wished. We had changed our plans to suit the day. We had, for the space of a whole glorious autumn, been time-rich.

THIRTY-FOUR

WINDY CRAG: EBB OF THE TIDE

THE last full day of fall broke after a night of pounding rain. We saw the sun rise that morning 180 miles from the sequoias, 150 miles from the otter surf, 2,800 miles by airline—or 20,000 as we had wandered—from our starting point on Monomoy. The date was the twentieth of December. The place was the Point Reyes Peninsula thirty miles north of the Golden Gate.

On opposite sides of the continent, Cape Cod stretches to the east and Point Reyes extends to the west. At Monomoy low dunes faced the Atlantic. Here the outer tip of the point met the sea in a towering 600-foot cliff that thrust out into the Pacific like the prow of some immense ship of rock, continually battered by the surf and surrounded by the wind.

The better part of that day, Nellie and I roamed over this peninsula with three western friends, Woody Williams, Don Greame Kelley and his wife, Marion. We picnicked on fried chicken among driftwood on the beach where a hollow in the headlands protected us from the wind. We wandered across miles of green, rolling, almost treeless downs, pasture land, foggy land where, after the rain, fenceposts were sometimes so thickly clad in swollen moss and lichens they rose beside the road like green candles coated with drippings of wax. On the granite slope of Inverness Ridge just west of Tomales Bay—that slender arm of the sea that penetrates the peninsula for more than fifteen miles and half severs it from the mainland—we came to a grove of pines. They were flat-topped. Their bark was deeply furrowed. And encircling their branches, even their trunks, were curious bracelets of cones.

These were the rare bishop pines. Remnants of a once-widespread species, they now occur in disconnected "islands" along the western coast as far south as Baja California. Scientists believe they originated in Pleistocene times in areas sheared off from the mainland by fault lines in the earth's crust. Cones of these trees have been found in the La Brea tar pits beside the skeletons of woolly mammoths and sabre-toothed tigers. Usually these cones develop early, when the tree is twelve or fifteen years old, sometimes even when it is only five or six. They appear first on the trunk. Later they form in circles around the main branches, as many as five to a circle with commonly two or three of these cone-bracelets to a branch. Some that we saw were green with moss. Others were bearded with lichen. They had been attached to the branches apparently for decades. For this tree is one of the "fire type" pines. It requires the heat of a forest conflagration to produce the slow opening of the cones and the shedding of the seeds. These seeds germinate rapidly in ashy soil. Thus, all at one time, they replant a stand of pines destroyed by fire.

Wherever we went among these pines of ancient lineage we heard an ancient sound, the low murmur of the distant surf. It was a sound that steadily rose in volume as we all worked our way out toward the high, gale-swept crag of the point late that afternoon.

Point Reyes is one of the windiest spots in all America. The year around, the average velocity here is more than twenty miles an hour. Once for six consecutive days, and another time for nine days, the wind blew fifty miles an hour. For a period of twenty-four hours the average stood at eighty miles. And once for five minutes it held at 110 miles. The peak velocity recorded at the point is 120 miles an hour.

For more than nine months of every year, the wind sweeps in from the sea out of the northwest.

On this afternoon it blew from that direction. And as our road climbed, the wind velocity increased. By the time we came out on the top of the lofty headland we were in the midst of a fifty-mile-an-hour gale. It shook the twisted cypresses that flared inland from the cliff edge. It keened among low-set telephone wires. It pounded along the roofs of the squat cluster of houses occupied by lighthouse men. Looking between the writhing trees we saw the straight line of the ten-mile beach that runs north from below the cliff banded on the seaward side with a wide white ribbon of tumbling surf.

Since 1870 the famous Point Reyes lighthouse has occupied a ledge some 300 feet down the face of the precipice. It is reached by an exposed wooden stairway of 433 steps that angles steeply down with a thin pipe railing on one side for support. Before we started this sheer descent, we caught our breath in the lee of sandstone formations eroded like rocks in the desert by centuries of wind. The Point Reyes Peninsula rests on a granite foundation of quartz diorite. But the point itself is largely made up of boulder conglomerate crossbedded with sandstone.

As we descended step by step the gusts battered us, took away our breath, ballooned our coats, forced us against the rail, while all the time the taut telephone wires descending to the lighthouse just above our heads screeched in a rising and falling wail. From time to time a fine sprinkling of spindrift struck our faces fully 500 feet above the sea. And always the gusts were filled with the wild roaring of the surf. We passed brilliant splotches of red on the spray-wet rock formed of the same alga that had coated the cypress twigs of Point Lobos.

In the shelter of the lighthouse we regained our breath. The young Coast Guardsman on duty, A. D. Garrison, showed us the complicated lenses, formed of more than 1,000 pieces of glass, that once every five seconds from an hour before sunset to an hour after sunrise send forth a white stab of light visible twenty-four miles at sea. The lenses were ground in Paris in 1867. They came around Cape Horn in a sailing vessel. And they were transported to Point Reyes by ox cart. For more than eighty years they have warned ships away from the perilous rocks of the point.

The screeching and bellowing of the wind outside was never stilled. The gusts increased in violence. They seemed to shake the very lighthouse. Whenever I thrust my head around the corner of the building to glimpse the enormous seas that shattered far below, my breath was forced back down my throat. Over and over again, as though I were diving under-water, I fought my way to the railing to peer downward at the churning, detonating tumult directly below. Gust-blown spray ran like thin shadows of clouds across the hills and valleys of the waves. At times I would see an incoming roller meet some deeply submerged rock and shatter with a tongue of foam that shot back, fanned out, shining white in the depths of the water. It was like watching the explosion of a mine or depth charge in the sea below.

These waves crashing against Point Reyes struck like liquid battering rams. Each cubic foot of water weighs more than sixty-two pounds. Once, on the coast of Scotland, scientists measured the force of incoming waves in calm and storm. They found that in fine weather they struck with a force of about 600 pounds to the square foot. But during storms the crash of the combers dealt the shore a blow of more than a ton to every square foot. The power of the waves that hit Point Reyes at such times is as great as though line after line of heavy destroyers heading toward the shore side by side at forty knots hurled themselves against the rock at ten-second intervals.

Off Point Reyes the floor of the sea slopes steeply down-ward for a mile or more until it reaches a depth of about 200 feet. Then it decreases its descent to about twenty feet to the mile until, some twenty miles offshore, it reaches the edge of a great submarine bench and plunges abruptly downward. Even in storms, wave motion rarely extends to a depth of more than 200 feet. Each wave advances across the shallowing sea toward the mainland with all its particles turning with a circular motion like revolving wheels. As it approaches the shore the friction of the bottom retards the lower particles. The upper portion of the moving wave begins to advance faster than the lower portion. The front grows steadily steeper. Finally the top curls over. The wave breaks.

Some years ago one of the lighthouse men made pets of two young ravens. On days of relative calm he would scale slices of bread from the cliff-side and watch the birds plunge downward and catch the food in the air before it struck the water. Looking down now, the only birds I saw were the cormorants that sometimes flew from rock to rock amid the spray, carried sidewise a full quarter of a mile on every downwind turn. Most of the birds that day had taken shelter on the lee side of the point where, in the spring of 1579, the high bluffs of the curving bay had reminded Sir Francis Drake of the white cliffs of Dover when he landed here to repair the *Golden Hinde*.

During recent weeks numerous whales had spouted off the point, plowing through heavy seas on their migration south. Among the birds, in these last days of fall, the black brant were bringing up the tail-end of the coastwise movement. They represented the last ripple of the great avian tide of autumn that we had seen in its beginnings on Monomoy.

Thirty miles to the southwest—like low, dark haystacks on the horizon—I could make out the Farallon Islands. Bare and waterless, jagged peaks thrust above the waves, these islands have been the nesting ground of murres and other sea birds for uncounted centuries. And here, less than 100 years ago, the eggers plied their trade, robbing tens of thousands of nests to supply the San Francisco market. Forty-niners paid as much as a dollar apiece for the Farallon eggs. During one two-month period in 1854 more than 500,000 were collected and sold by a single company. It is estimated that in the fifty years before this vicious traffic was abolished 12,000,000 dozen eggs were taken from the cliffs of the islands. Today the whole Farallon group is a closely guarded refuge where birds of the sea find sanctuary.

Looking down from my wind-buffeted eyrie I could note but little difference in the tumultuous seas below as the water fell away to its farthest ebb. On Monomoy we had seen the full tide, the turn of the tide, the beginning of the season. Here at Point Reyes we saw the ebb of the tide—the ebb of the season's tide, the ebb of migration's tide, the ebb tide of our travels. And in the early setting of the December sun, far to the south, we saw the tide of light, too, fall back to its lowest ebb of the year.

All the while we had been working west through the advancing autumn, the northern hemisphere had been slowly "tilting away from the sun." The days had been growing shorter. On this afternoon sunset came at 5:05 P.M. Although Point Reyes is the foggiest spot on the whole California coast, the skies were clear. Only a low bank of clouds stretched along the western horizon. It flamed in the sunset and all the great expanse of tumbling, wind-worried water between was touched with dull reflections of the flame. With silent emotion we watched the sun disappear and the colors fade. This was the sundown of the day and the sundown of the season. All across the land the glory of an American autumn had come and now had almost gone. The "third act of the eternal play" was nearly completed. And never again would we know another autumn like this.

In fading light we struggled through the gale up the long stairs to the protection of the cypress trees. We rode away down the steep descent and out across the rolling downs where hills and hollows were losing their individuality in the universal enveloping dusk. The evening closed in, the last evening of fall, the one the country people of England used to call Winter's Eve.

The next morning Nellie and I returned to the bishop pines. We wandered in sunshine through the grove accompanied wherever we went by the thin sound of wind among the needles and the low, endless murmur of the outer surf. Here, so far from home, we came to the end of our autumn journey, to the final moments of fall. We followed the hands of my watch as they moved early that afternoon from 1:30 to 1:40 to 1:44—the last minute of autumn, the dividing line of the seasons. At that moment on this day of the longest shadows, this shortest day of all, this twenty-first of December, the year reached its winter solstice. The sun, shining from farthest south in the heavens, "stood still" before beginning its long, slow climb to the zenith of June. One instant it was autumn, the next it was winter. In this moment in the sunshine, between breaths, fall had slipped away.

INDEX